mothers • brothers • sisters
AND OTHERS

Enjoy!
Linda Hofstetter

A Collection of Loved Recipes for You and Your Family
by LINDA HOFSTETTER

Pictured on the cover: Left to right: Linda at the KOLR 10 Brunch Contest; Ken and Steve Hofstetter; Linda Hofstetter and sister Jean Frankhouser; JchnAnn Corder, Lisa and Alleta Bergmanis.

This book is dedicated to all the

mothers • brothers • sisters

AND OTHERS

who make our life so good.

Personally to my husband Steve, who is always there supporting me and to my dear sister, Katherine Deihl, who departed this life and left us far too soon.

Sisters they are blessed with an extra sense that whispers when the other needs them.

ANNIE DANIELSON

While some of this publication contain some of Linda's original recipes, there is no attempt to label them all as such. Some have been adapted from other cooks or cookbooks and some simply old favorites—source unknown.

Steve and Linda Hofstetter

♥ My Sisters ♥

My sister, Katherine Deihl

My Family

Brent, Linda and Steve

Brooke, Linda and Brendan

Brooke with Grandma Linda

Brooke and Brendan

Dad with the girls

Brooke and Brendan with Grandpa Steve

4

Bless the **food** before us,
the **family** beside us,
and the **love** between us.
Amen.

Clarence and Eulah Becker

Clarence Becker

Grandma and Grandpa Becker

Me and my sisters

Grandma and Grandpa Belcher

Linda's family at milestone birthday

Food, Friends, Family

Cherry Crunch {page 129}

The Hofstetter sisters
Georgia, Shirley and Margaret

Steph and the boys

Steve, Sarah, Samantha and Scott Hofstetter

Grandma Beckley

Bo and Jeane Gordon

Kiddy cookies

Chocolat wafer Cookies
small marshmellows
Candy canes
poder suger
Milk

Crush Chocolate cookies in a large mixing bowl add 2 crushed candy canes and 1 cup of little marshmellow Mix with enough milk to hold together Roll mixture size balls. Then roll the balls in powder suger

Linda with Grandma Franklin

Linda with Chef Brian Romano of the Cook's Kettle in Springfield, Missouri

Brent's original Kiddy Cookie Recipe {page 116}

Friends are the family you choose.

Beverly with Noelle

Jan, Ellie and Misty

Chili served over tamales {page 111}

7

appetizers, drinks, etc.
PAGE 17

sides & salads
PAGE 43

the main event
PAGE 77

desserts & other sweet treats
PAGE 115

Table of Contents

Dedication 2
Introduction 13
The Importance of the Apron 14

Appetizers, Drinks, Etc. (Page 17)

Yummy Sandwiches 18	Hot Artichoke Augratin with French Bread Dippers 31
Mulled Cider 19	Frozen Fruit Cups 32
Raspberry Lemonade 20	Cheese Rolls 33
Russian Tea 21	Korean Egg Rolls 34
Homemade Cappuccino 22	Marcie's Spiced Pecans 36
Dill Dip 23	Marilyn's Spiced Pecans 37
Reuben Dip 24	Meng Cheese 38
Spicy Hot Pretzels 25	Summer Sausage 39
Party Fodder 26	Fruit Dip 40
Sticky Wings 27	Caramel Dip 40
Reindeer Munch 28	Cheese Tid-Bits 41
Cream Cheese Mints 29	Rainy's Meatballs 42
Baked Cream Cheese Appetizer 30	

table of contents

Sides and Salads (Page 43)

Corn Casserole 44	Greek Pasta Salad 61
Pat Darnell's Creamy Hot Bacon Salad 45	Asparagus Picnic Salad 62
French Dressing 46	Garlic-Cheese Biscuits 63
Plum Sauce 47	Whole-Wheat Bread 64
Jeane's Chicken Salad 48	Hash Brown Casserole 65
Shrimp Salad 49	Frozen Champagne Salad 66
Madison's Salad 50	Apple Snicker Salad I 67
Broccoli Salad 51	Apple Snicker Salad II 68
Cauliflower and Broccoli Salad 52	Easy Dinner Rolls 69
Layered Salad 53	Yellow Squash Casserole 70
Dorito Taco Salad 54	Potato Salad 71
Chinese Coleslaw 55	Deviled Eggs 72
Grandma Beckley's Cranberry Salad 56	"Hot" Macaroni 73
Linda's Version of the Cranberry Salad 57	Karen's Creamy Macaroni Salad 74
Cucumber and Onions 58	Grape Salad 75
Pea Salad or Red Bean Salad 59	Cherry Pie Filling Salad 76
Vegetable Salad 60	

Main Event (Page 77)

Spinach Pie 78	French Toast 81
Chicken Hot Dish 79	Plaza Steak Soup 82
Chuck Roast and Vegetables 80	Herbed Vegetable Beef Soup 83

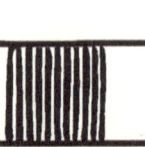

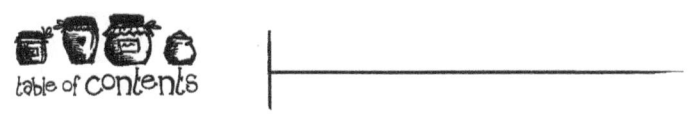

table of contents

Chicken Enchilada Soup 84	Prime Rib 99
Broccoli Cheese Soup 85	Tortilla Soup 100
Deviled Beef Patties 86	Steve and Linda's Chicken Noodle Soup 101
Ham Balls 87	Bar-B-Que 102
Cheesy Zucchini Lasagna 88	Crock Pot Roast-Beef 103
Roasted Veggie Lasagna 89	Reuben Casserole 104
South of the Border Lasagna 90	Creamy Fettuccine Alfredo 105
Lobster House Flounder Parmesan 91	Steve's Fra Diavolo 106
Crustless Crab Quiche 92	Dalton's Prize-Winning Chili Con Carne 108
Ham and Beans(cooked in the oven) 93	Hofstetter's Prize Winning Chili Recipe 110
Jan's Pimento Cheese 94	White Chili 111
Spicy Pimento Cheese 95	Chicken Enchiladas 112
Smoky Salmon Fillets 96	Chicken Pot Pie 113
Leo's Clam Chowder 97	Mom's (Me) Meatloaf 114
Beef Brisket 98	Glaze 114

Desserts and Other Sweet Treats (Page 115)

Kiddy Cookies 116	Vanilla Sauce 120
Rhubarb Custard Pie 117	Russian Tea Cakes 121
Mom's Bread Pudding 118	Snicker Pie 122
Sauce 119	Low-Fat Key Lime Pie 123
Lava Sauce 119	Chocolate Fondue 124
Bread Pudding 120	Lemonade Cake 125

table of contents

Desserts and Other Sweet Treats continued

Grandma Linda's Baseball Cookies......... 126
Ginger Snaps........................ 128
Cherry Crunch....................... 129
Raisin Pie.......................... 130
Pineapple Upside Down Cake........... 131
White Wedding Cake Cupcakes.......... 132
Buttercream Frosting for Wedding Cake Cupcakes (and variations)...................... 133
White Chocolate Cream Cheese Frosting.... 134
German Apple Cake................... 135
Peach Pie Dessert.................... 136
Carrot Cake......................... 137
Baby Food Carrot Cake................ 138
Cream Cheese Frosting................ 139
Glorified Brownies................... 140
Peanut Butter Bars................... 141
Mother's Soft Pies................... 142
Meringue............................ 143
Grandma Witt's Sugar Cookies.......... 144
Joni's Mom's Cut-Out Cookies.......... 145

Brown Sugar Dumplings............... 146
Salad Dressing Cake.................. 147
Low-fat Coffee Cake.................. 148
Angel Food Cake..................... 149
Toffee Bars......................... 150
Snickerdoodles...................... 151
Lost Snickerdoodle Recipe............. 152
Springerle Cookies................... 153
Red Velvet Cupcakes.................. 154
Praline Sauce for Ice Cream........... 155
Pecan Pie........................... 155
Katherine's Home Made Ice Cream....... 156
Sweet Potato Pie..................... 157
Pecan Pralines...................... 158
Rum Balls........................... 159
Mississippi Mud Cake................. 160
Cherry Fruit Cake.................... 161
Oatmeal Cake........................ 162
Peach Pie........................... 164

Index 165

Closing Blessing 169

mothers • brothers • sisters
AND OTHERS

A collection of food, friends, and family

BY **LINDA HOFSTETTER**

IN THIS CRAZY WORLD IN WHICH WE LIVE, life gets so hectic that we sometimes do not slow down to enjoy our families and friends, and when we do it is usually to share a meal. How many times do we meet friends for lunch, have that special dinner for our kids and grandkids (their favorite—their choice), or just slow down enough to have an evening meal with our husband to go over the events of the day.

So with all this in mind I have compiled several of my favorite recipes to read, to make, and to savor.

I have retired, and it has always been my dream to write a cookbook. I have been blessed to have lots of friends and family who have shared their culinary talents and treats with me. So it is with great pleasure that I present these stories and recipes to tempt you to prepare and have them with your mothers, brothers, sisters, and others. So you too can make memories and have stories to pass along.

♥ Linda

P.S. Special thanks go to my friend Lisa Bergmanis for helping proofread, Roxie Kelley for having her cookbook writing class and getting me on track with my book, and to Amanda DeGraffenreid at DeGraf Design (www.degrafdesign.com) for her expertise in graphic design for the beautiful cover and page designs. Thanks also to all my friends and family in their encouragement in this project.

The Importance of the Apron

This poem was shared at a tea hosted by the local PEO group. There was a member that had a collection of aprons that she shared with the group along with this oh so true story. It so reminds me of my grandmas.

I don't think our kids know what an apron is. The principle use of Grandma's apron was to protect the dress underneath because she only had a few. It was also because it was easier to wash aprons than dresses, and aprons used less material.

It was wonderful for drying children's tears, and on occasion was even used for cleaning dirty ears. From the chicken coop, the apron was used for carrying eggs, fussy chicks, and sometimes half-hatched eggs to be finished in a warm oven. When company came, those aprons were ideal hiding places for shy kids. And when the weather was cold, Grandma wrapped it around her arms. Those big old aprons wiped many a perspiring brow bent over the hot wood stove and served as potholders for removing pans from the oven.

Chips and kindling wood were brought into the kitchen in that apron. From the garden, it carried all sorts of vegetables. After the peas had been shelled, it carried out the hulls.

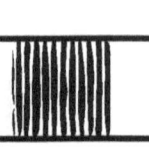

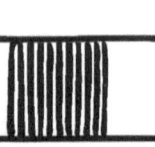

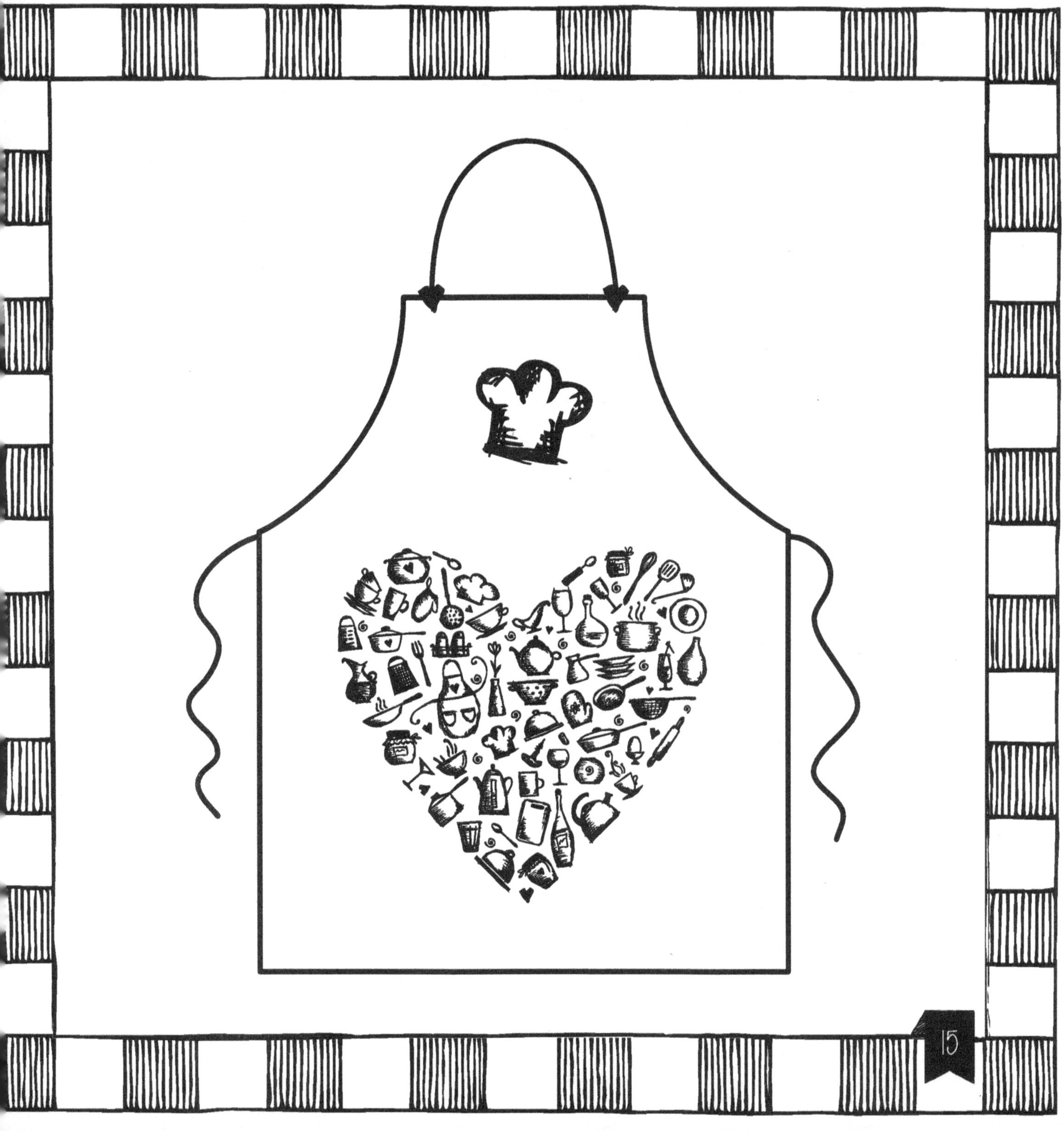

The Importance of the Apron cont.

In the fall, the apron was used to bring in apples that had fallen from the trees in the orchard. When unexpected company drove up the road, it was surprising how much furniture that old apron could dust in a matter of seconds. When dinner was ready, Grandma walked out onto the porch, waved her apron, and the menfolk knew it was time to come from the fields for dinner. It will be a long time before someone invents something that will replace that "old-time apron" that served so many purposes.

THINK ABOUT IT: Grandma used to set her hot baked apple pie on the window sill to cool. Her granddaughters set theirs on the window sill to thaw. There are health nuts today who would go crazy trying to figure out how many germs were on that apron. The only thing ever caught from an apron was — **A LOT OF LOVE!**

ANONYMOUS

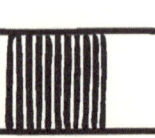

Raspberry Lemonade {page 20}

appetizers, drinks, etc.

17

appetizers, drinks, etc.

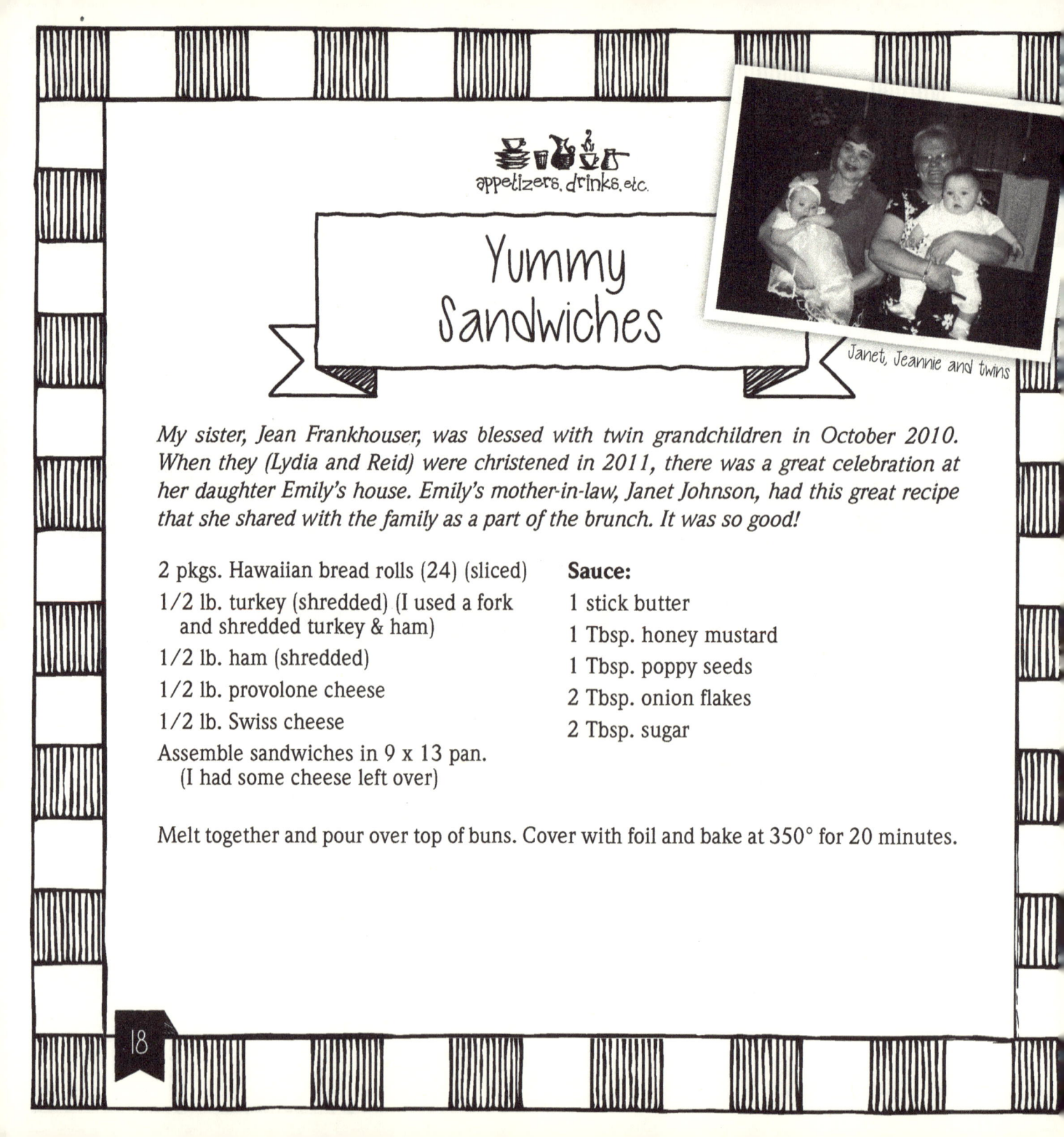

Yummy Sandwiches

Janet, Jeannie and twins

My sister, Jean Frankhouser, was blessed with twin grandchildren in October 2010. When they (Lydia and Reid) were christened in 2011, there was a great celebration at her daughter Emily's house. Emily's mother-in-law, Janet Johnson, had this great recipe that she shared with the family as a part of the brunch. It was so good!

2 pkgs. Hawaiian bread rolls (24) (sliced)
1/2 lb. turkey (shredded) (I used a fork and shredded turkey & ham)
1/2 lb. ham (shredded)
1/2 lb. provolone cheese
1/2 lb. Swiss cheese
Assemble sandwiches in 9 x 13 pan. (I had some cheese left over)

Sauce:
1 stick butter
1 Tbsp. honey mustard
1 Tbsp. poppy seeds
2 Tbsp. onion flakes
2 Tbsp. sugar

Melt together and pour over top of buns. Cover with foil and bake at 350° for 20 minutes.

appetizers, drinks, etc.

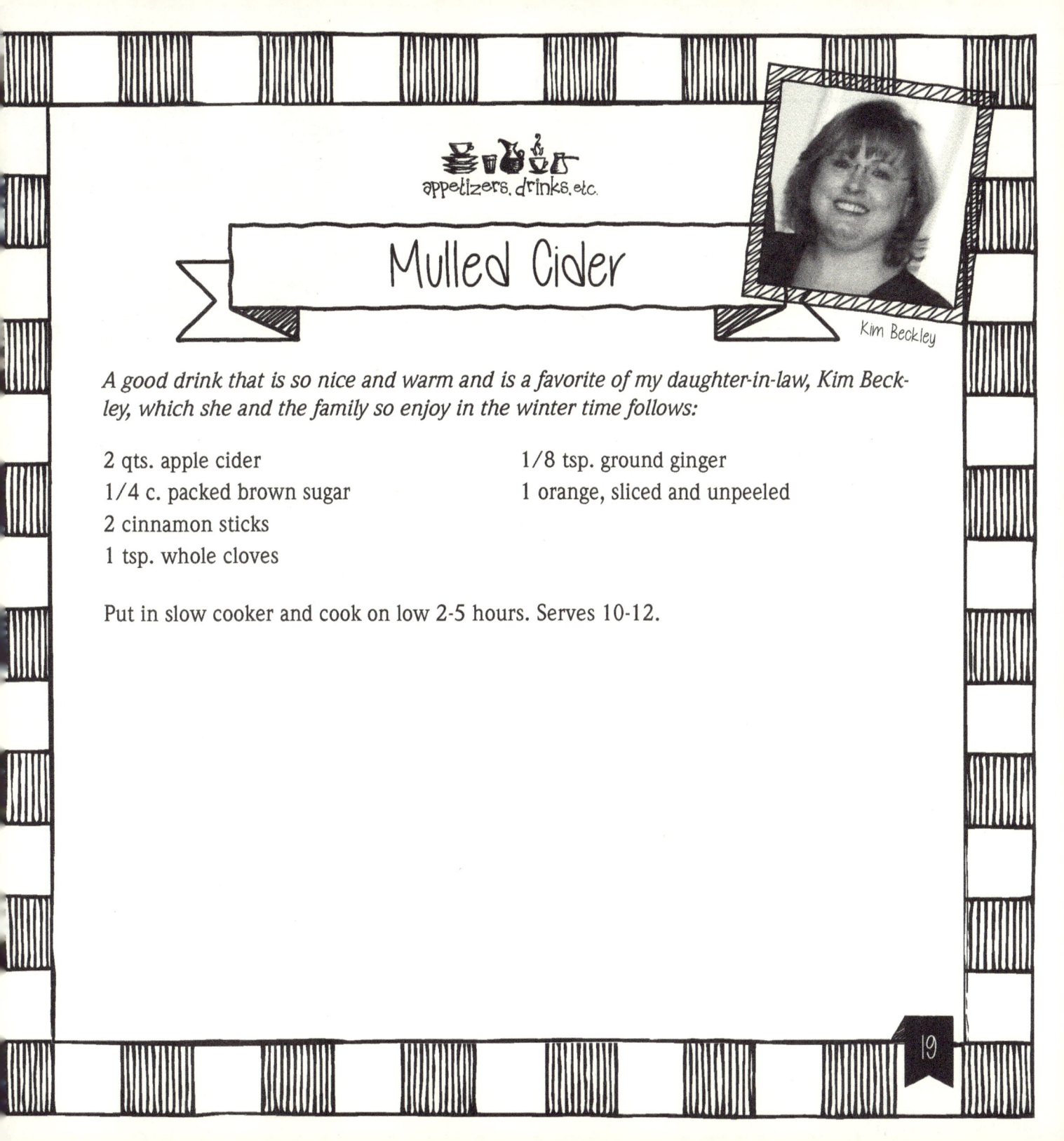

Mulled Cider

Kim Beckley

A good drink that is so nice and warm and is a favorite of my daughter-in-law, Kim Beckley, which she and the family so enjoy in the winter time follows:

2 qts. apple cider
1/4 c. packed brown sugar
2 cinnamon sticks
1 tsp. whole cloves

1/8 tsp. ground ginger
1 orange, sliced and unpeeled

Put in slow cooker and cook on low 2-5 hours. Serves 10-12.

appetizers, drinks, etc.

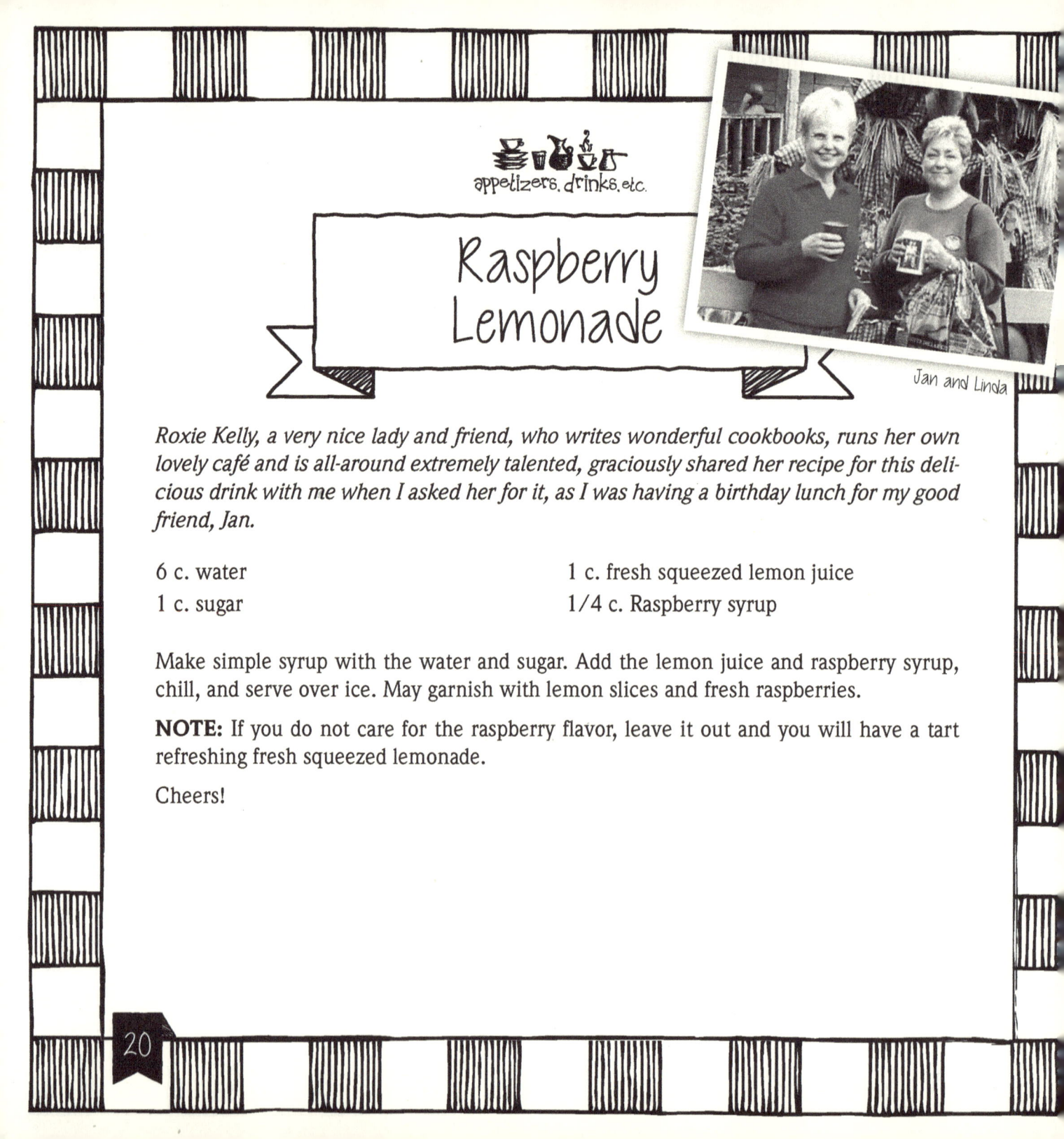

Raspberry Lemonade

Jan and Linda

Roxie Kelly, a very nice lady and friend, who writes wonderful cookbooks, runs her own lovely café and is all-around extremely talented, graciously shared her recipe for this delicious drink with me when I asked her for it, as I was having a birthday lunch for my good friend, Jan.

6 c. water
1 c. sugar
1 c. fresh squeezed lemon juice
1/4 c. Raspberry syrup

Make simple syrup with the water and sugar. Add the lemon juice and raspberry syrup, chill, and serve over ice. May garnish with lemon slices and fresh raspberries.

NOTE: If you do not care for the raspberry flavor, leave it out and you will have a tart refreshing fresh squeezed lemonade.

Cheers!

appetizers, drinks, etc.

Russian Tea

This is a great instant hot tea that is so good to sip in the winter. It is from Steve's sister-in-law, Marilyn, from South Carolina.

2 c. Tang
1/2 c. instant tea
1 tsp. cinnamon
1/2 tsp. of powdered cloves
1 tsp. lemon peel (optional)

Mix all ingredients, keep in tight container. Use two heaping teaspoons of mix per mug of boiling water.

appetizers, drinks, etc.

Homemade Cappuccino

One Christmas my Mom was given this mix as a wonderful gift from her friend, Judy Dye. The recipe was tied to the container, and we make it over and over to enjoy during the frosty days of fall and winter.

- 1 c. dry coffee creamer (any flavor). I like Amaretto or Hazelnut.
- 1 c. instant cocoa mix
- 2/3 c. instant coffee crystals
- 1/2 c. sugar
- 1/2 tsp. cinnamon

Mix all ingredients well. Use 3 heaping teaspoons in 1 cup of hot water. Adjust to your taste.

appetizers, drinks, etc.

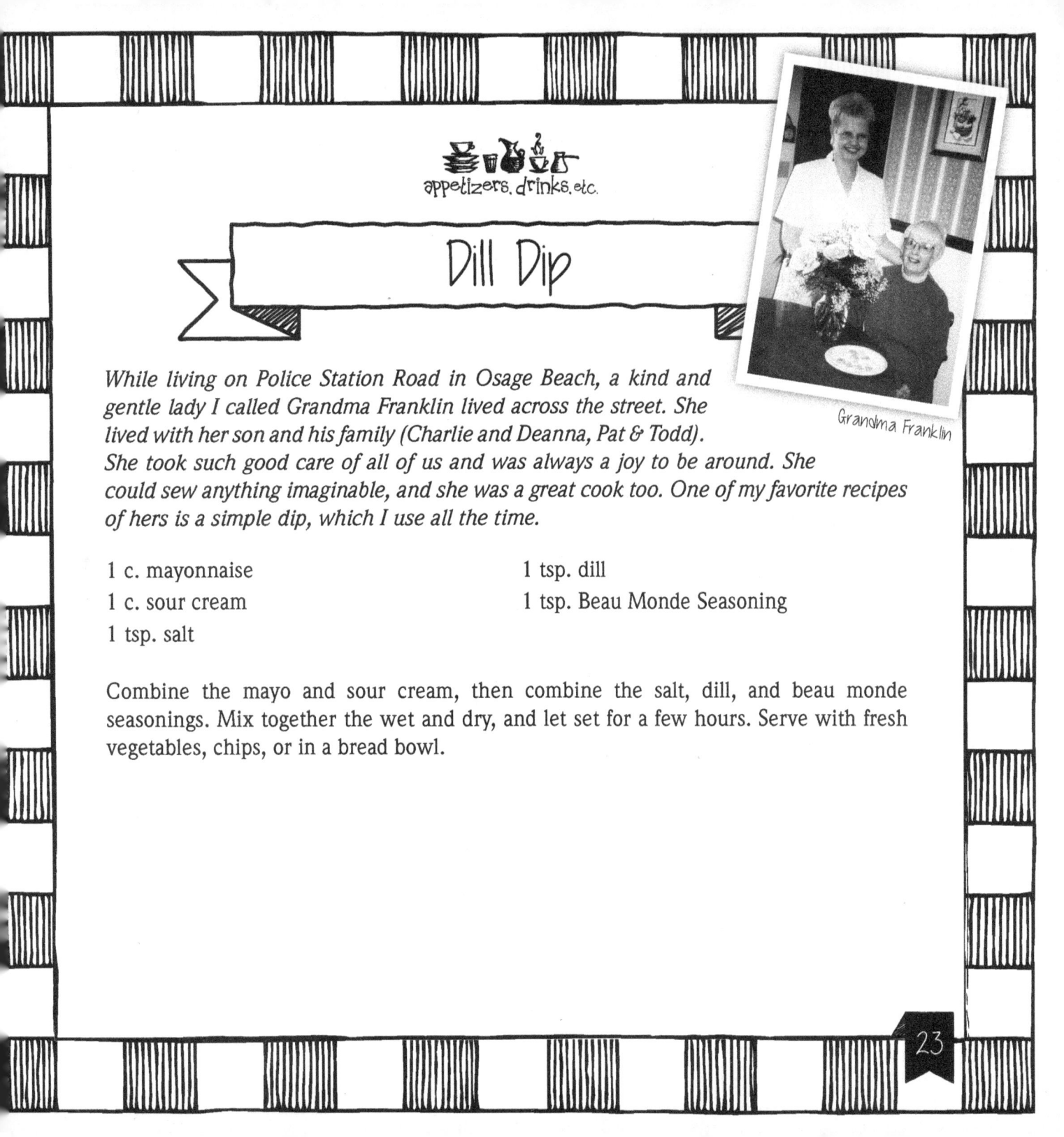

Dill Dip

Grandma Franklin

While living on Police Station Road in Osage Beach, a kind and gentle lady I called Grandma Franklin lived across the street. She lived with her son and his family (Charlie and Deanna, Pat & Todd). She took such good care of all of us and was always a joy to be around. She could sew anything imaginable, and she was a great cook too. One of my favorite recipes of hers is a simple dip, which I use all the time.

1 c. mayonnaise
1 c. sour cream
1 tsp. salt
1 tsp. dill
1 tsp. Beau Monde Seasoning

Combine the mayo and sour cream, then combine the salt, dill, and beau monde seasonings. Mix together the wet and dry, and let set for a few hours. Serve with fresh vegetables, chips, or in a bread bowl.

appetizers, drinks, etc.

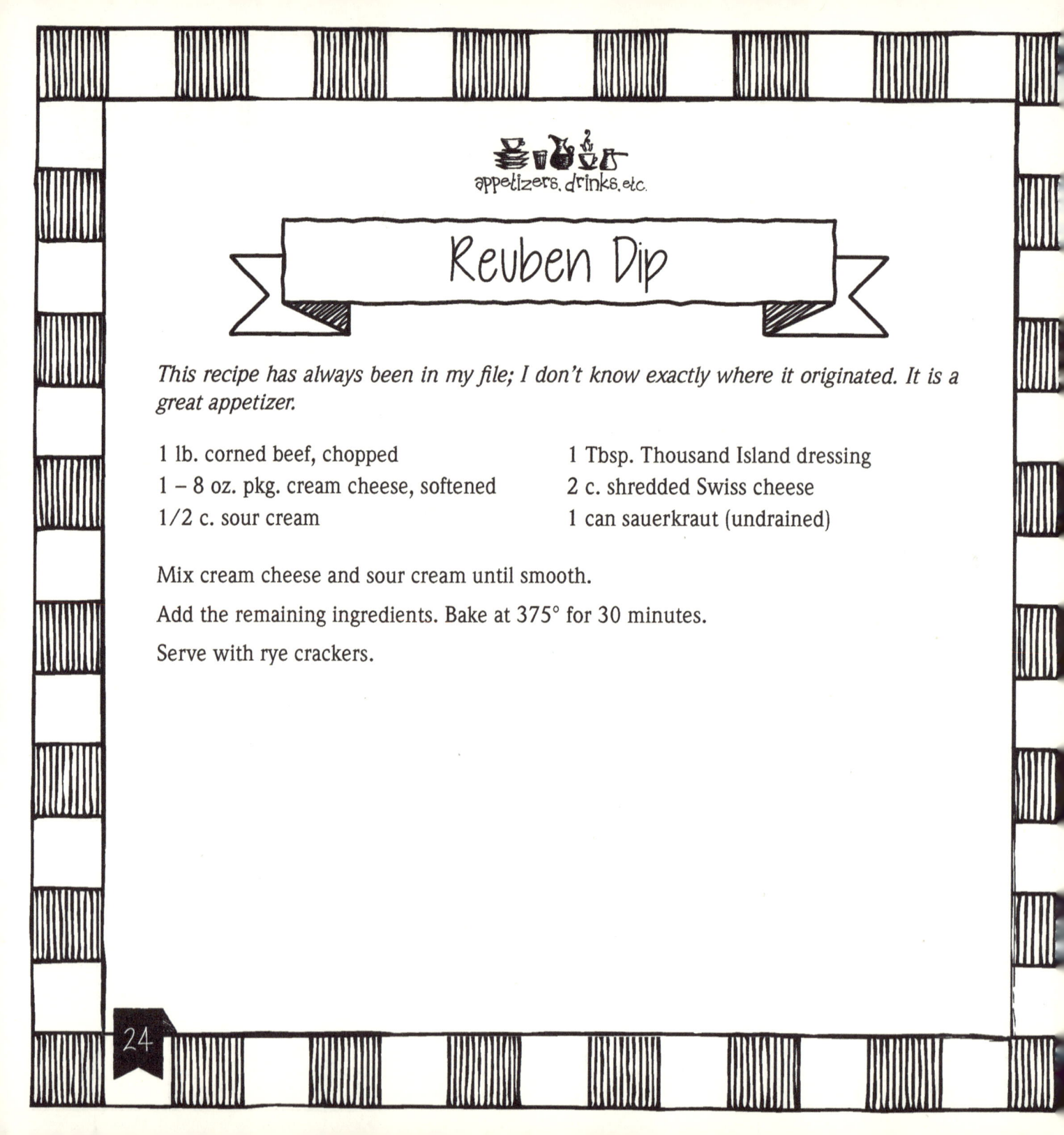

Reuben Dip

This recipe has always been in my file; I don't know exactly where it originated. It is a great appetizer.

1 lb. corned beef, chopped
1 – 8 oz. pkg. cream cheese, softened
1/2 c. sour cream
1 Tbsp. Thousand Island dressing
2 c. shredded Swiss cheese
1 can sauerkraut (undrained)

Mix cream cheese and sour cream until smooth.

Add the remaining ingredients. Bake at 375° for 30 minutes.

Serve with rye crackers.

appetizers, drinks, etc.

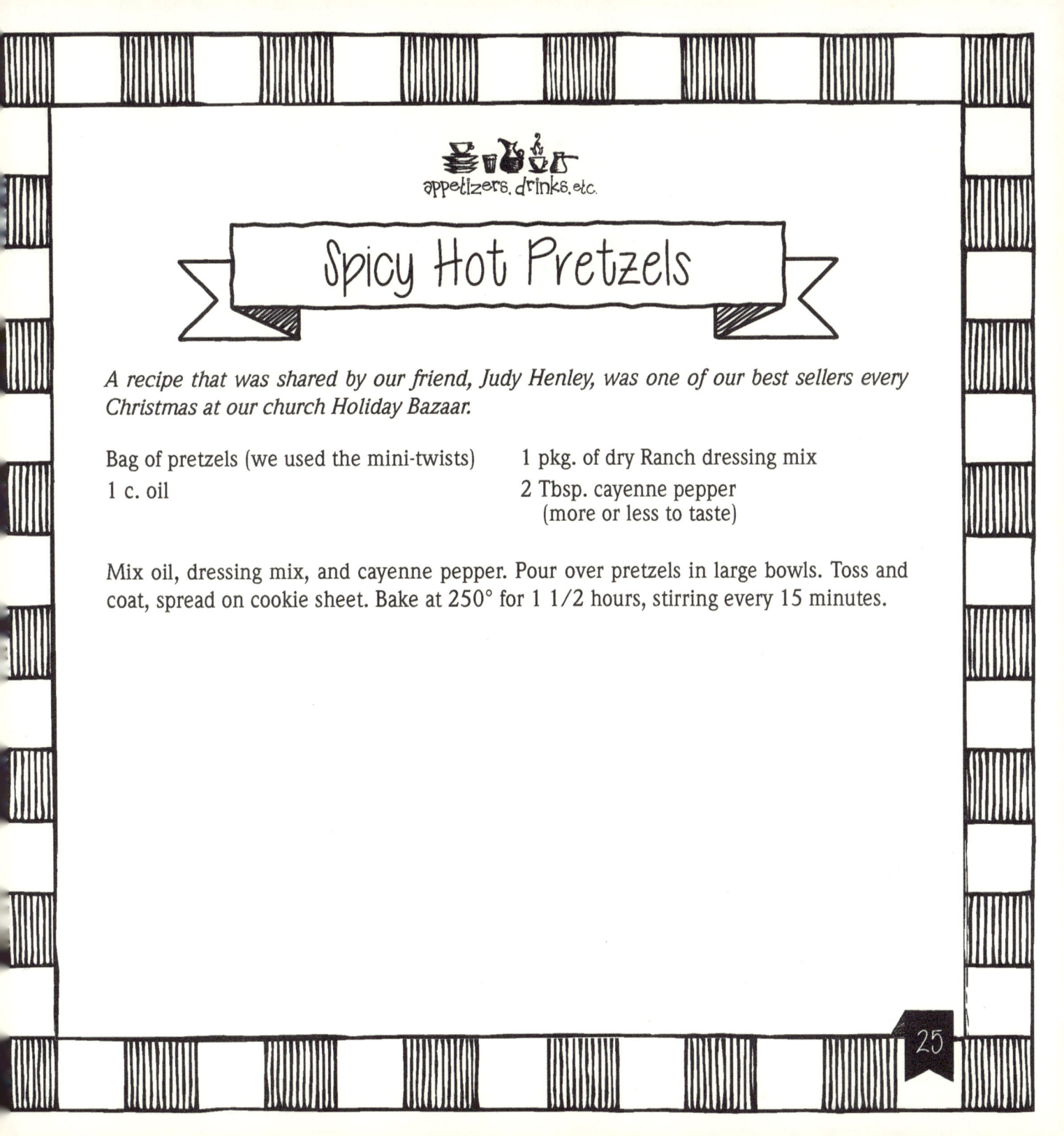

Spicy Hot Pretzels

A recipe that was shared by our friend, Judy Henley, was one of our best sellers every Christmas at our church Holiday Bazaar.

Bag of pretzels (we used the mini-twists)
1 c. oil
1 pkg. of dry Ranch dressing mix
2 Tbsp. cayenne pepper (more or less to taste)

Mix oil, dressing mix, and cayenne pepper. Pour over pretzels in large bowls. Toss and coat, spread on cookie sheet. Bake at 250° for 1 1/2 hours, stirring every 15 minutes.

appetizers, drinks, etc.

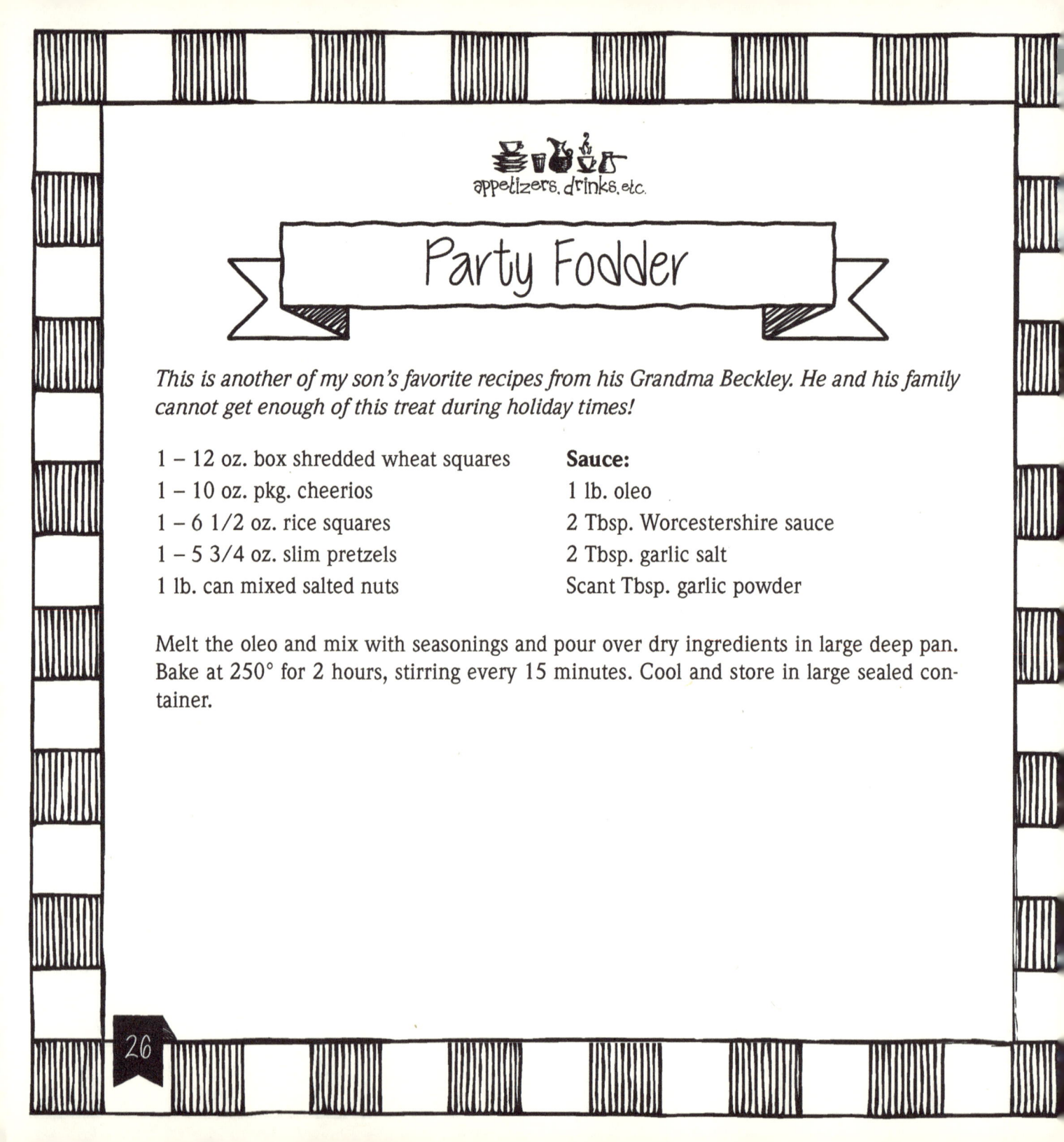

Party Fodder

This is another of my son's favorite recipes from his Grandma Beckley. He and his family cannot get enough of this treat during holiday times!

1 – 12 oz. box shredded wheat squares
1 – 10 oz. pkg. cheerios
1 – 6 1/2 oz. rice squares
1 – 5 3/4 oz. slim pretzels
1 lb. can mixed salted nuts

Sauce:
1 lb. oleo
2 Tbsp. Worcestershire sauce
2 Tbsp. garlic salt
Scant Tbsp. garlic powder

Melt the oleo and mix with seasonings and pour over dry ingredients in large deep pan. Bake at 250° for 2 hours, stirring every 15 minutes. Cool and store in large sealed container.

appetizers, drinks, etc.

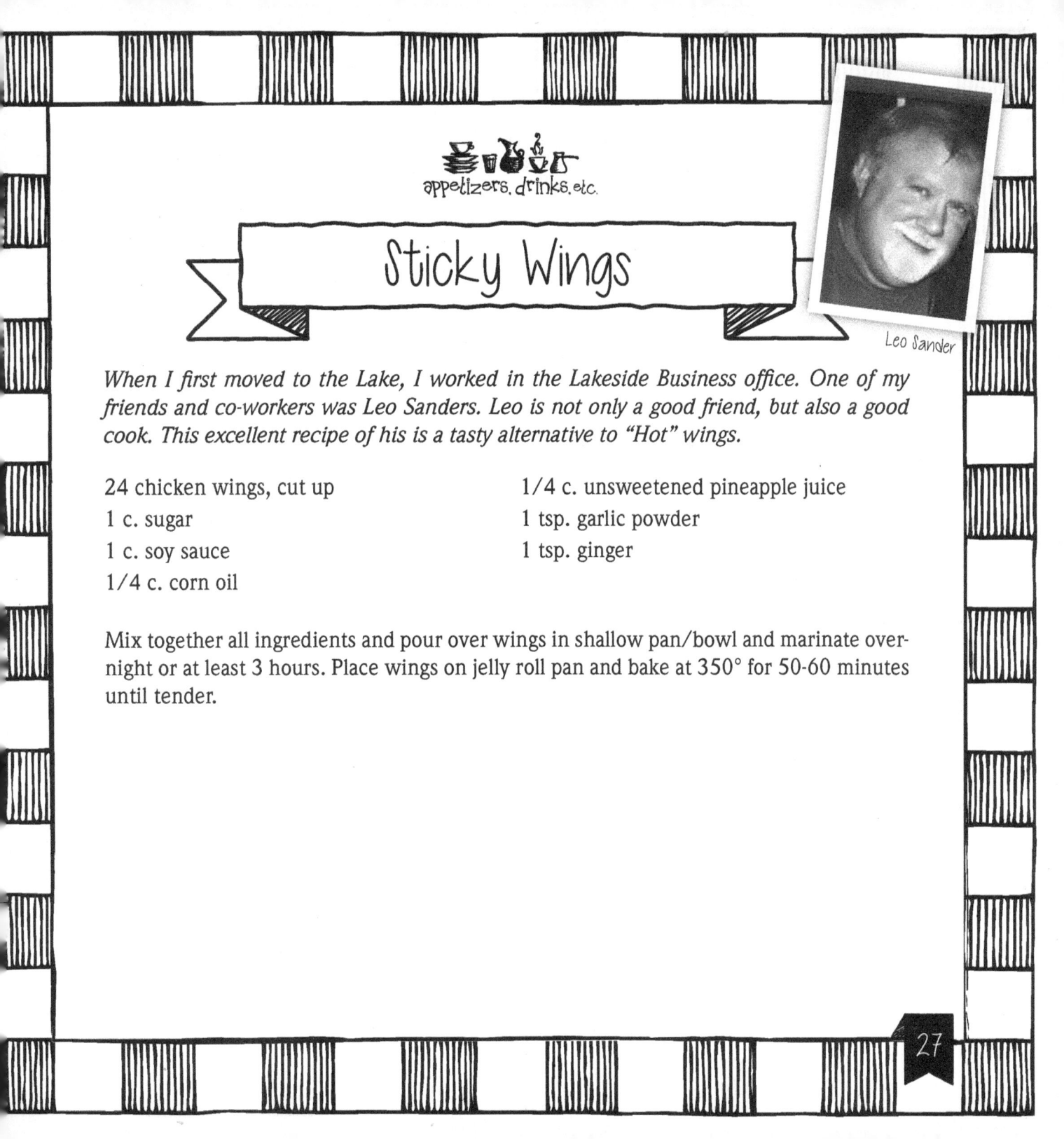

Sticky Wings

Leo Sander

When I first moved to the Lake, I worked in the Lakeside Business office. One of my friends and co-workers was Leo Sanders. Leo is not only a good friend, but also a good cook. This excellent recipe of his is a tasty alternative to "Hot" wings.

24 chicken wings, cut up
1 c. sugar
1 c. soy sauce
1/4 c. corn oil

1/4 c. unsweetened pineapple juice
1 tsp. garlic powder
1 tsp. ginger

Mix together all ingredients and pour over wings in shallow pan/bowl and marinate overnight or at least 3 hours. Place wings on jelly roll pan and bake at 350° for 50-60 minutes until tender.

appetizers, drinks, etc.

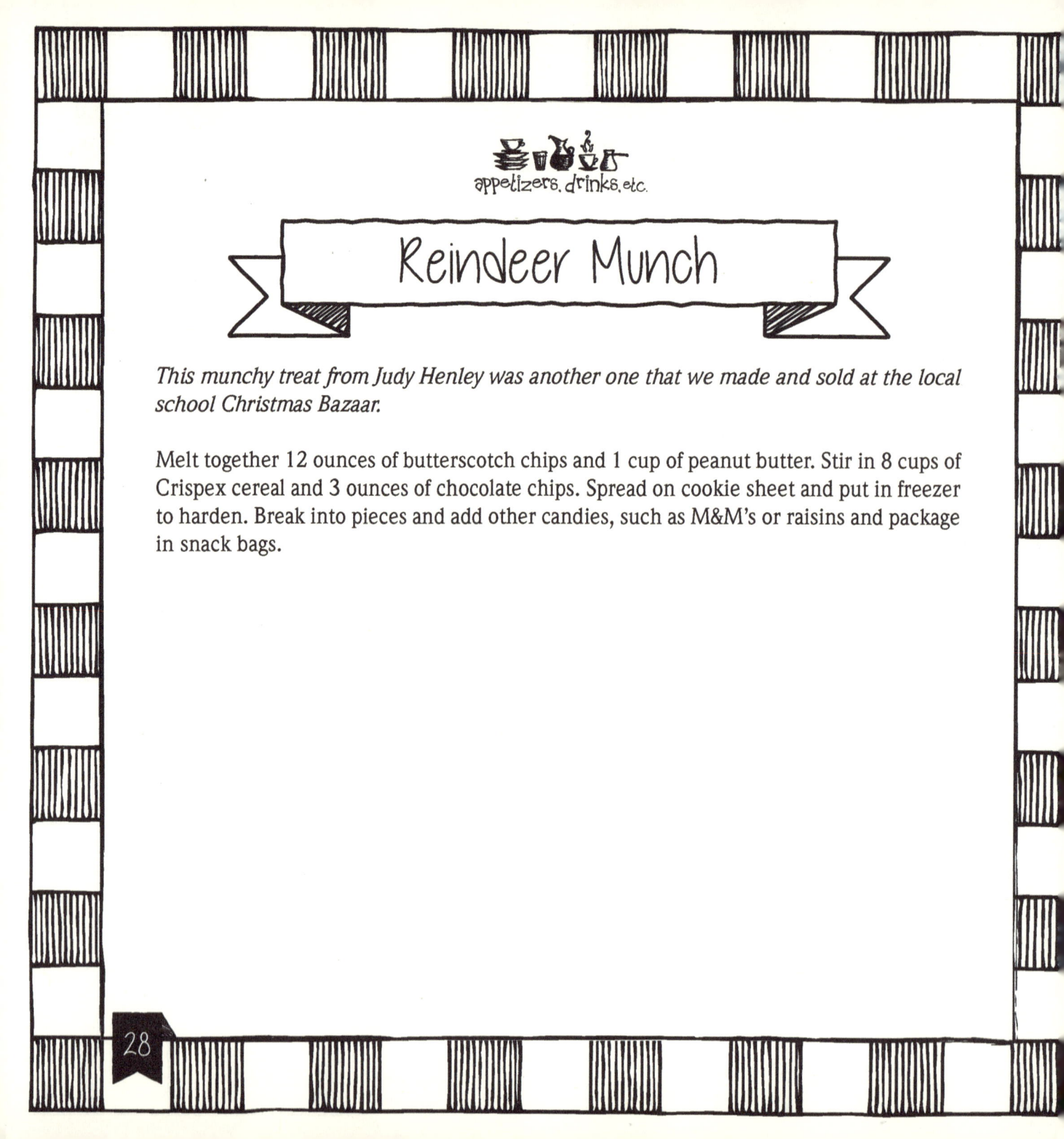

Reindeer Munch

This munchy treat from Judy Henley was another one that we made and sold at the local school Christmas Bazaar.

Melt together 12 ounces of butterscotch chips and 1 cup of peanut butter. Stir in 8 cups of Crispex cereal and 3 ounces of chocolate chips. Spread on cookie sheet and put in freezer to harden. Break into pieces and add other candies, such as M&M's or raisins and package in snack bags.

appetizers, drinks, etc.

Cream Cheese Mints

I have made these mints several times for various fun occasions. You can tint them to fit the color scheme of showers, weddings, parties, etc.

4 oz. cream cheese (room temperature)
1 2/3 c. powdered sugar
1/8-1/4 tsp. oil of peppermint

Gel food coloring
Granulated sugar
Flexible rubber mint molds

Mix together cream cheese, powdered sugar, peppermint, and food coloring. Shape into small balls, roll in granulated sugar and press into mint mold. After filling molds, pop out, store chilled in container, between wax paper, until ready to serve.

appetizers, drinks, etc.

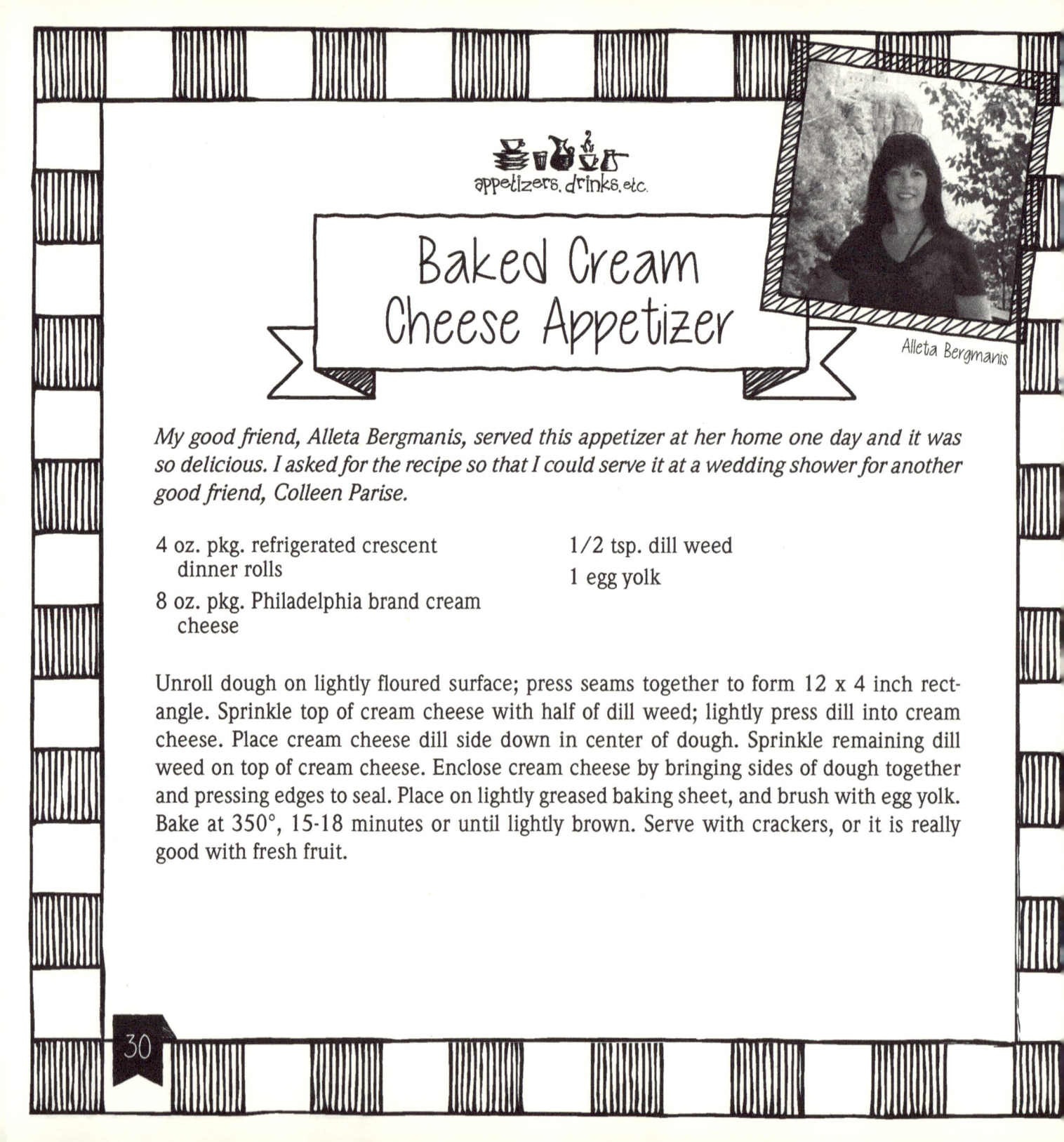

Baked Cream Cheese Appetizer

Alleta Bergmanis

My good friend, Alleta Bergmanis, served this appetizer at her home one day and it was so delicious. I asked for the recipe so that I could serve it at a wedding shower for another good friend, Colleen Parise.

- 4 oz. pkg. refrigerated crescent dinner rolls
- 8 oz. pkg. Philadelphia brand cream cheese
- 1/2 tsp. dill weed
- 1 egg yolk

Unroll dough on lightly floured surface; press seams together to form 12 x 4 inch rectangle. Sprinkle top of cream cheese with half of dill weed; lightly press dill into cream cheese. Place cream cheese dill side down in center of dough. Sprinkle remaining dill weed on top of cream cheese. Enclose cream cheese by bringing sides of dough together and pressing edges to seal. Place on lightly greased baking sheet, and brush with egg yolk. Bake at 350°, 15-18 minutes or until lightly brown. Serve with crackers, or it is really good with fresh fruit.

appetizers, drinks, etc.

Hot Artichoke Augratin with French Bread Dippers

When I first moved to the Lake of the Ozarks, my first supervisor at the Lakeside Business office was Joyce Rader. She shared this delicious warm dip recipe that was loved by everyone at the office. There are additional recipes throughout the book that Joyce gave to me over the years.

- 1/2 c. slivered blanched almonds
- 1 can (14 oz.) artichoke hearts, drained and finely chopped
- 1 c. grated parmesan cheese
- 1 c. mayonnaise

Preheat oven to 350°. Place almonds in shallow baking pan. Place in preheated oven for 5 minutes turning once until lightly brown. Cool in pan on wire rack. Combine artichokes, cheese, and mayonnaise in a medium bowl, stirring well. Spoon into a shallow 2 cup baking dish. Bake at 350° for 30 minutes or until bubbly. Remove, sprinkle with toasted almonds, and serve with toasted French bread cut in 1/2-inch strips.

Linda and Joyce Rader

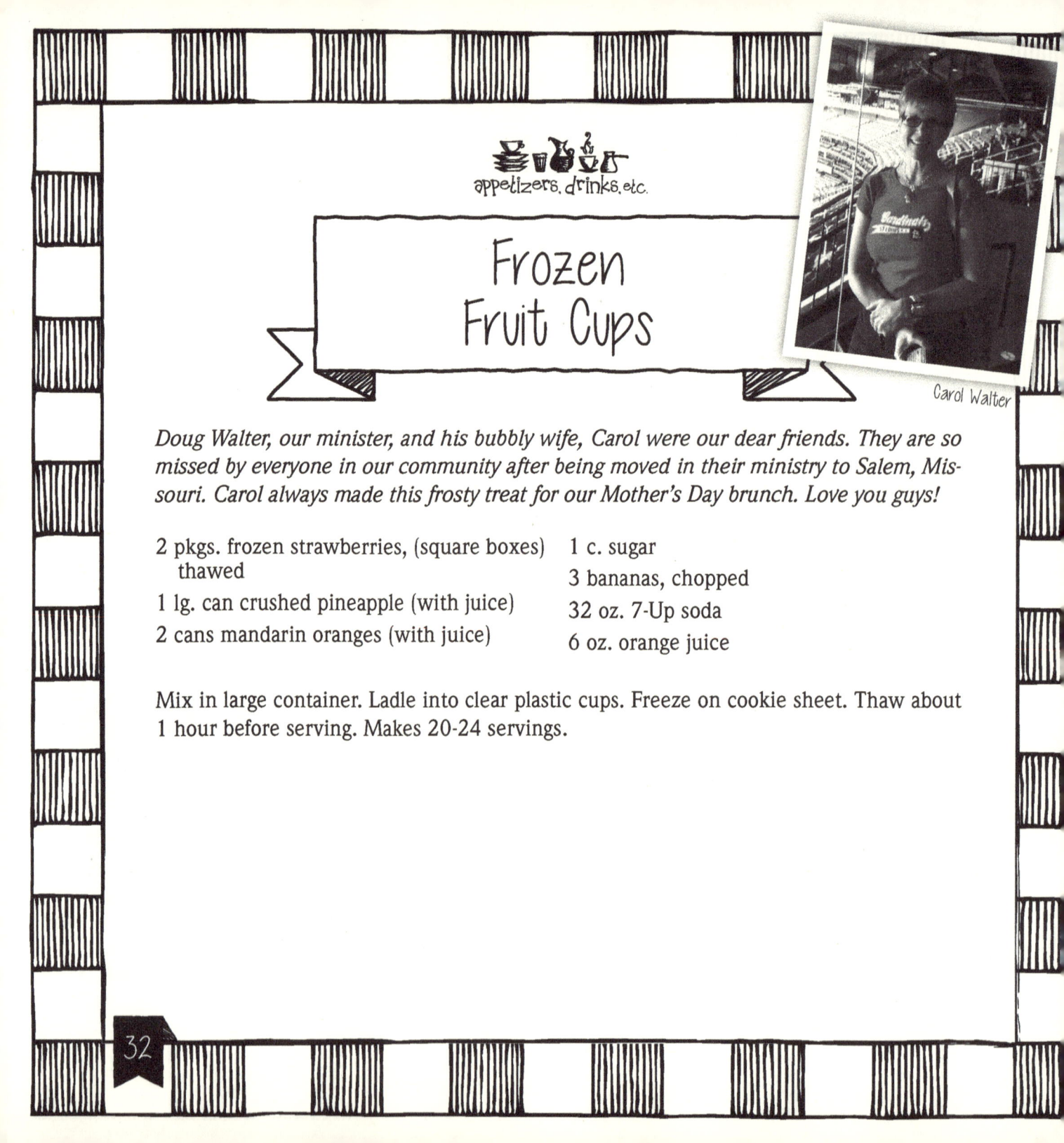

appetizers, drinks, etc.

Frozen Fruit Cups

Carol Walter

Doug Walter, our minister, and his bubbly wife, Carol were our dear friends. They are so missed by everyone in our community after being moved in their ministry to Salem, Missouri. Carol always made this frosty treat for our Mother's Day brunch. Love you guys!

- 2 pkgs. frozen strawberries, (square boxes) thawed
- 1 lg. can crushed pineapple (with juice)
- 2 cans mandarin oranges (with juice)
- 1 c. sugar
- 3 bananas, chopped
- 32 oz. 7-Up soda
- 6 oz. orange juice

Mix in large container. Ladle into clear plastic cups. Freeze on cookie sheet. Thaw about 1 hour before serving. Makes 20-24 servings.

appetizers, drinks, etc.

Cheese Rolls

My sister, Katherine and her husband, Ron ran Village Cheese and Wine Shop in Mexico, MO. Every year at Christmas there were hundreds of gift baskets made. We worked morning, noon, and night until the job was complete. One of the most requested items in the basket was Mom's (Eulah Becker) cheese rolls. This is the wonderful recipe.

Leave at room temperature until soft:

- 3 – 8 oz. pkgs. cream cheese
- 2 c. grated blue cheese
- 2 c. grated sharp cheddar cheese

Mix well into the cheese:

- 1 Tbsp. garlic salt
- 2 Tbsp. Worcestershire sauce
- 1/2 to 1/3 c. grated onion, juice included (I leave out, because I don't like onions)

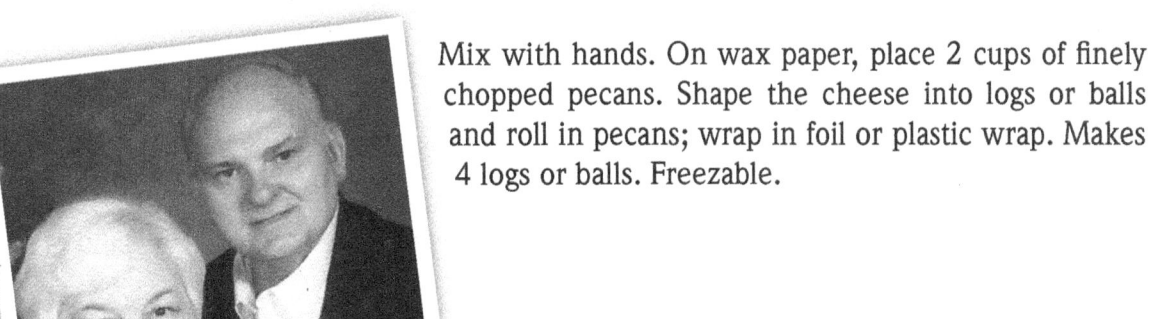

Mix with hands. On wax paper, place 2 cups of finely chopped pecans. Shape the cheese into logs or balls and roll in pecans; wrap in foil or plastic wrap. Makes 4 logs or balls. Freezable.

Katherine and Ron

appetizers, drinks, etc.

Korean Egg Rolls

My husband, Steve, had friends in Clayton, Illinois. They were Mark and Helen Kim from Korea. Mark was a Presbyterian minister. They shared this appetizer with him, and it is a great recipe to make with and for friends as it makes quite a large amount.

Filling:
- 1 1/2 lbs. ground pork (do not use sausage)
- 1/2 lb. hamburger
- 4 eggs
- 1 tsp. sesame oil
- 3 Tbsp. soy sauce
- 2 c. shredded cabbage
- 1 c. chopped onion

If the pre-cut, smaller wonton skins (approximately 3 x 3) are not available, purchase the large skins and cut into 4 squares. Wontons are usually in the fresh produce area at your local grocer. Small wontons come about 50 in a package. One recipe makes approximately 200 egg rolls.

Arrange a group of skins so that 1/4-inch of 2 sides is exposed as shown in diagram.

Beat 1 egg, then with a basting brush, brush the exposed edges of the skins with beaten egg (for sealing purposes).

Place about 1/2 teaspoon of meat mixture in center of skin, fold into a triangle and press edges together.

Fry in sesame oil in electric skillet (350°) until golden brown.

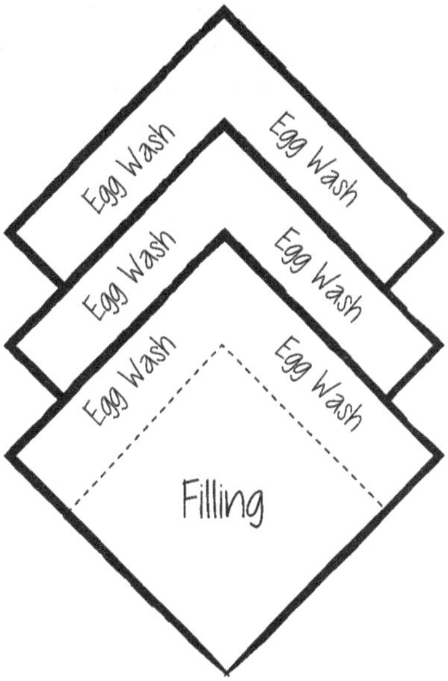
Egg Wash
Egg Wash
Egg Wash
Egg Wash
Egg Wash
Egg Wash
Filling

Cooked Egg rolls can be frozen. To serve, take from freezer, place on cookie sheet, and place in preheated 350 degree oven for 8-10 minutes. Do not heat in microwave.

Sauce:

1 c. yellow mustard

2 tsp. soy sauce

1/2 tsp. vinegar – small amount

1 1/2 c. sugar

Mix to taste. It will take a lot of sugar. If the sauce has too much of mustard or vinegar taste, add more soy sauce and sugar.

appetizers, drinks, etc.

Marcie's Spiced Pecans

I have two recipes for Spiced Pecans. The first is sugar and spice given to me by my friend, Marcie Vansyoc, a sweetheart of a person from Camdenton, Missouri. The other is a more savory version from my sister-in-law in South Carolina, Marilyn Hofstetter.

1 egg white
1 tsp. salt
4 c. pecan halves

1/2 c. sugar
1/2 tsp. cinnamon

Beat the egg white and salt together with a fork in a large bowl. Add the pecan halves and toss lightly until well coated. Mix together the sugar and cinnamon and sprinkle over pecans, tossing well. Bake on a cookie sheet sprayed with PAM in a 225 degree oven for 1 hour. Nuts should look dry and aren't sticky when done. Cool on brown paper.

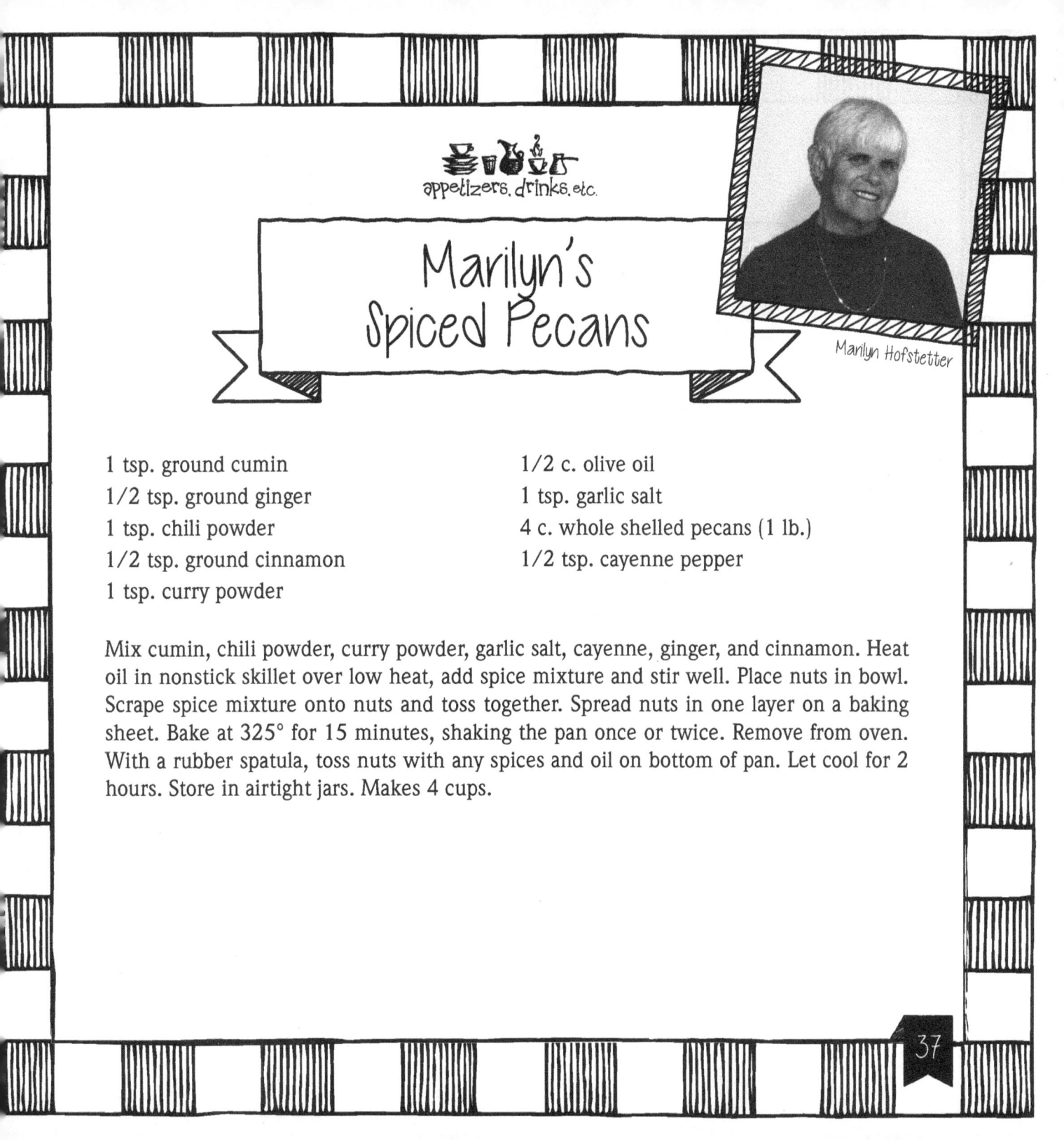

appetizers, drinks, etc.

Marilyn's Spiced Pecans

Marilyn Hofstetter

1 tsp. ground cumin
1/2 tsp. ground ginger
1 tsp. chili powder
1/2 tsp. ground cinnamon
1 tsp. curry powder

1/2 c. olive oil
1 tsp. garlic salt
4 c. whole shelled pecans (1 lb.)
1/2 tsp. cayenne pepper

Mix cumin, chili powder, curry powder, garlic salt, cayenne, ginger, and cinnamon. Heat oil in nonstick skillet over low heat, add spice mixture and stir well. Place nuts in bowl. Scrape spice mixture onto nuts and toss together. Spread nuts in one layer on a baking sheet. Bake at 325° for 15 minutes, shaking the pan once or twice. Remove from oven. With a rubber spatula, toss nuts with any spices and oil on bottom of pan. Let cool for 2 hours. Store in airtight jars. Makes 4 cups.

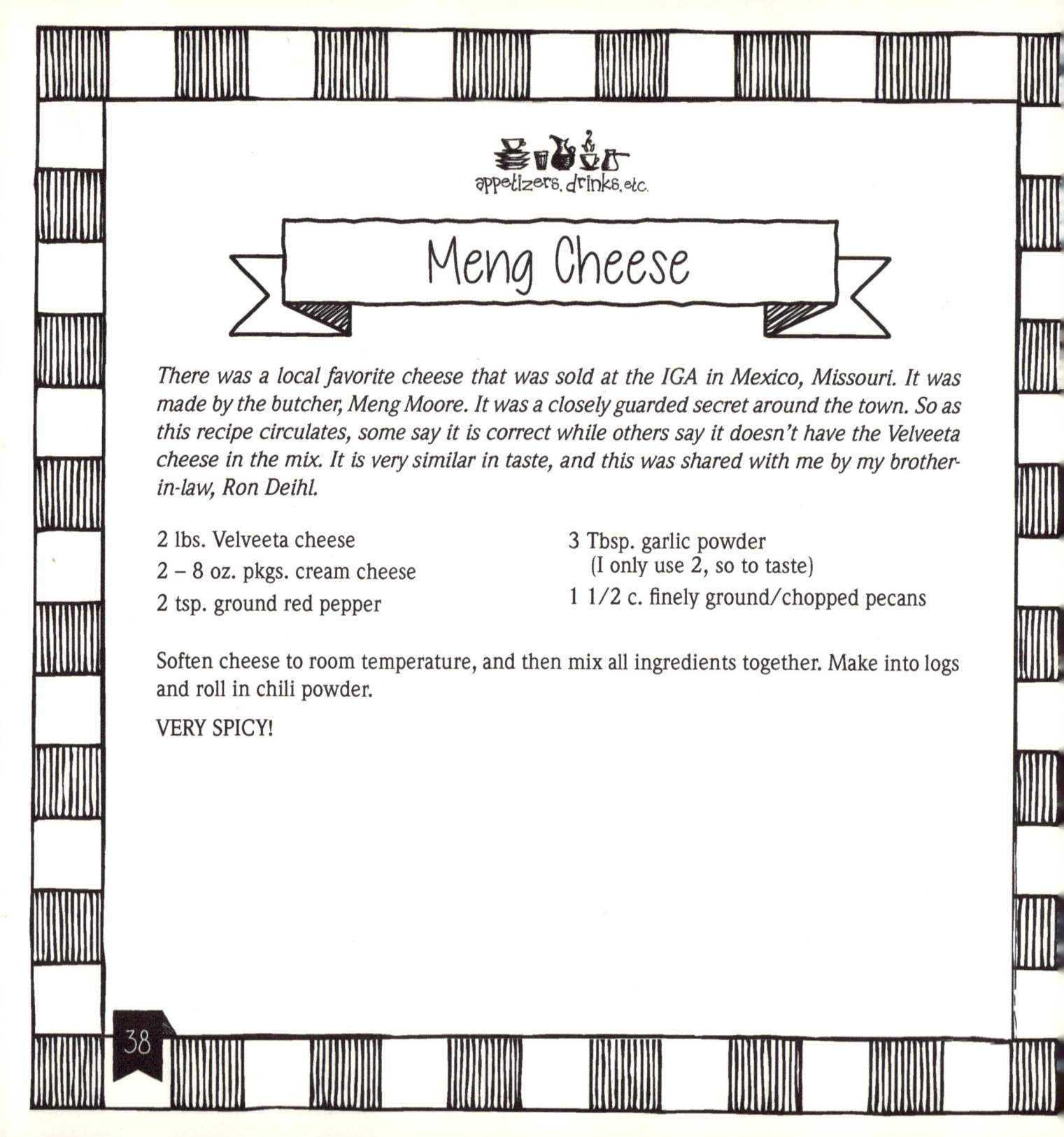

appetizers, drinks, etc.

Meng Cheese

There was a local favorite cheese that was sold at the IGA in Mexico, Missouri. It was made by the butcher, Meng Moore. It was a closely guarded secret around the town. So as this recipe circulates, some say it is correct while others say it doesn't have the Velveeta cheese in the mix. It is very similar in taste, and this was shared with me by my brother-in-law, Ron Deihl.

- 2 lbs. Velveeta cheese
- 2 – 8 oz. pkgs. cream cheese
- 2 tsp. ground red pepper
- 3 Tbsp. garlic powder (I only use 2, so to taste)
- 1 1/2 c. finely ground/chopped pecans

Soften cheese to room temperature, and then mix all ingredients together. Make into logs and roll in chili powder.

VERY SPICY!

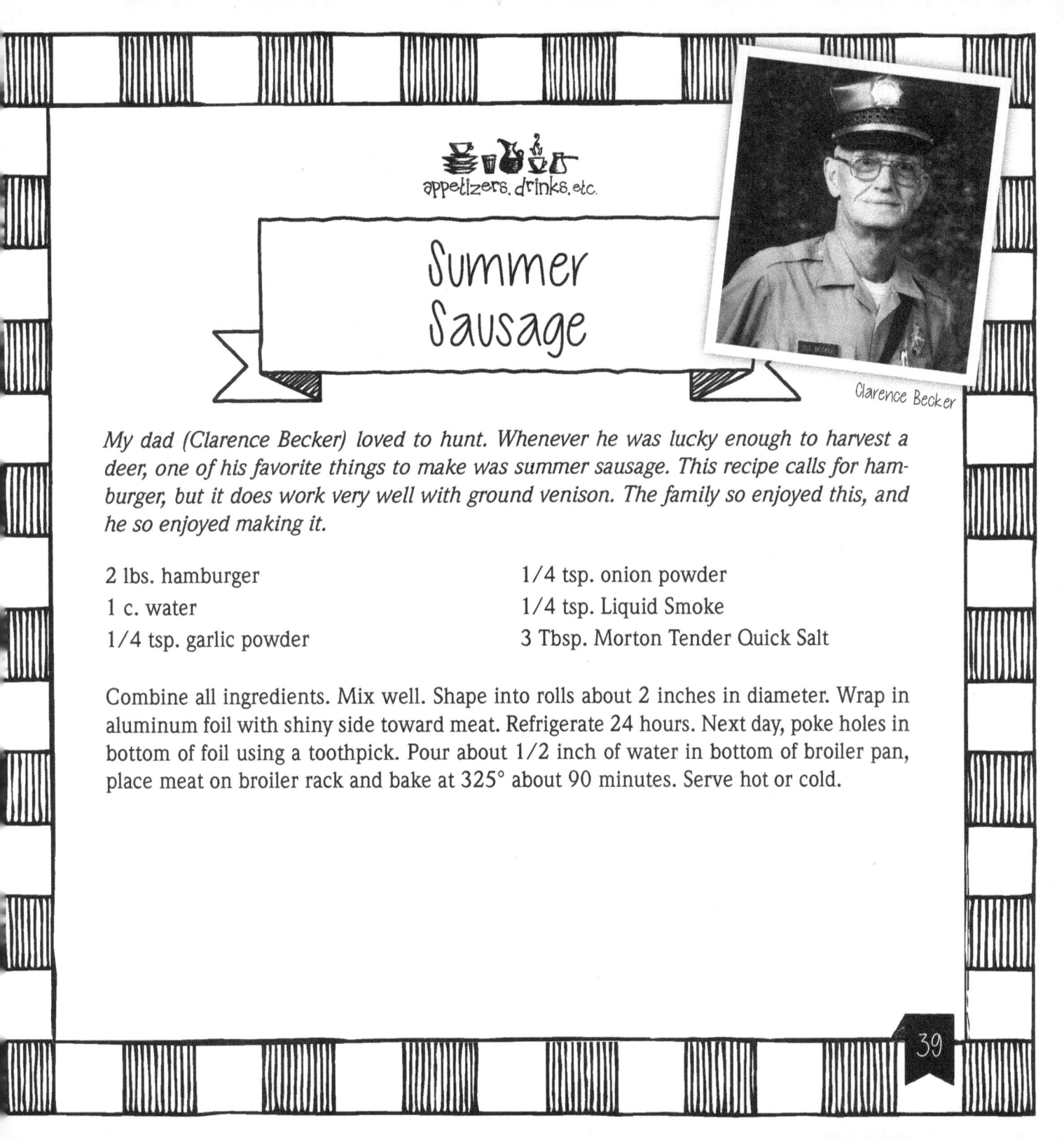

appetizers, drinks, etc.

Summer Sausage

Clarence Becker

My dad (Clarence Becker) loved to hunt. Whenever he was lucky enough to harvest a deer, one of his favorite things to make was summer sausage. This recipe calls for hamburger, but it does work very well with ground venison. The family so enjoyed this, and he so enjoyed making it.

- 2 lbs. hamburger
- 1 c. water
- 1/4 tsp. garlic powder
- 1/4 tsp. onion powder
- 1/4 tsp. Liquid Smoke
- 3 Tbsp. Morton Tender Quick Salt

Combine all ingredients. Mix well. Shape into rolls about 2 inches in diameter. Wrap in aluminum foil with shiny side toward meat. Refrigerate 24 hours. Next day, poke holes in bottom of foil using a toothpick. Pour about 1/2 inch of water in bottom of broiler pan, place meat on broiler rack and bake at 325° about 90 minutes. Serve hot or cold.

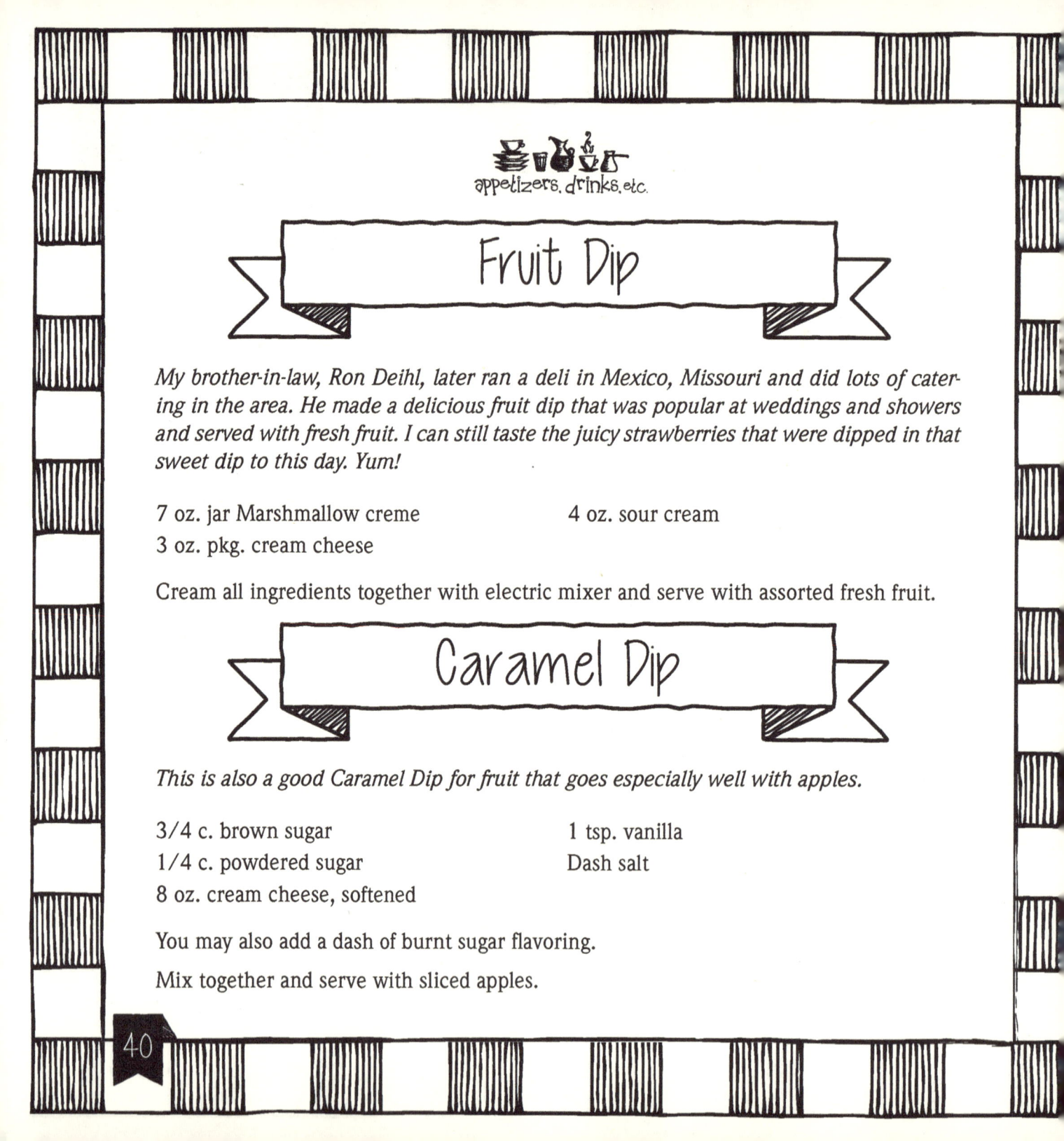

appetizers, drinks, etc.

Fruit Dip

My brother-in-law, Ron Deihl, later ran a deli in Mexico, Missouri and did lots of catering in the area. He made a delicious fruit dip that was popular at weddings and showers and served with fresh fruit. I can still taste the juicy strawberries that were dipped in that sweet dip to this day. Yum!

7 oz. jar Marshmallow creme
3 oz. pkg. cream cheese
4 oz. sour cream

Cream all ingredients together with electric mixer and serve with assorted fresh fruit.

Caramel Dip

This is also a good Caramel Dip for fruit that goes especially well with apples.

3/4 c. brown sugar
1/4 c. powdered sugar
8 oz. cream cheese, softened
1 tsp. vanilla
Dash salt

You may also add a dash of burnt sugar flavoring.

Mix together and serve with sliced apples.

appetizers, drinks, etc.

Cheese Tid-Bits

Marge and Linda

My good friend, Marge Winters, was one of the best cooks I have ever known. She always had a recipe and a great meal to be shared. She was a great friend and confidant. This recipe is for a tasty appetizer which she always kept on hand to serve with a frosty beverage when anyone stopped by to visit.

1/2 lb. grated extra-sharp cheddar cheese
1/2 b. butter
2 c. flour
1 tsp. salt
Dash red pepper (to taste)
2 3/4 c. Rice Krispies

Let cheese and butter soften, cream together. Add flour, salt, red pepper and knead. Add Rice Krispies and make into small balls. Bake at 375° for 15 minutes. These stay crisp for a long time in a Tupperware container. (Refrigerate or freeze until ready to use.)

appetizers, drinks, etc.

Rainy's Meatballs

Rainy Turner Burris

I had a wonderful friend, Rainy Turner Burris. Rainy had a contagious laugh and was always fun to be around. She liked to make a crock pot of meatballs with this wonderful sauce on them. They were one of my son Brent's favorites, and he was never shy about asking her to bring them when she was coming to visit. Our dear friend passed away suddenly in 2012, and her laugh and smile will be forever remembered.

Lg. pkg. frozen meatballs
Sauce:
1 lb. can of cranberry sauce
12 oz. jar chili sauce
1 Tbsp. lemon juice
2 Tbsp. brown sugar

Put meatballs in crock pot, mix all sauce ingredients together and pour over meatballs; cook in crock pot until heated through and serve hot.

Jeane's Chicken Salad {page 48}

sides & salads

43

sides & salads

Corn Casserole

My husband Steve, had a wonderful sister, also named Linda. She raised five wonderful children, who still to this day, miss her so much. Prior to Linda's passing in 2001, she made every family gathering for holidays and celebrations a time for making special memories. Linda never failed to make Corn Casserole, a favorite side dish of her brother and family.

1 can corn, drained
2 cans creamed corn
1 egg, beaten
1 tsp. sugar
1/2 c. milk
1 sleeve of crackers, crushed
2 Tbsp. butter, cut into pats

Mix together the cans of corn, egg, sugar, milk, and crushed crackers. Pour in a greased 8 x 11 casserole dish and top with pats of butter. Bake at 350° for 45 minutes, until set in the middle and golden brown.

Ken, Linda, Steve

sides & salads

Pat Darnell's Creamy Hot Bacon Salad

Jan Parish's friend, Pat Darnell (formerly of Springfield, MO and now of Anaconda, MT) one day hosted a lovely luncheon for Jenny Tracey (a dear friend who passed away with lung cancer), and she served this delicious salad.

Ingredients:

- 1 bag of Romaine style lettuce (washed, drained and chilled)
- Assorted veggies of choice, cleaned and chilled (i.e. broccoli, cauliflower, tomatoes, red onions, etc.
- 3-4 pieces of bacon, cut up fine and fried crisp
- Browned croutons in butter—use approximately 1/2 c. croutons and 1/4 c. butter
- Nuts of choice - almonds, walnuts, or pecans. Approximately 1/2 cup nuts coarsely chopped in sugar and butter. Use 2 to 3 tablespoons of sugar and 1/4 stick of butter (combined and sautéed in skillet).

Combine all the above and then add the dressing.

Dressing:

- 3/4 c. mayonnaise
- 1/3 c. cider vinegar
- 1/3 c. sugar

Mix, then cook until ready to boil. Serve warm over salad. Dressing can be made ahead and heated at last minute, if desired.

sides & salads

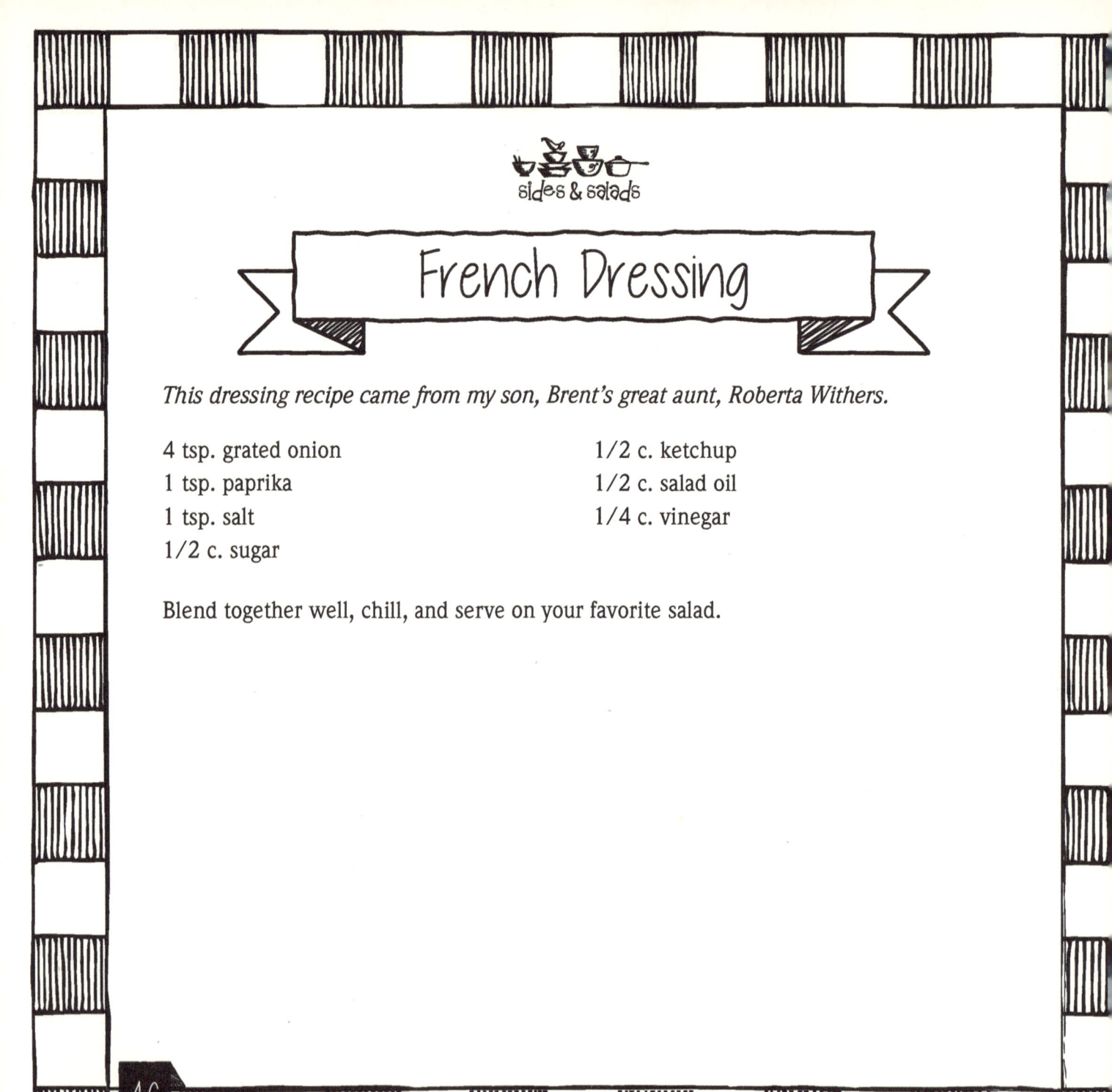

French Dressing

This dressing recipe came from my son, Brent's great aunt, Roberta Withers.

4 tsp. grated onion
1 tsp. paprika
1 tsp. salt
1/2 c. sugar
1/2 c. ketchup
1/2 c. salad oil
1/4 c. vinegar

Blend together well, chill, and serve on your favorite salad.

sides & salads

Plum Sauce

I love a good plum sauce to be served over grilled pork tenderloin. So after experimenting, I came up with this mixture.

1/2 jar Red Plum jam
1/8 c. lemon juice
1/8 c. orange juice
1/4 c. soy sauce
2 Tbsp. brown sugar
2 Tbsp. catsup

1 tsp. yellow mustard
1/2 tsp. chili powder
1/4 tsp. ginger
Dash cayenne pepper
Corn starch to thicken

Heat together and serve over your grilled tenderloin.

sides & salads

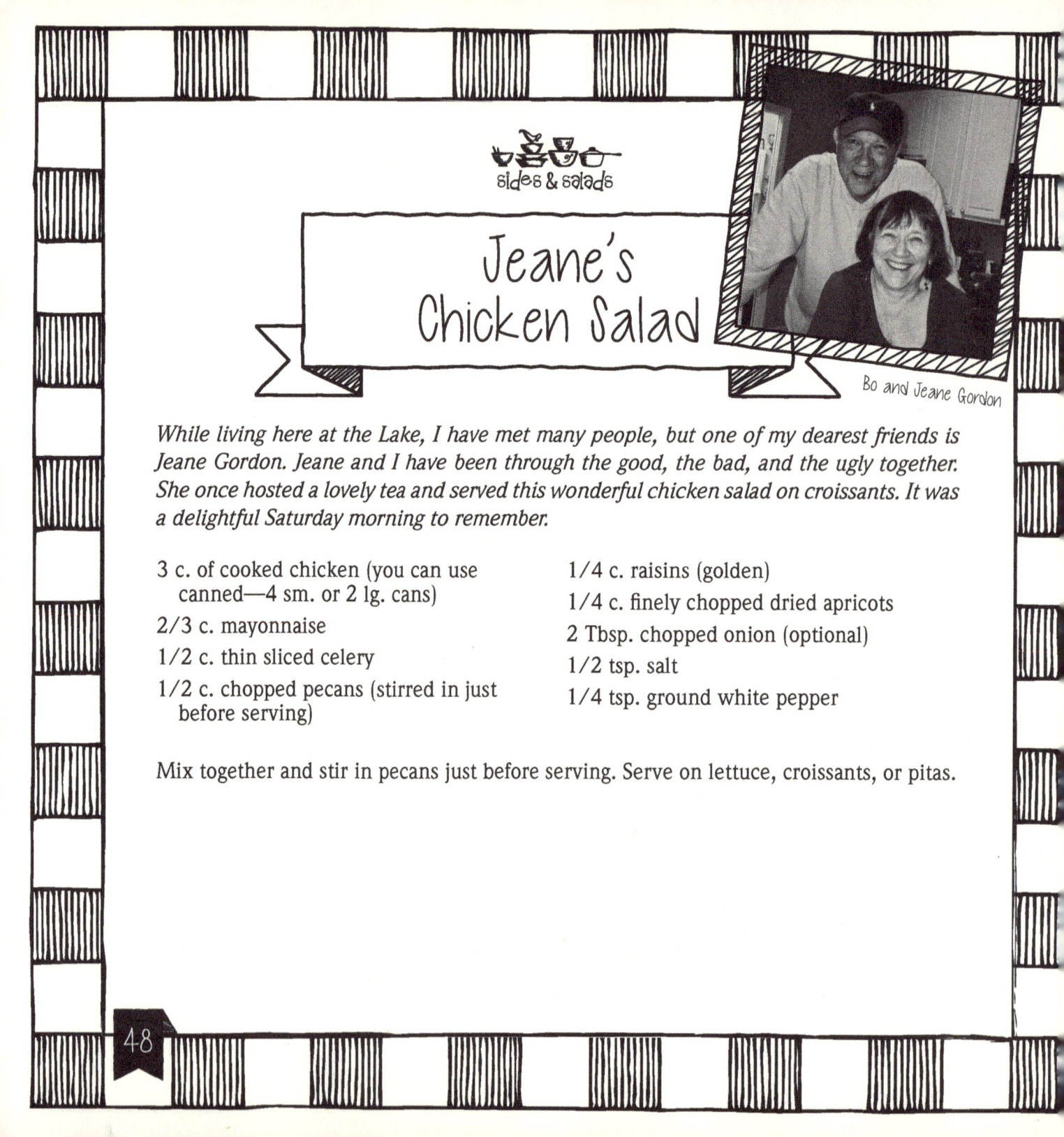

Jeane's Chicken Salad

Bo and Jeane Gordon

While living here at the Lake, I have met many people, but one of my dearest friends is Jeane Gordon. Jeane and I have been through the good, the bad, and the ugly together. She once hosted a lovely tea and served this wonderful chicken salad on croissants. It was a delightful Saturday morning to remember.

- 3 c. of cooked chicken (you can use canned—4 sm. or 2 lg. cans)
- 2/3 c. mayonnaise
- 1/2 c. thin sliced celery
- 1/2 c. chopped pecans (stirred in just before serving)
- 1/4 c. raisins (golden)
- 1/4 c. finely chopped dried apricots
- 2 Tbsp. chopped onion (optional)
- 1/2 tsp. salt
- 1/4 tsp. ground white pepper

Mix together and stir in pecans just before serving. Serve on lettuce, croissants, or pitas.

sides & salads

Shrimp Salad

Marge also made this cool shrimp salad, and it is great to serve in the summer. You can pretty much add or subtract whatever you like to this salad to suit your taste.

1 lb. shell macaroni, cooked and drained.

Add cooked shrimp, diced celery, onions, chopped tomatoes, radishes, green olives, or whatever you have. Add mayonnaise till creamy. Top with 8 hard-boiled eggs crumbled.

Enjoy!

Marge Winters

sides & salads

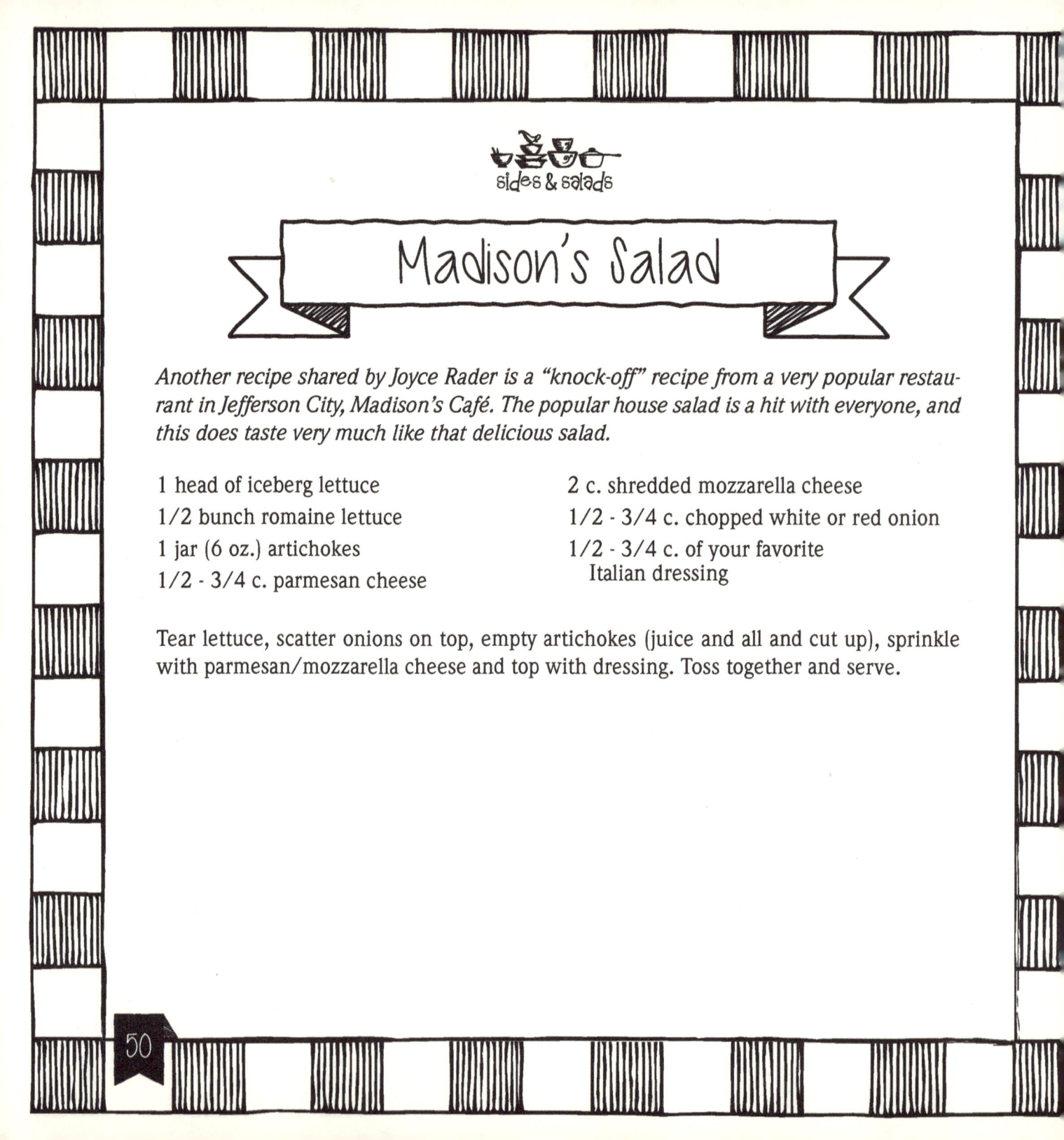

Madison's Salad

Another recipe shared by Joyce Rader is a "knock-off" recipe from a very popular restaurant in Jefferson City, Madison's Café. The popular house salad is a hit with everyone, and this does taste very much like that delicious salad.

1 head of iceberg lettuce
1/2 bunch romaine lettuce
1 jar (6 oz.) artichokes
1/2 - 3/4 c. parmesan cheese
2 c. shredded mozzarella cheese
1/2 - 3/4 c. chopped white or red onion
1/2 - 3/4 c. of your favorite Italian dressing

Tear lettuce, scatter onions on top, empty artichokes (juice and all and cut up), sprinkle with parmesan/mozzarella cheese and top with dressing. Toss together and serve.

sides & salads

Broccoli Salad

This favorite Broccoli Salad recipe of mine is very versatile. You can add what you like in this recipe, or leave out what you don't. You can also do 1/2 broccoli and 1/2 cauliflower if you like. This is so delicious, and no matter what you mix in, always use the same dressing, and it is great!

4-5 c. broccoli florets
1 c. raisins
1/2 c. sunflower kernels
1/4 c. chopped red onion
1/2 jar real bacon bits

4 oz. grated cheddar cheese
Dressing:
1 c. mayonnaise
1/4 c. sugar
2 tsp. vinegar

Mix salad ingredients together and chill; add dressing just before serving.

sides & salads

Cauliflower and Broccoli Salad

Another salad recipe which is similar, but has both broccoli and cauliflower was frequently brought to our office. So I'm not sure which one of the girls it belonged to, but it was always a favorite.

One head cauliflower
One bunch of broccoli
One medium purple onion (I leave out—once again onion is not for me)

One small jar of pimento

Cut cauliflower, broccoli, and onion, in bite-size pieces, and add pimento.

Toss with dressing recipe that follows:

Dressing
1 c. mayonnaise
1/2 c. sugar
1 Tbsp. mustard
1/2 c. vinegar
1/2 c. oil
Salt and pepper to taste

Combine and mix well, toss with your vegetables, chill and serve.

sides & salads

Layered Salad

My sister, Katherine Deihl, made this delicious salad for family gatherings. She was a great cook and always had the best family gatherings. Miss you Katherine.

1 head lettuce – broken in small pieces
1 head cauliflower
1/3 c. onion, chopped
1 c. crumbled bacon
Layer in glass bowl.

Mix together for dressing:
1 1/2 c. mayonnaise
1/2 c. sugar
Spread on top of salad ingredients.

Then sprinkle with:
1/3 c. cheddar cheese.

Chill and serve. Can be made the day ahead.

Katherine, Jeannie, Karen, Linda

sides & salads

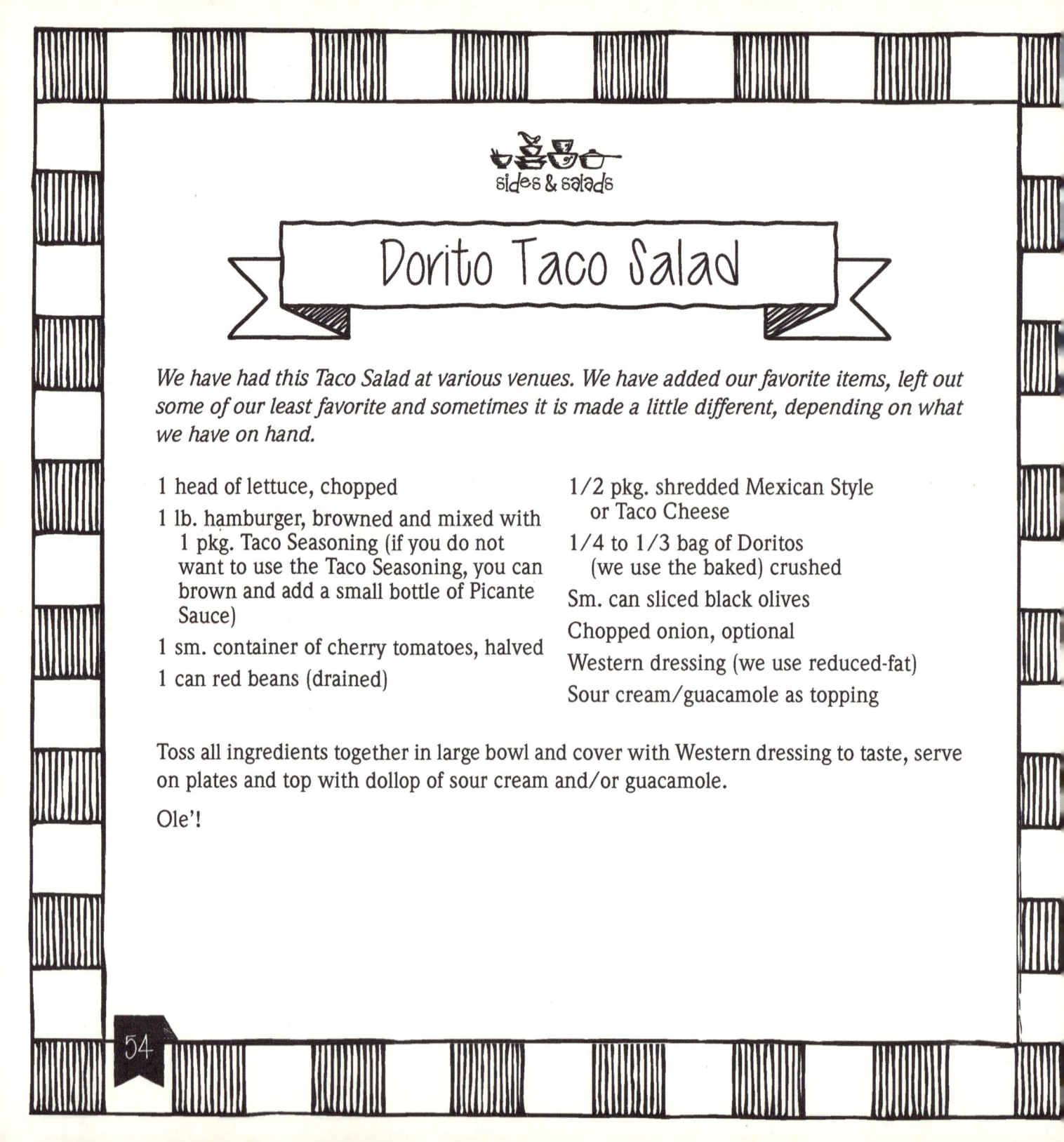

Dorito Taco Salad

We have had this Taco Salad at various venues. We have added our favorite items, left out some of our least favorite and sometimes it is made a little different, depending on what we have on hand.

- 1 head of lettuce, chopped
- 1 lb. hamburger, browned and mixed with 1 pkg. Taco Seasoning (if you do not want to use the Taco Seasoning, you can brown and add a small bottle of Picante Sauce)
- 1 sm. container of cherry tomatoes, halved
- 1 can red beans (drained)
- 1/2 pkg. shredded Mexican Style or Taco Cheese
- 1/4 to 1/3 bag of Doritos (we use the baked) crushed
- Sm. can sliced black olives
- Chopped onion, optional
- Western dressing (we use reduced-fat)
- Sour cream/guacamole as topping

Toss all ingredients together in large bowl and cover with Western dressing to taste, serve on plates and top with dollop of sour cream and/or guacamole.

Ole'!

sides & salads

Chinese Coleslaw

My nephew Chad had a friend several years back who always brought this delicious Coleslaw to family gatherings.

Chop together:

1 head of cabbage   2 bunches of green onions

Then mix with the following:

Brown in butter, 2 pkgs. of Ramen noodles crumbled, sesame seeds (to taste), and 3 oz. almonds.

Dressing: 3 Tbsp. soy sauce
3/4 c. oil   1/2 c. sugar

Stir together and toss with salad 20 minutes before serving.

sides & salads

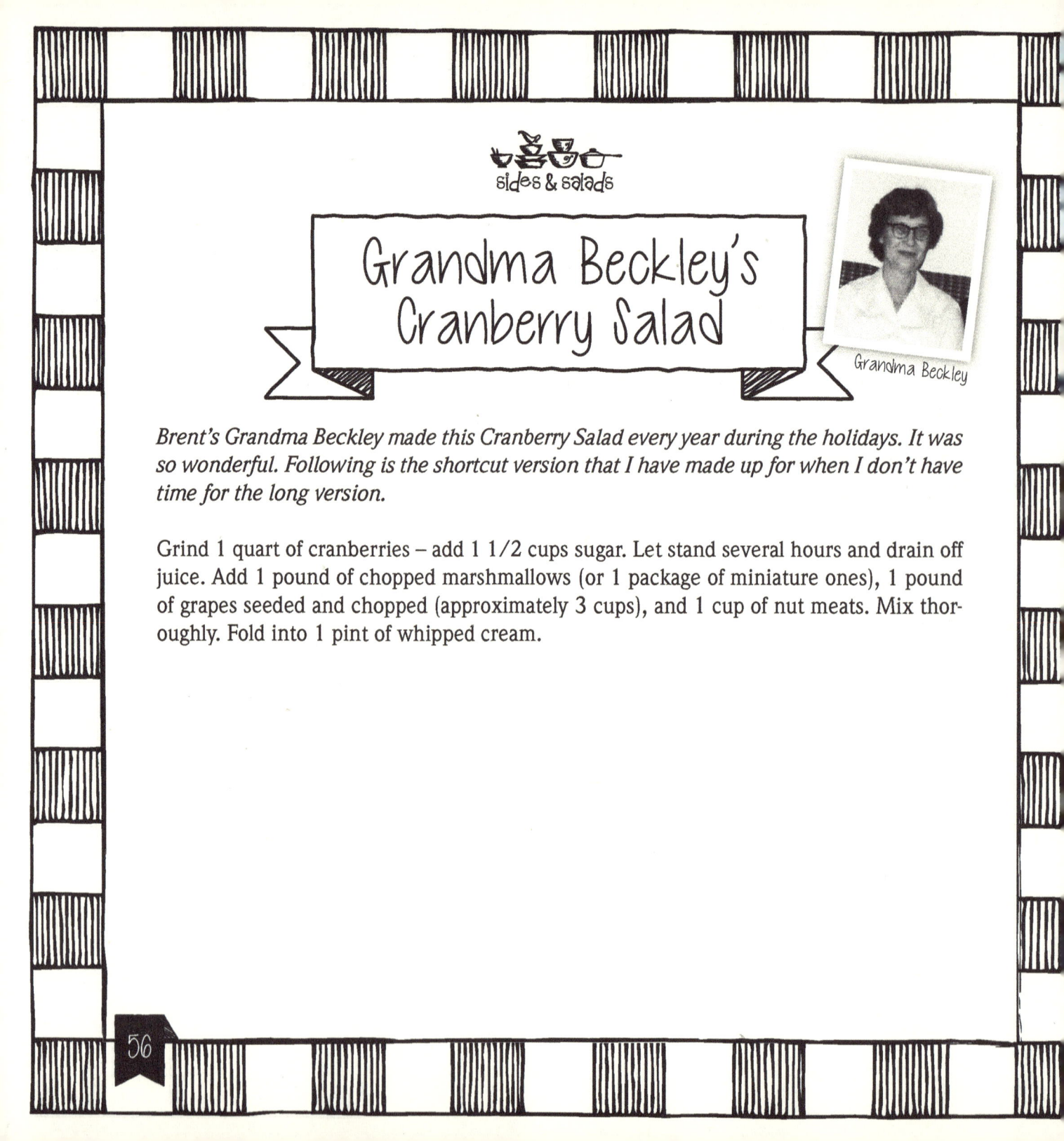

Grandma Beckley's Cranberry Salad

Grandma Beckley

Brent's Grandma Beckley made this Cranberry Salad every year during the holidays. It was so wonderful. Following is the shortcut version that I have made up for when I don't have time for the long version.

Grind 1 quart of cranberries – add 1 1/2 cups sugar. Let stand several hours and drain off juice. Add 1 pound of chopped marshmallows (or 1 package of miniature ones), 1 pound of grapes seeded and chopped (approximately 3 cups), and 1 cup of nut meats. Mix thoroughly. Fold into 1 pint of whipped cream.

sides & salads

Linda's Version of the Cranberry Salad

This recipe is a shortcut from the lengthy one of the previous holiday salad.

8 oz. container Cool-Whip, thawed
1 1/2 c. seedless red grapes, halved
1/2 bag mini-marshmallows

14 oz. can whole cranberry sauce
3/4 c. chopped pecans

Mix all the ingredients together, chill, and serve.

sides & salads

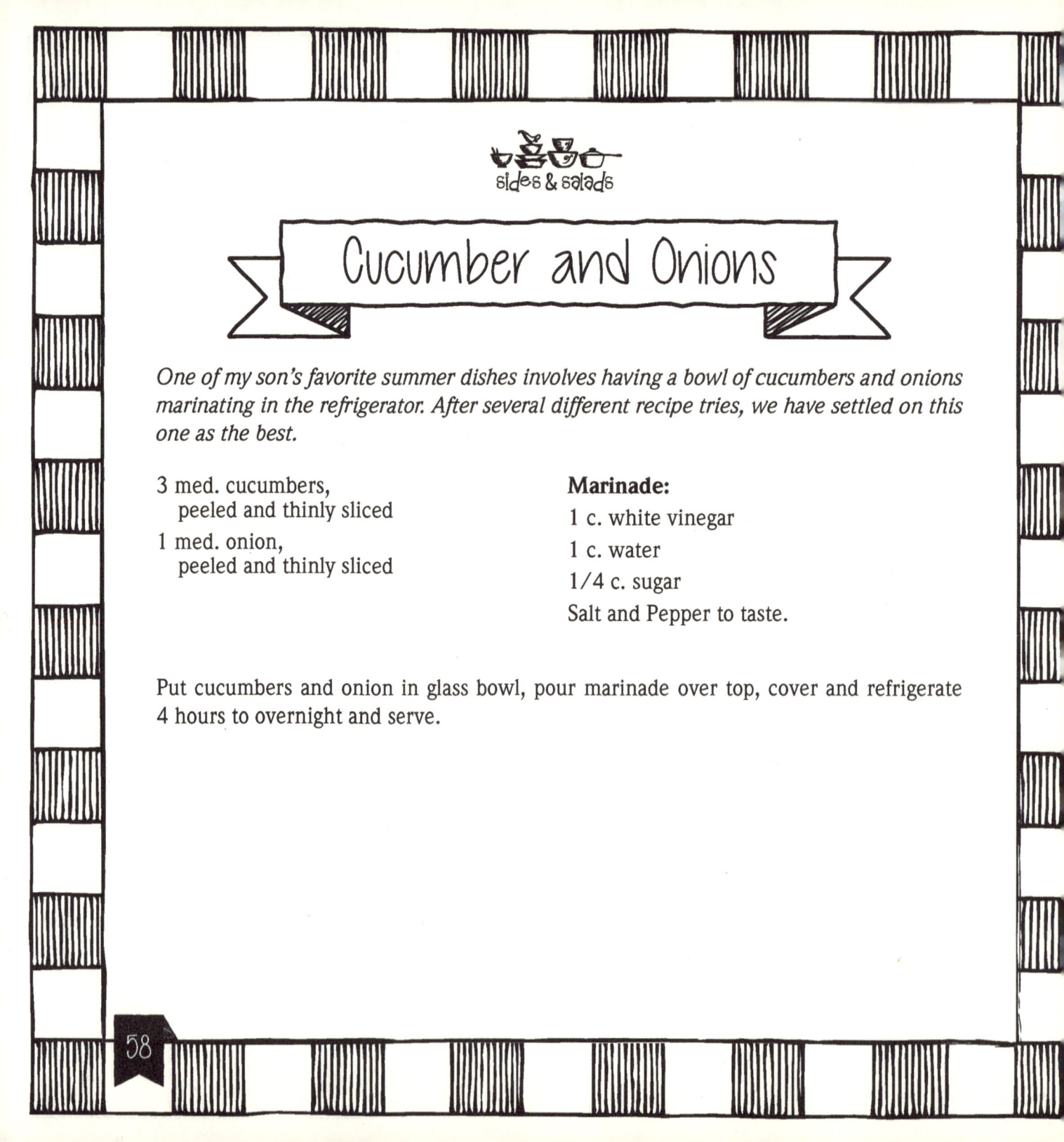

Cucumber and Onions

One of my son's favorite summer dishes involves having a bowl of cucumbers and onions marinating in the refrigerator. After several different recipe tries, we have settled on this one as the best.

3 med. cucumbers, peeled and thinly sliced
1 med. onion, peeled and thinly sliced

Marinade:
1 c. white vinegar
1 c. water
1/4 c. sugar
Salt and Pepper to taste.

Put cucumbers and onion in glass bowl, pour marinade over top, cover and refrigerate 4 hours to overnight and serve.

sides & salads

Pea Salad or Red Bean Salad

My Steve loves Pea Salad and Red Bean Salad. So we make it several different ways, but one that is really fresh tasting is made with frozen peas.

- 1 box of frozen peas – 10 oz. – thawed (if you do not have frozen peas, use a can of the LeSeuer peas, drained)
- 3 gherkin pickles – chopped, more or less to taste
- 1 boiled egg, chopped
- 2 oz. Velveeta, small cubes
- 2/3 c. mayonnaise
- Salt/pepper to taste

Mix all ingredients together, chill, and serve.

You can turn this into red bean salad by omitting the peas and substituting a can of red beans.

sides & salads

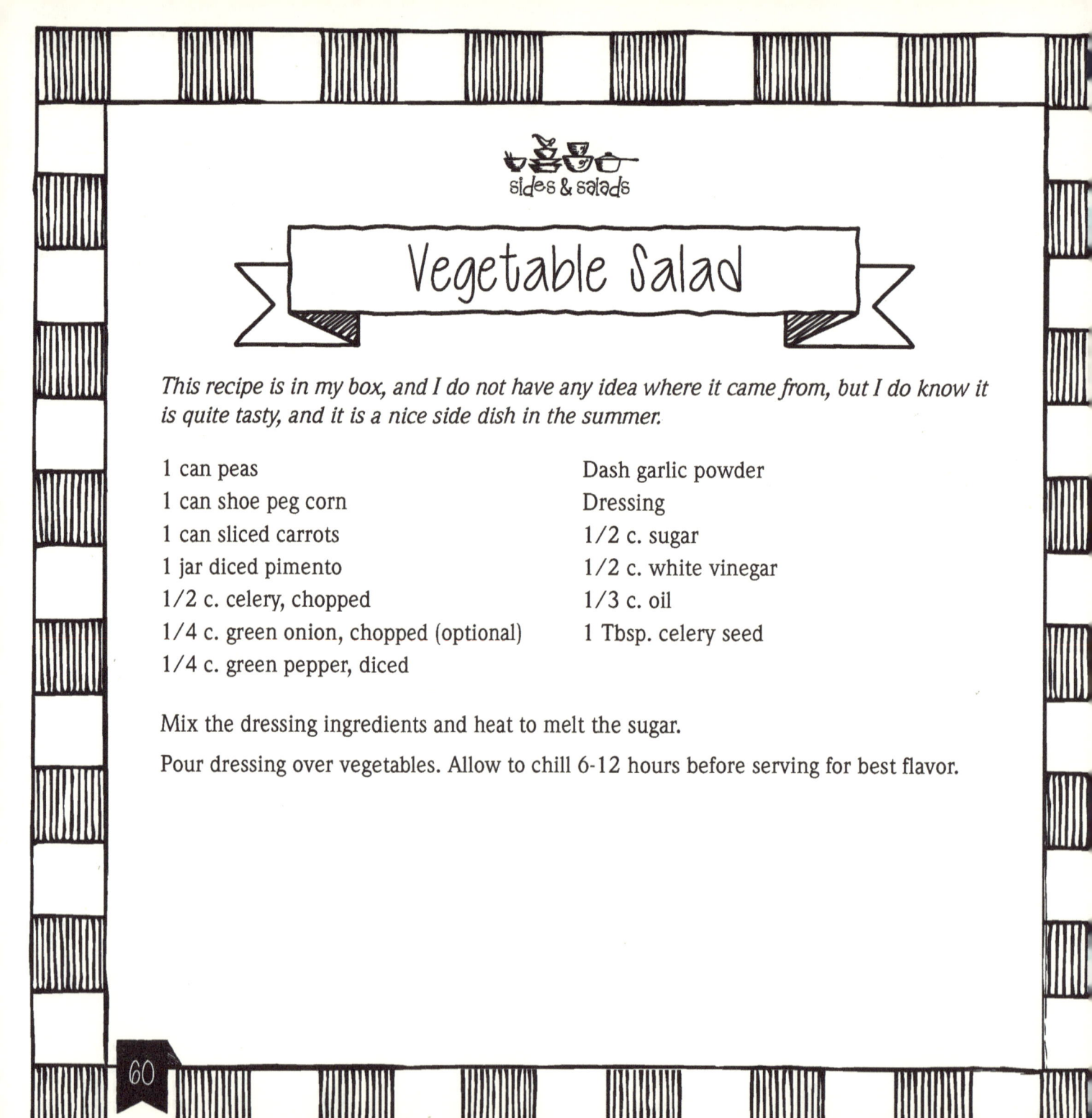

Vegetable Salad

This recipe is in my box, and I do not have any idea where it came from, but I do know it is quite tasty, and it is a nice side dish in the summer.

- 1 can peas
- 1 can shoe peg corn
- 1 can sliced carrots
- 1 jar diced pimento
- 1/2 c. celery, chopped
- 1/4 c. green onion, chopped (optional)
- 1/4 c. green pepper, diced
- Dash garlic powder
- Dressing
- 1/2 c. sugar
- 1/2 c. white vinegar
- 1/3 c. oil
- 1 Tbsp. celery seed

Mix the dressing ingredients and heat to melt the sugar.

Pour dressing over vegetables. Allow to chill 6-12 hours before serving for best flavor.

sides & salads

Greek Pasta Salad

Jan, Ellie and Misty

My friend, Jan, has a lovely daughter, Misty Horn. Misty is a mother who always loves to have dinner on the table every evening to greet her family. This recipe is a great salad/side dish that is so good on those hot summer nights.

10 oz. pkg. linguine, cooked
1 can lg. black olives, sliced
3-4 Roma tomatoes
1 cucumber, diced
green onions, sliced
1 pkg. feta cheese with basil, crumbled

Dressing
1/4 c. olive oil
3 Tbsp. mayonnaise
2 Tbsp. of Cavender Greek Seasoning
2 Tbsp. lemon juice

Combine all of salad ingredients.

Mix dressing.

Combine, chill, and serve.

sides & salads

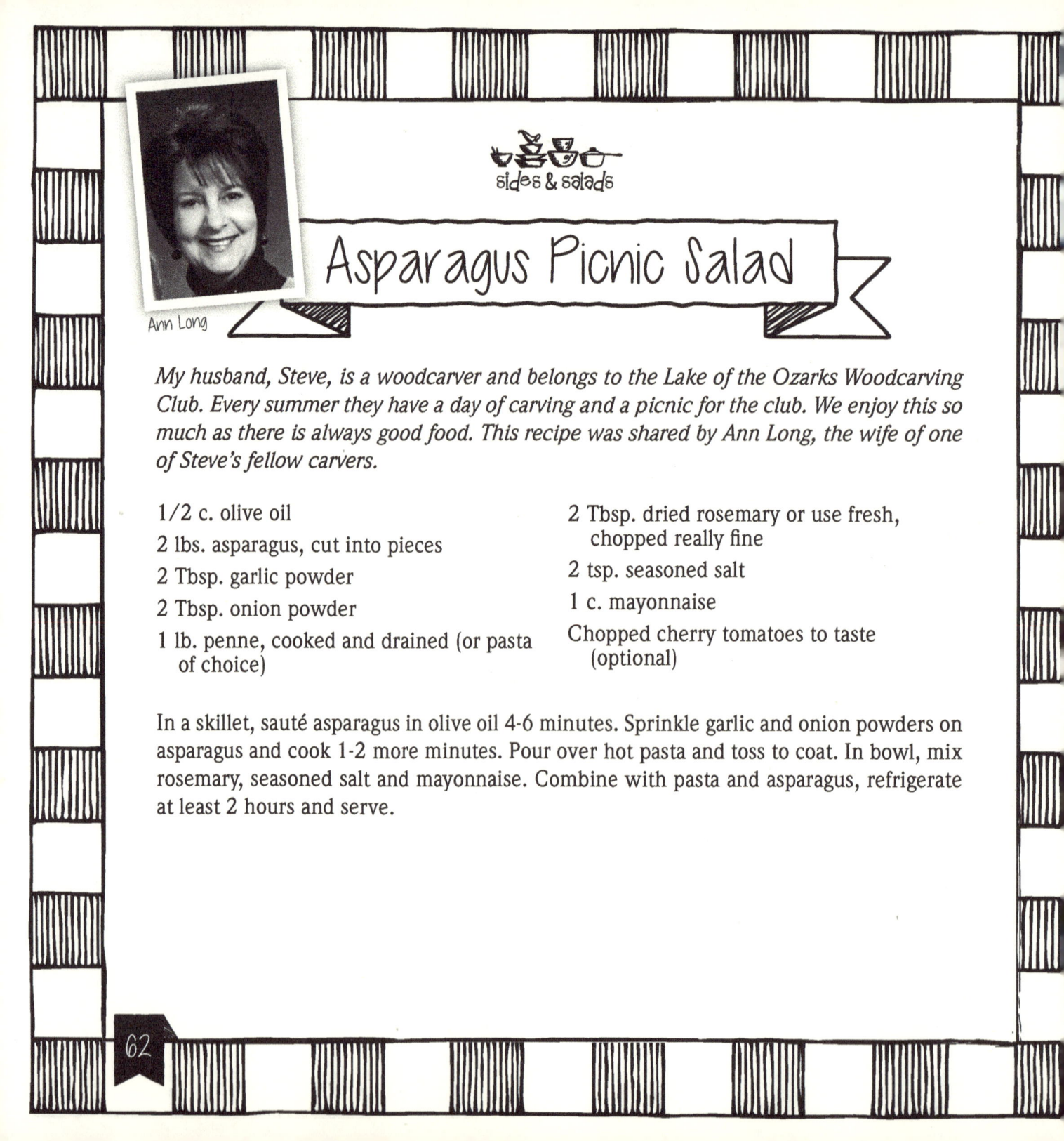

Asparagus Picnic Salad

Ann Long

My husband, Steve, is a woodcarver and belongs to the Lake of the Ozarks Woodcarving Club. Every summer they have a day of carving and a picnic for the club. We enjoy this so much as there is always good food. This recipe was shared by Ann Long, the wife of one of Steve's fellow carvers.

- 1/2 c. olive oil
- 2 lbs. asparagus, cut into pieces
- 2 Tbsp. garlic powder
- 2 Tbsp. onion powder
- 1 lb. penne, cooked and drained (or pasta of choice)
- 2 Tbsp. dried rosemary or use fresh, chopped really fine
- 2 tsp. seasoned salt
- 1 c. mayonnaise
- Chopped cherry tomatoes to taste (optional)

In a skillet, sauté asparagus in olive oil 4-6 minutes. Sprinkle garlic and onion powders on asparagus and cook 1-2 more minutes. Pour over hot pasta and toss to coat. In bowl, mix rosemary, seasoned salt and mayonnaise. Combine with pasta and asparagus, refrigerate at least 2 hours and serve.

sides & salads

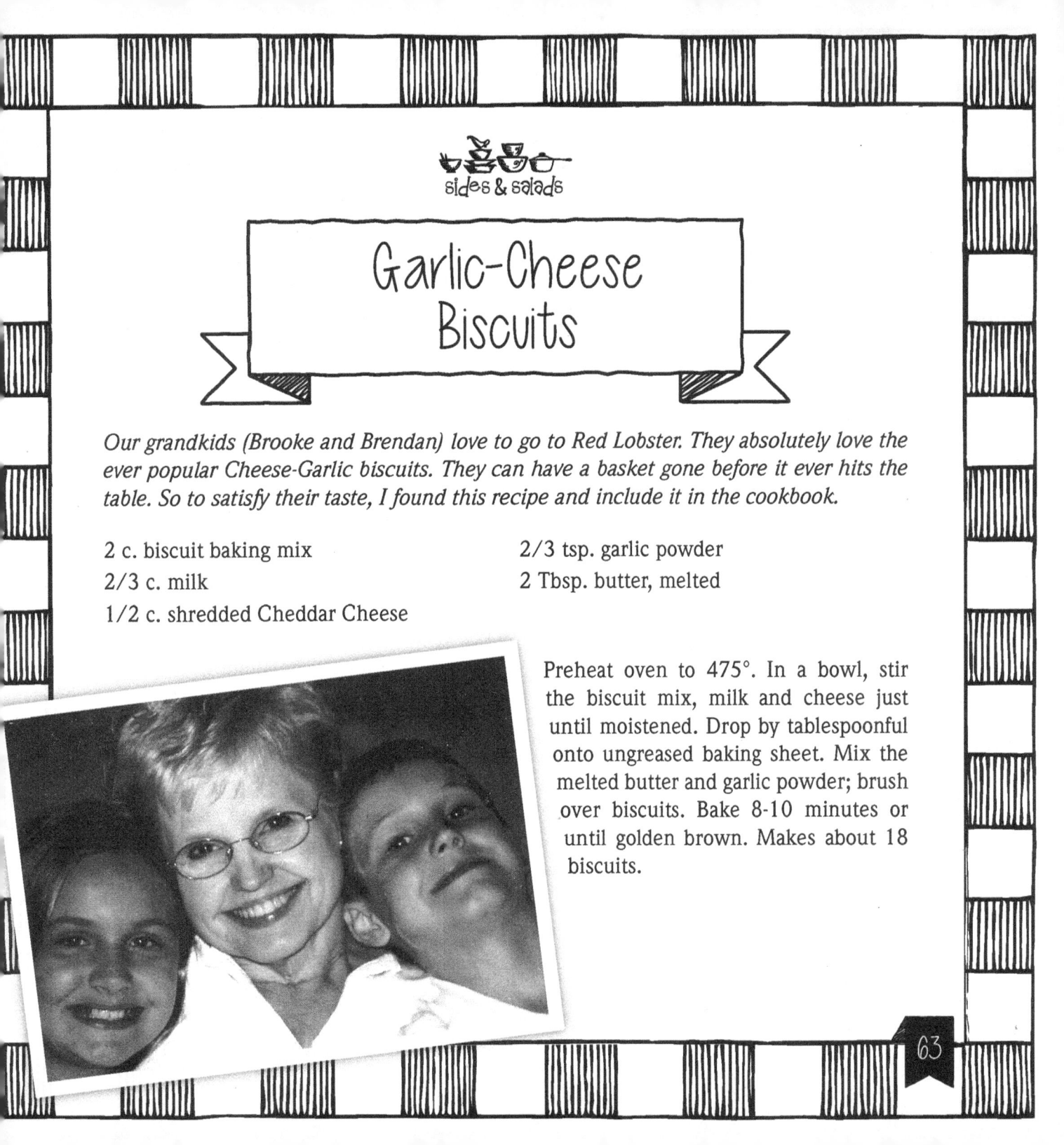

Garlic-Cheese Biscuits

Our grandkids (Brooke and Brendan) love to go to Red Lobster. They absolutely love the ever popular Cheese-Garlic biscuits. They can have a basket gone before it ever hits the table. So to satisfy their taste, I found this recipe and include it in the cookbook.

2 c. biscuit baking mix
2/3 c. milk
1/2 c. shredded Cheddar Cheese

2/3 tsp. garlic powder
2 Tbsp. butter, melted

Preheat oven to 475°. In a bowl, stir the biscuit mix, milk and cheese just until moistened. Drop by tablespoonful onto ungreased baking sheet. Mix the melted butter and garlic powder; brush over biscuits. Bake 8-10 minutes or until golden brown. Makes about 18 biscuits.

sides & salads

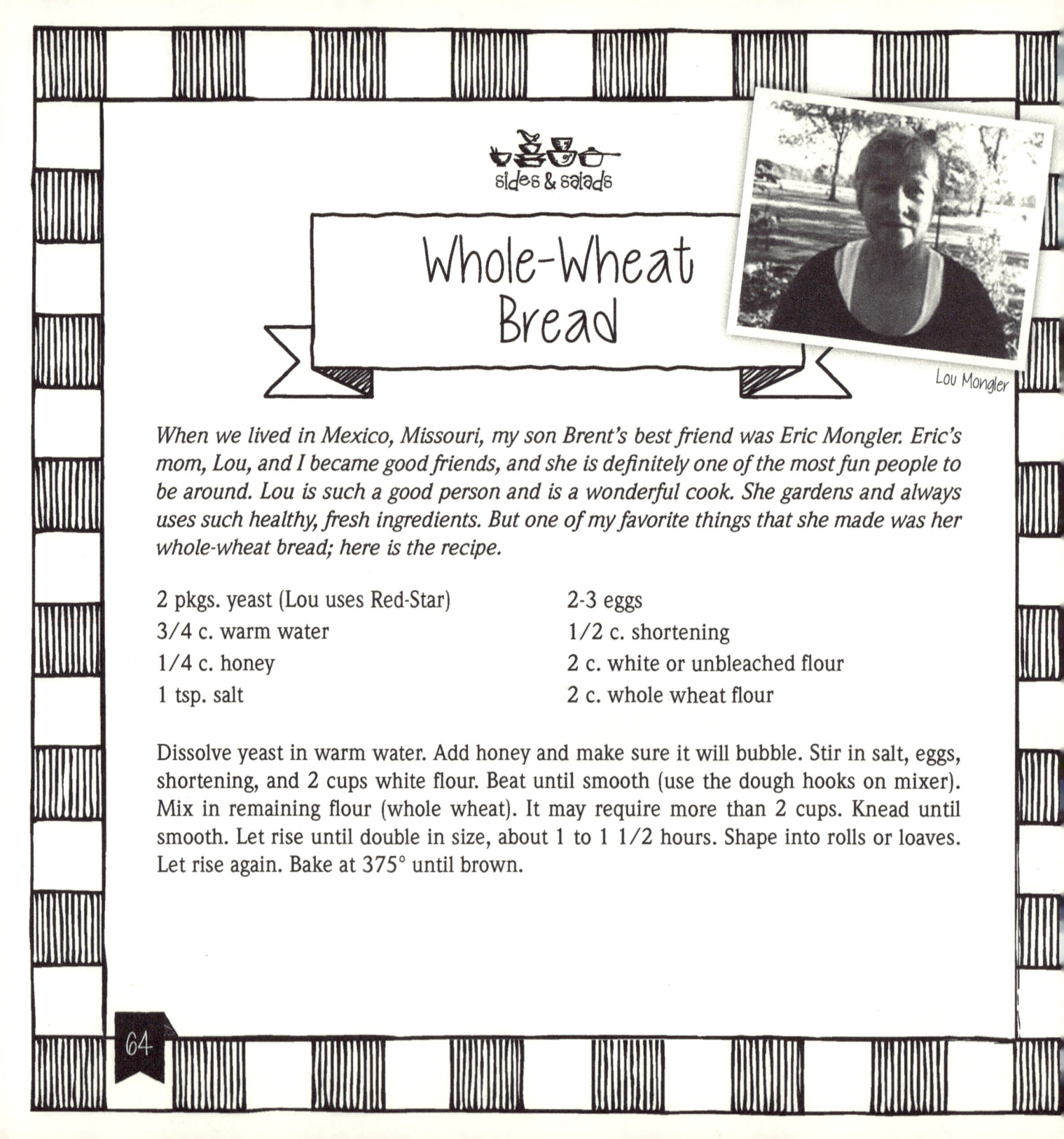

Whole-Wheat Bread

Lou Mongler

When we lived in Mexico, Missouri, my son Brent's best friend was Eric Mongler. Eric's mom, Lou, and I became good friends, and she is definitely one of the most fun people to be around. Lou is such a good person and is a wonderful cook. She gardens and always uses such healthy, fresh ingredients. But one of my favorite things that she made was her whole-wheat bread; here is the recipe.

2 pkgs. yeast (Lou uses Red-Star)
3/4 c. warm water
1/4 c. honey
1 tsp. salt
2-3 eggs
1/2 c. shortening
2 c. white or unbleached flour
2 c. whole wheat flour

Dissolve yeast in warm water. Add honey and make sure it will bubble. Stir in salt, eggs, shortening, and 2 cups white flour. Beat until smooth (use the dough hooks on mixer). Mix in remaining flour (whole wheat). It may require more than 2 cups. Knead until smooth. Let rise until double in size, about 1 to 1 1/2 hours. Shape into rolls or loaves. Let rise again. Bake at 375° until brown.

sides & salads

Hash Brown Casserole

This recipe is always requested and always eaten, and is a great dish to bring to gatherings. Where I first got this recipe is hard to say, but it is a keeper.

1 pkg. frozen hash brown potatoes, thawed
1 stick butter, melted
Chopped onion to taste, optional
1 can cream of chicken soup
1 pkg. shredded cheddar cheese
8 oz. sour cream
Salt and pepper

Mix together and put in greased 9 x 13 baking dish.

Topping:
1 stick butter
2 c. crushed corn flakes

Melt butter and combine with crushed corn flakes and cover casserole.

Bake at 350° for 35 minutes, or until golden brown and bubbly.

sides & salads

Frozen Champagne Salad

We had a wonderful neighbor in Osage Beach, MO, named Lelle Unzicker; she was such a joy and always had time and a story to share, as any retired teacher would. When my son, Brent, graduated from high school, we had a great celebration for friends and family and Mrs. Unzicker brought this delicious frozen salad to share. It was an immediate hit and has been adopted by our family as a favorite dish to this day.

- 8 oz. pkg. cream cheese, softened
- 3/4 c. sugar
- 10 oz. pkg. frozen strawberries, thawed, fruit and juice
- 1 lg. can crushed pineapple, drained
- 1/2 c. chopped nuts (optional-I have a niece that doesn't like them)
- 9 oz. tub Cool-Whip, thawed

Whip cream cheese until fluffy. Mix together sugar, strawberries, pineapple, and cool whip. Combine mixture with cream cheese. Pour into 9 x 13 pan and freeze. Set out about 15 minutes ahead of serving to soften. Cut into squares and serve.

Grandma Becker and Brent

sides & salads

Apple Snicker Salad I

Grandma Joyce and Sarah

Over the 4th of July 2012, our granddaughter, Sarah Hofstetter, was visiting from Hampton, Illinois. She shared this delicious sweet salad with us for dinner one evening. It was given to her by her Grandma Joyce.

4 apples (2 gala and 2 granny smith)
Bag of mini-marshmallows (use as many as desired)
2 (8 oz.) tubs of cool whip, thawed
Bag of fun size Snickers (cut into bite-size pieces)
Cinnamon as desired
Sprinkle salt only once on top – very lightly

Slice apples to small dice. Cut Snickers into small bite-size pieces. Add marshmallows and cool whip. Stir in slowly, allowing it to be on every surface of food. Once very well stirred, sprinkle with the cinnamon and salt and VOILA! A tasty salad.

Samantha and Sarah

sides & salads

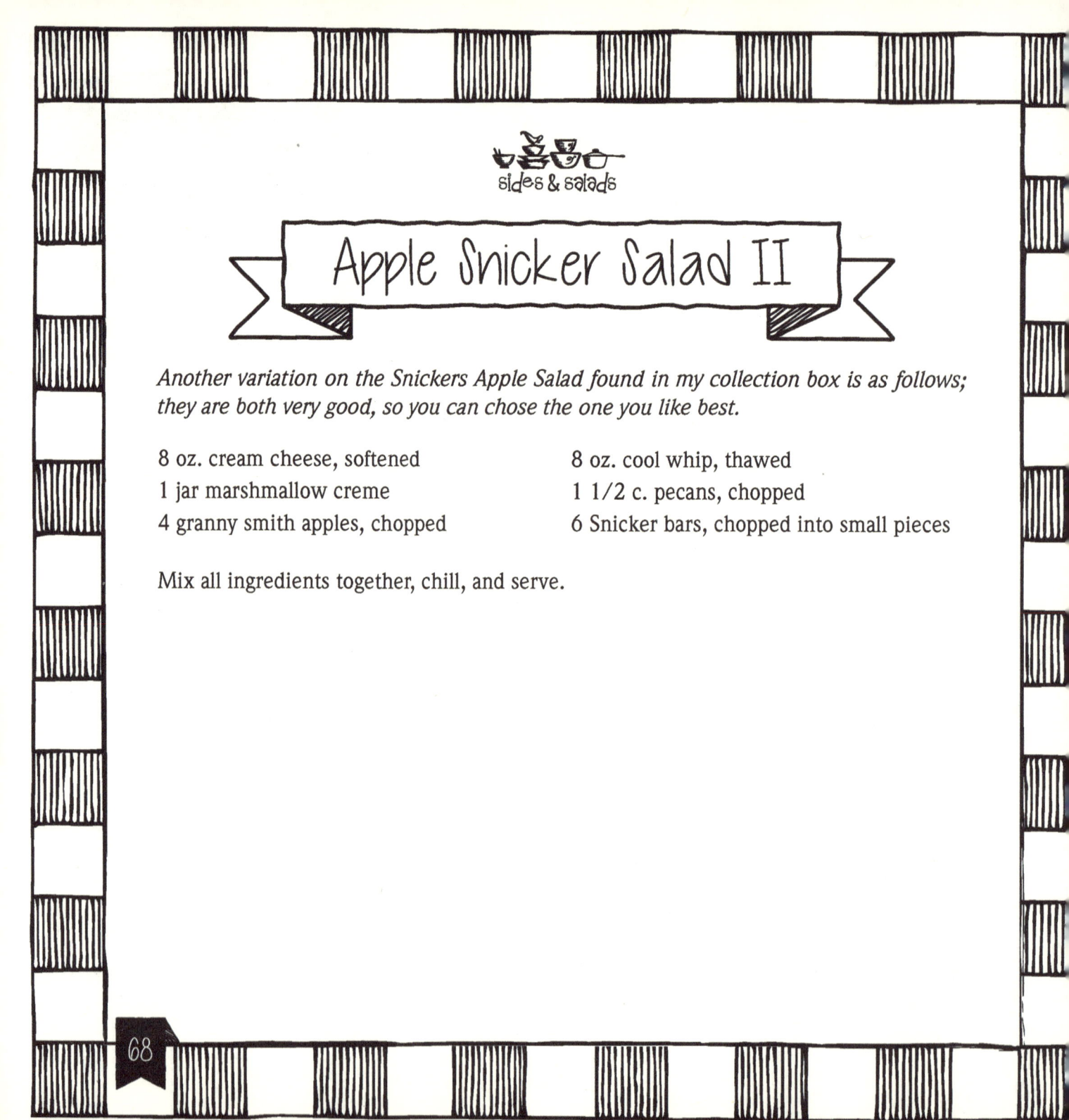

Apple Snicker Salad II

Another variation on the Snickers Apple Salad found in my collection box is as follows; they are both very good, so you can chose the one you like best.

- 8 oz. cream cheese, softened
- 1 jar marshmallow creme
- 4 granny smith apples, chopped
- 8 oz. cool whip, thawed
- 1 1/2 c. pecans, chopped
- 6 Snicker bars, chopped into small pieces

Mix all ingredients together, chill, and serve.

sides & salads

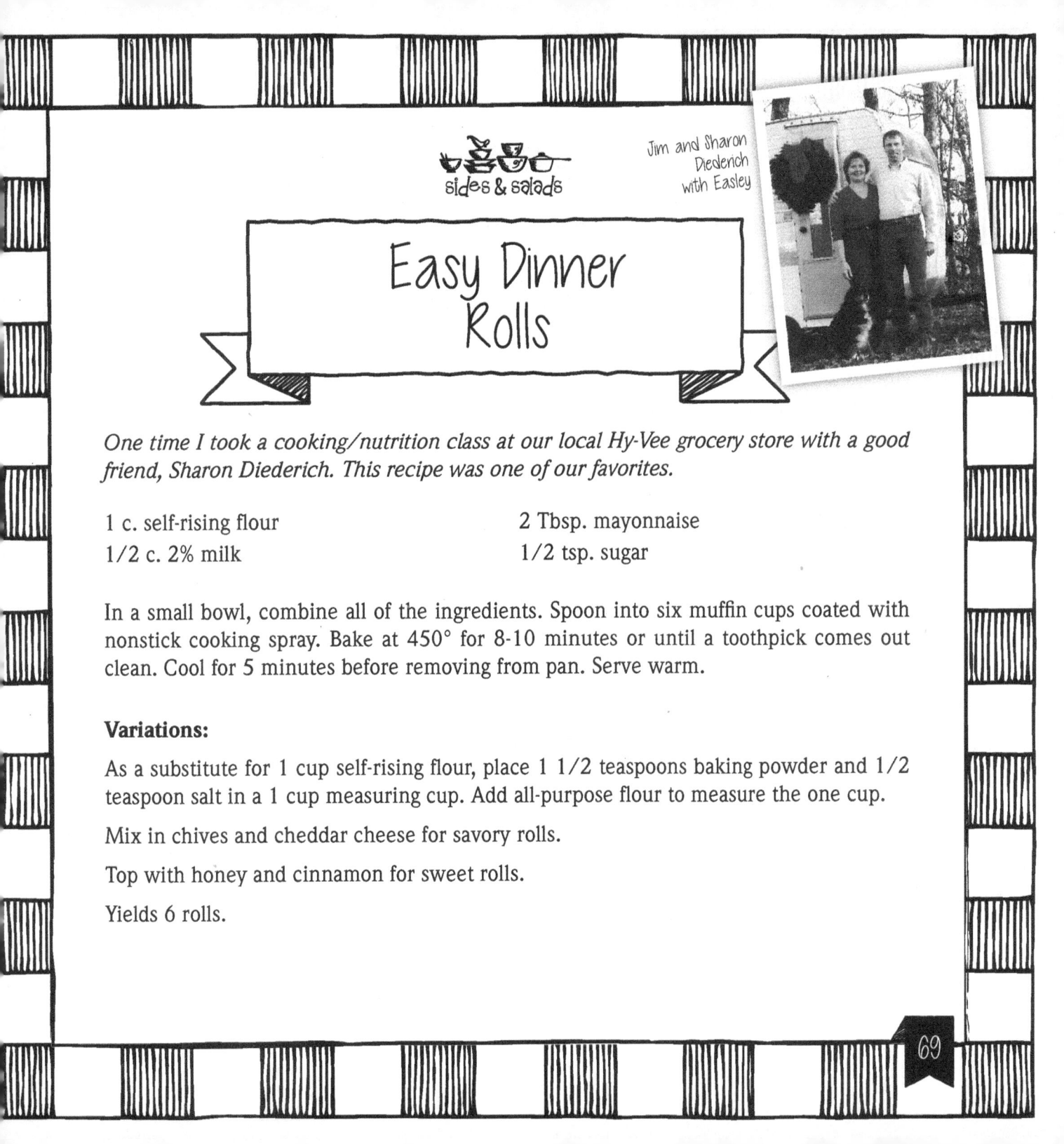

Jim and Sharon Diederich with Easley

Easy Dinner Rolls

One time I took a cooking/nutrition class at our local Hy-Vee grocery store with a good friend, Sharon Diederich. This recipe was one of our favorites.

1 c. self-rising flour
1/2 c. 2% milk

2 Tbsp. mayonnaise
1/2 tsp. sugar

In a small bowl, combine all of the ingredients. Spoon into six muffin cups coated with nonstick cooking spray. Bake at 450° for 8-10 minutes or until a toothpick comes out clean. Cool for 5 minutes before removing from pan. Serve warm.

Variations:

As a substitute for 1 cup self-rising flour, place 1 1/2 teaspoons baking powder and 1/2 teaspoon salt in a 1 cup measuring cup. Add all-purpose flour to measure the one cup.

Mix in chives and cheddar cheese for savory rolls.

Top with honey and cinnamon for sweet rolls.

Yields 6 rolls.

sides & salads

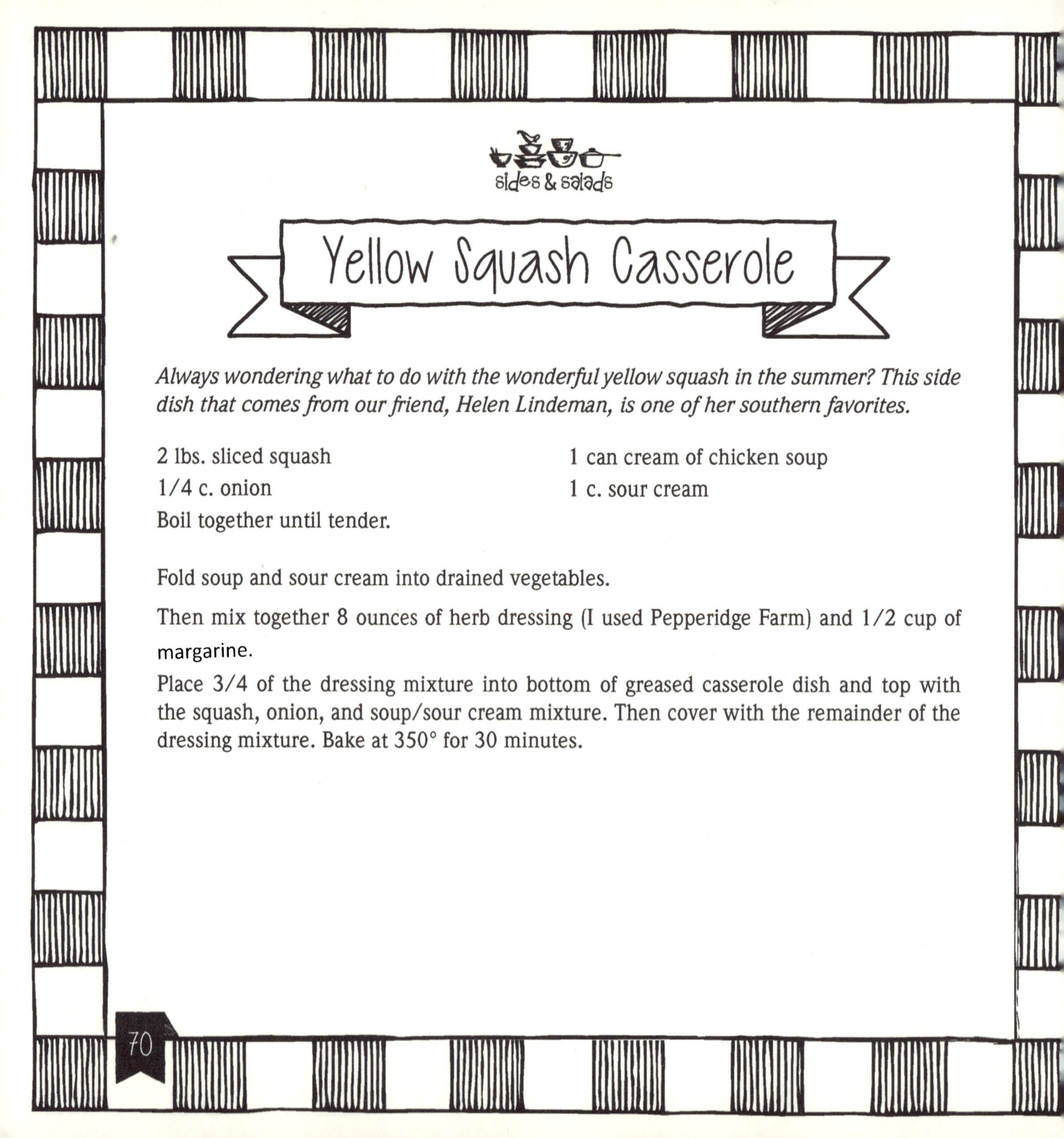

Yellow Squash Casserole

Always wondering what to do with the wonderful yellow squash in the summer? This side dish that comes from our friend, Helen Lindeman, is one of her southern favorites.

2 lbs. sliced squash
1/4 c. onion
Boil together until tender.

1 can cream of chicken soup
1 c. sour cream

Fold soup and sour cream into drained vegetables.

Then mix together 8 ounces of herb dressing (I used Pepperidge Farm) and 1/2 cup of margarine.

Place 3/4 of the dressing mixture into bottom of greased casserole dish and top with the squash, onion, and soup/sour cream mixture. Then cover with the remainder of the dressing mixture. Bake at 350° for 30 minutes.

sides & salads

Potato Salad

Everyone loves my potato salad. I have always made it just by sight, so I have now tried measuring things to bring it all together. With lots of tweaking and tasting, this is how it is made; of course you can adjust to your taste, with a little less of this and a little more of that.

- 5 lbs. red potatoes (cooked in a large pan with skins on until fork tender, then drain and cover with cold water, peel and dice and place in large bowl.)

Add the dressing:
- 2 c. of mayonnaise
- 2 Tbsp. mustard
- 1 tsp. sugar

Then stir in the following:
- 1/2 c. sweet pickle relish
- 1 c. chopped celery (or 1/2 c. onion and 1/2 c. celery if you prefer to have a little onion in your potato salad; I am not an onion person.)
- 4 boiled eggs, chopped

Mix thoroughly and chill well before serving.

Makes 8-10 generous servings.

sides & salads

Deviled Eggs

At Easter time you must always have deviled eggs, but my family always enjoys them, no matter what the season.

8 lg. eggs, boiled and peeled

Slice in half and mash the yolks, reserving the whites for filling.

With the mashed yolks, add the following ingredients:

1/2 tsp. sugar
1 scant tsp. yellow mustard
1/3 c. mayonnaise
1/8 tsp. white pepper
Salt to taste

Mix together well and fill reserved egg whites, chill and serve.

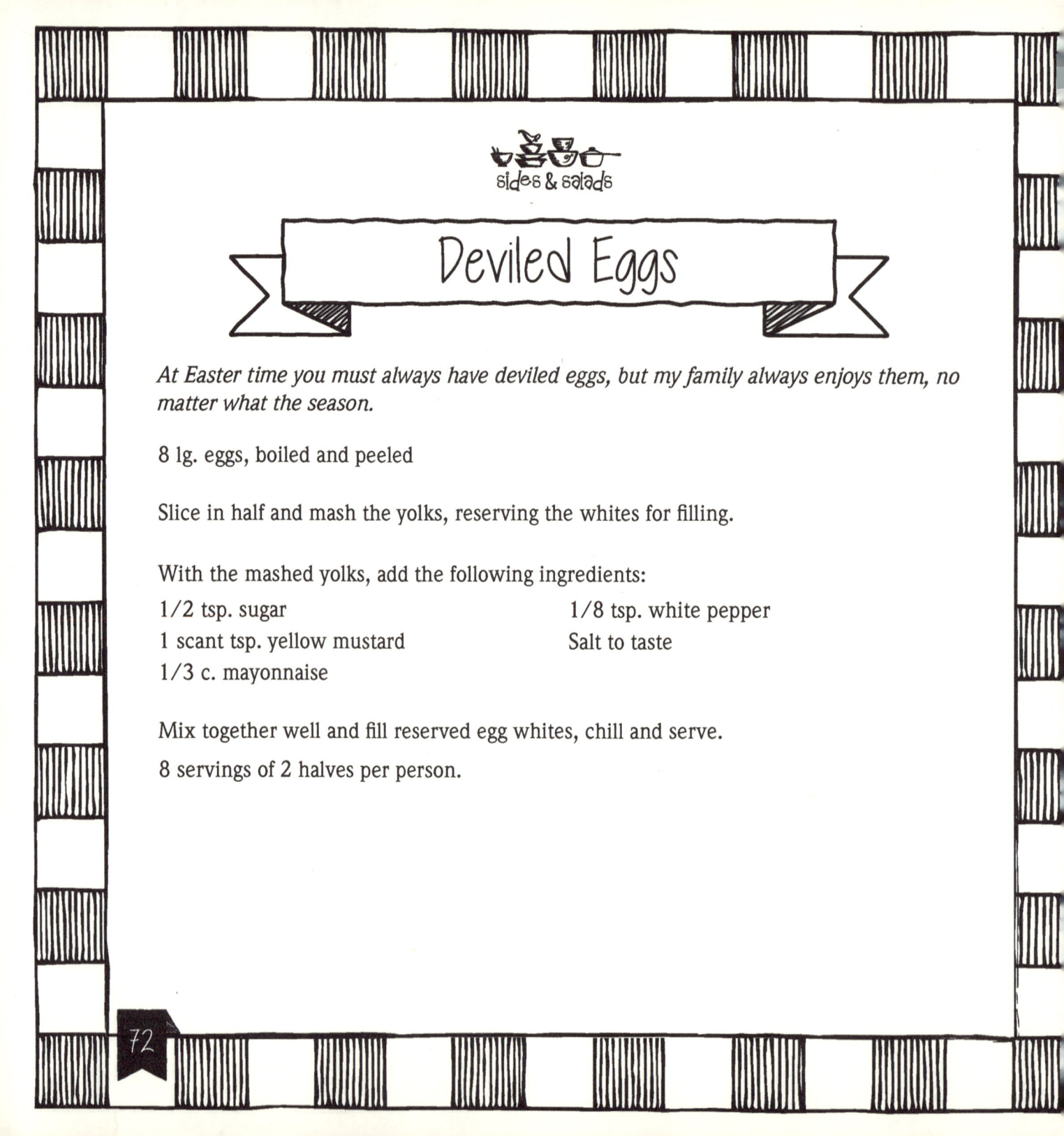

8 servings of 2 halves per person.

sides & salads

"Hot" Macaroni

Here is the recipe for one of my son's favorite side dishes, made by his Grandma Becker, who spoiled him a whole lot! It pairs well with the meatloaf recipe.

2 c. uncooked shell macaroni

Cook according to package directions. Drain, but do not rinse. Place back in pan and add the following:

1 can of tomato juice (11.5 ounce)
3 Tbsp. butter
1 tsp. sugar

1 tsp. pepper (more or less depending on how "hot" you like)
Salt to taste

Heat and cook until thick and creamy and little to no liquid remains.

Yum!

sides & salads

Karen's Creamy Macaroni Salad

Every summer when there is a family party or Bar-B-Que to attend, there is always a request for my sister, Karen Owen's, creamy pasta salad. It has just the right amount of summer vegetables, pasta, and creamy Miracle Whip. It is the perfect side with spicy Bar-B-Que.

1 1/2 c. uncooked Elbow macaroni
1/2 c. diced green pepper
1 c. sliced green olives with pimentos
2 c. diced tomatoes
2 c. Miracle Whip plus 1 Tbsp.
1/2 tsp. onion salt

Cook and drain, but do not rinse the macaroni.

Place all of prepared vegetables (green pepper, olives, and tomato) in a bowl with 1 Tablespoon of Miracle Whip and the onion salt, and allow to marinate while cooking the macaroni. Drain, but do not rinse the macaroni. Pour the hot macaroni into the bowl over the vegetables and add the 2 cups of Miracle Whip; mix together and chill before serving.

Karen, Katherine, Emily, Linda

sides & salads

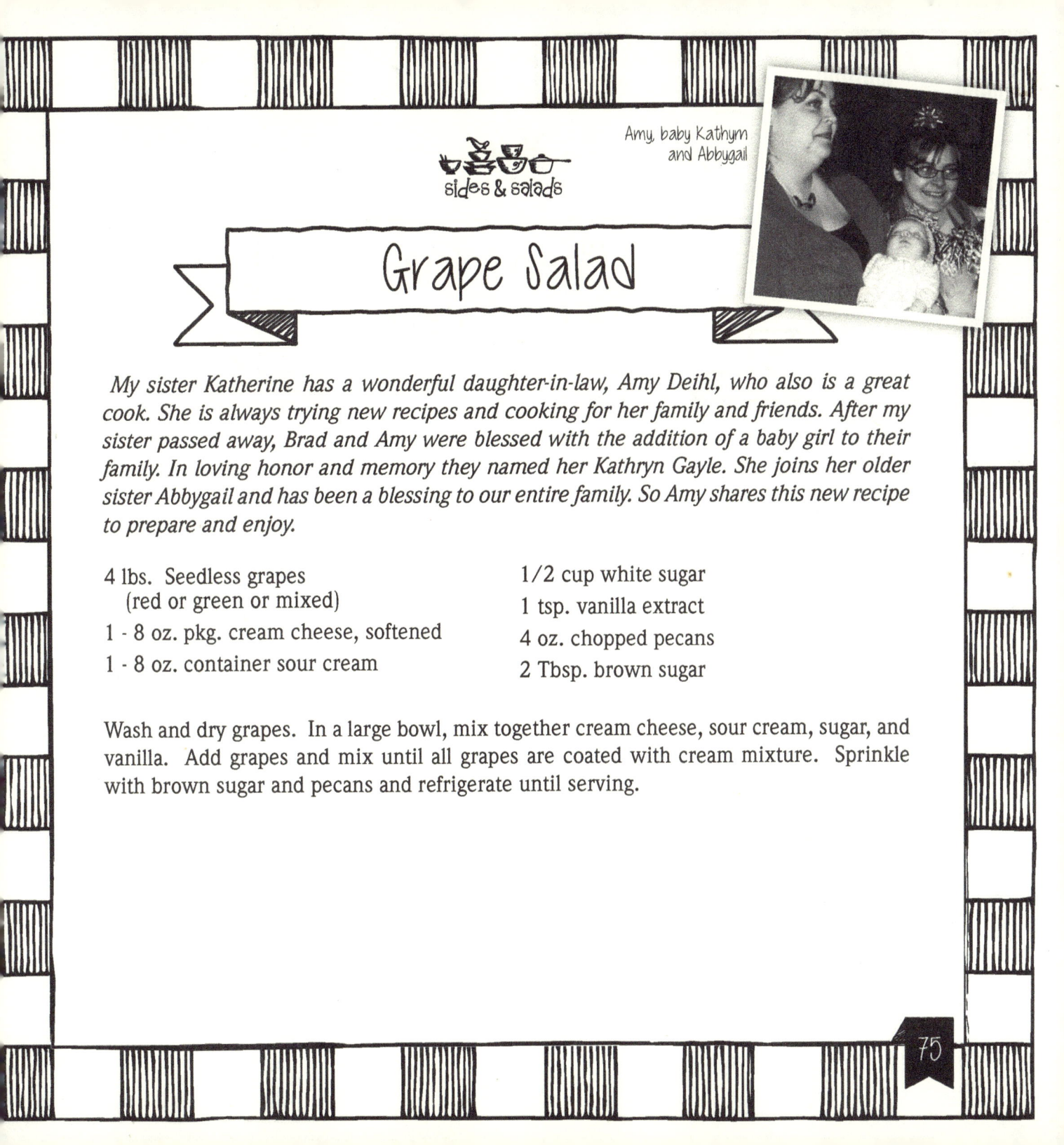

Grape Salad

Amy, baby Kathyrn and Abbygail

My sister Katherine has a wonderful daughter-in-law, Amy Deihl, who also is a great cook. She is always trying new recipes and cooking for her family and friends. After my sister passed away, Brad and Amy were blessed with the addition of a baby girl to their family. In loving honor and memory they named her Kathryn Gayle. She joins her older sister Abbygail and has been a blessing to our entire family. So Amy shares this new recipe to prepare and enjoy.

- 4 lbs. Seedless grapes (red or green or mixed)
- 1 - 8 oz. pkg. cream cheese, softened
- 1 - 8 oz. container sour cream
- 1/2 cup white sugar
- 1 tsp. vanilla extract
- 4 oz. chopped pecans
- 2 Tbsp. brown sugar

Wash and dry grapes. In a large bowl, mix together cream cheese, sour cream, sugar, and vanilla. Add grapes and mix until all grapes are coated with cream mixture. Sprinkle with brown sugar and pecans and refrigerate until serving.

sides & salads

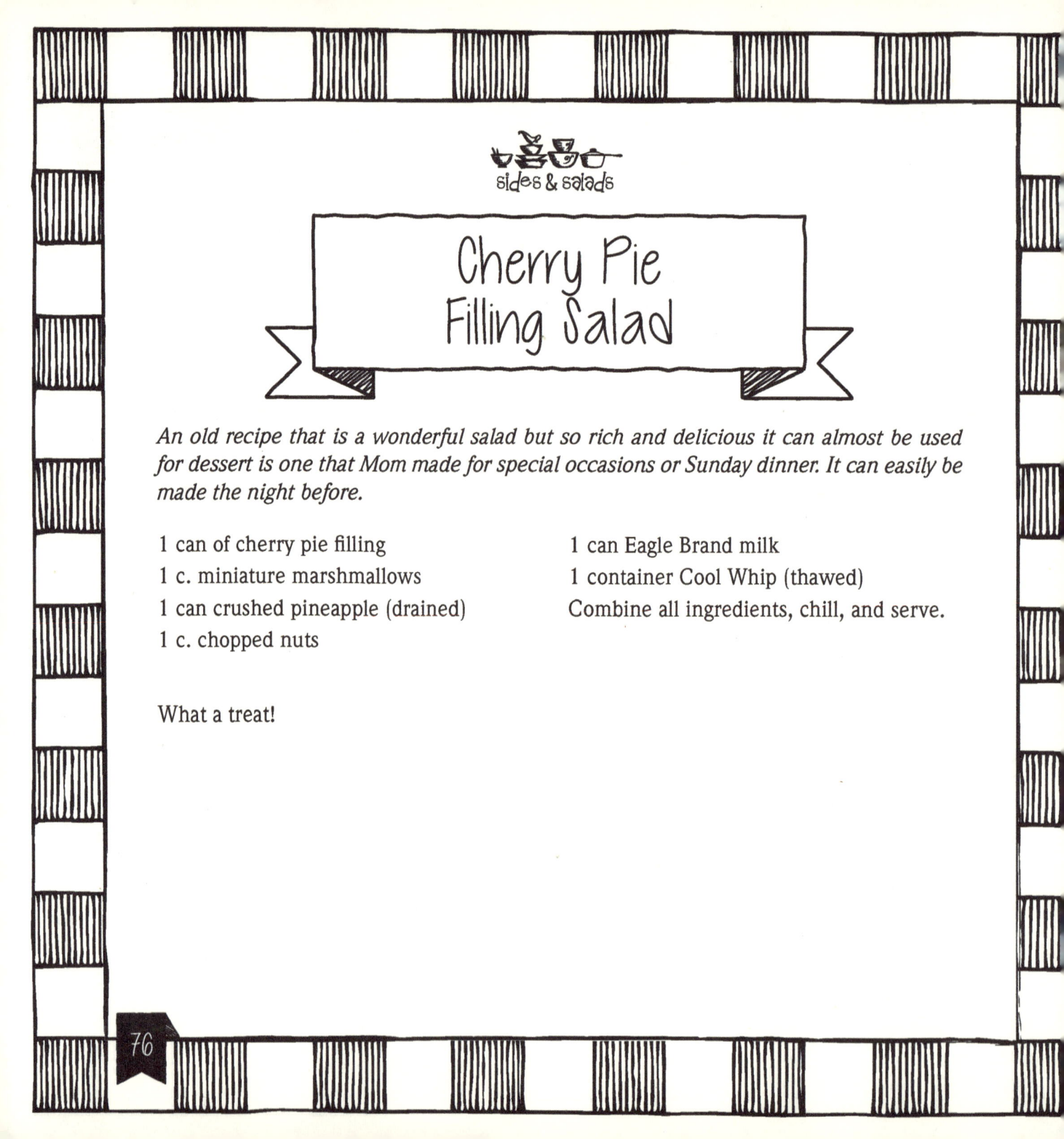

Cherry Pie Filling Salad

An old recipe that is a wonderful salad but so rich and delicious it can almost be used for dessert is one that Mom made for special occasions or Sunday dinner. It can easily be made the night before.

- 1 can of cherry pie filling
- 1 c. miniature marshmallows
- 1 can crushed pineapple (drained)
- 1 c. chopped nuts
- 1 can Eagle Brand milk
- 1 container Cool Whip (thawed)

Combine all ingredients, chill, and serve.

What a treat!

Spinach Pie {page 78}

the main event

the main event

Spinach Pie

This delicious recipe was given to me by my friend, Susan Bowden. She first served this at a Mother's Day Brunch at our church. It was a definite hit and was always requested. I always made sure it was served at my table in the following years. I entered this recipe in the KOLR 10 Brunch Recipe contest in March 2012, and it was judged by Chef Brian Romano of the Cook's Kettle in Springfield, Missouri to be one of the final four of the contest. It was so much fun and an honor to be a part of this experience. You'll want to try this yummy savory treat!

- 1 lb. Italian Sausage (sweet not spicy) removed from casing
- 6 eggs
- 2 – 10 oz. pkgs. Frozen spinach, thawed and drained
- 16 oz. Mozzarella cheese, shredded
- 2/3 c. Ricotta cheese
- 1/2 tsp. salt
- 1/8 tsp. pepper
- 1/8 tsp. garlic powder
- Pie crusts – enough for 2 pies (top and bottom)

Brown sausage in skillet about 10 minutes, drain grease. Reserve one egg yolk. In a large bowl, combine all the rest of the eggs, sausage, thawed spinach, mozzarella cheese, ricotta cheese, salt, pepper, and garlic powder and set aside.

Prepare pie crust and put in pie pans, spoon spinach mixture (divided between the two pies) in pie shells. Roll other pie crusts out and cover top of mixture, then seal edges. Slit top with knife. With the reserved egg yolk, add 1 Tablespoon water and brush tops with it. Bake at 375° for 1 hour and 15 minutes. Cool a bit before cutting. Make two 9" pies.

the main event

Chicken Hot Dish

The Lake Presbyterian Church always had an annual salad luncheon and this dish was served at the lovely affair. It is so good to prepare for a crowd and is often served at church dinners.

3 c. of cooked chicken, cubed
3 c. of herb flavored croutons
1 c. celery, chopped
7 oz. can water chestnuts, sliced

1 c. mayonnaise
(do not use salad dressing)
2 – 10 oz. cans Cream of Chicken Soup

Blend mayonnaise and soup, add all other ingredients, turn into a greased 9 x 13 pan, cover and refrigerate at least 3 hours or overnight. Bake at 350° covered, 30-40 minutes.

Note: Set on counter to bring to room temperature before baking.

You may also add chunks of zucchini for additional good taste.

the main event

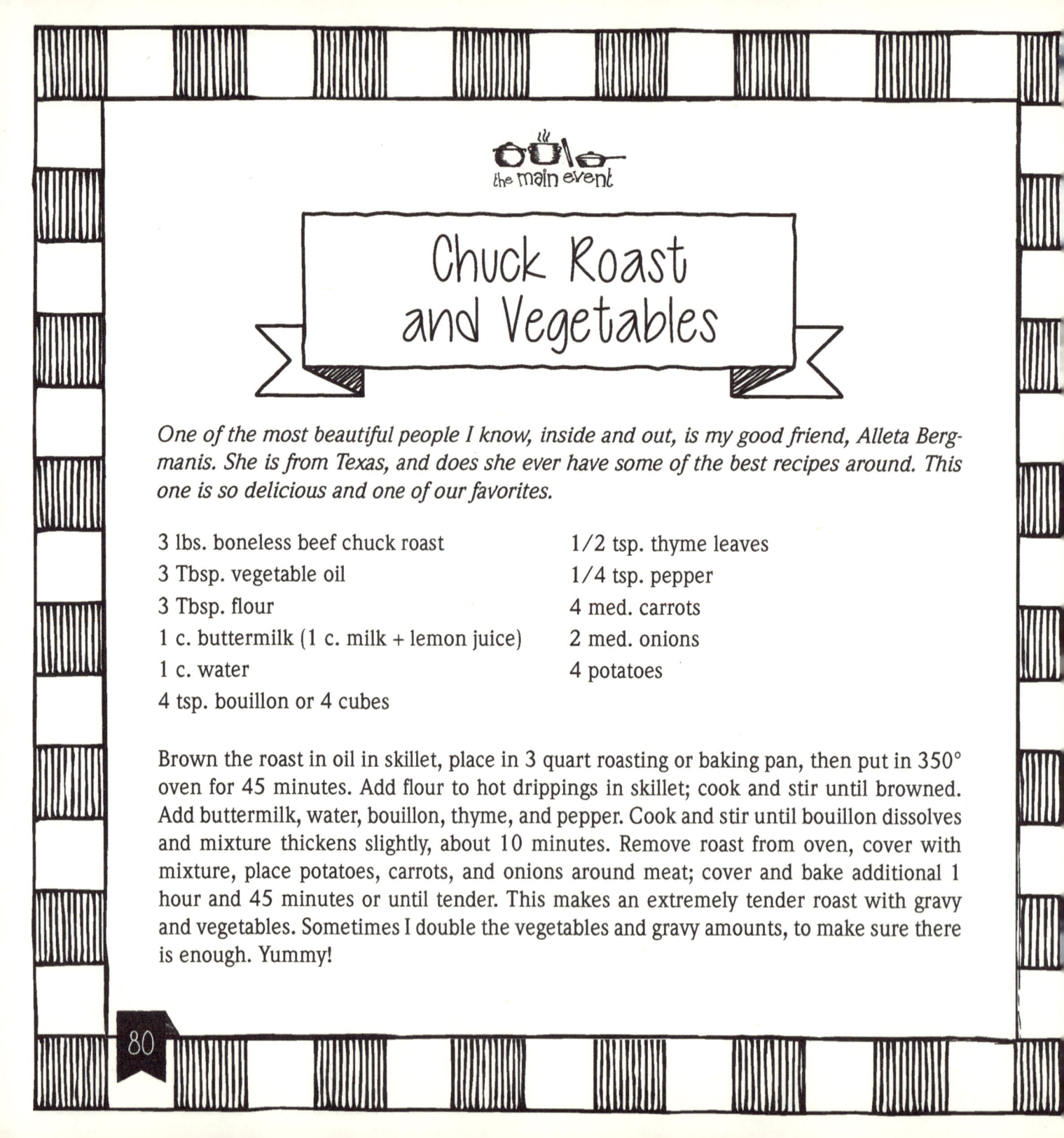

Chuck Roast and Vegetables

One of the most beautiful people I know, inside and out, is my good friend, Alleta Bergmanis. She is from Texas, and does she ever have some of the best recipes around. This one is so delicious and one of our favorites.

- 3 lbs. boneless beef chuck roast
- 3 Tbsp. vegetable oil
- 3 Tbsp. flour
- 1 c. buttermilk (1 c. milk + lemon juice)
- 1 c. water
- 4 tsp. bouillon or 4 cubes
- 1/2 tsp. thyme leaves
- 1/4 tsp. pepper
- 4 med. carrots
- 2 med. onions
- 4 potatoes

Brown the roast in oil in skillet, place in 3 quart roasting or baking pan, then put in 350° oven for 45 minutes. Add flour to hot drippings in skillet; cook and stir until browned. Add buttermilk, water, bouillon, thyme, and pepper. Cook and stir until bouillon dissolves and mixture thickens slightly, about 10 minutes. Remove roast from oven, cover with mixture, place potatoes, carrots, and onions around meat; cover and bake additional 1 hour and 45 minutes or until tender. This makes an extremely tender roast with gravy and vegetables. Sometimes I double the vegetables and gravy amounts, to make sure there is enough. Yummy!

the main event

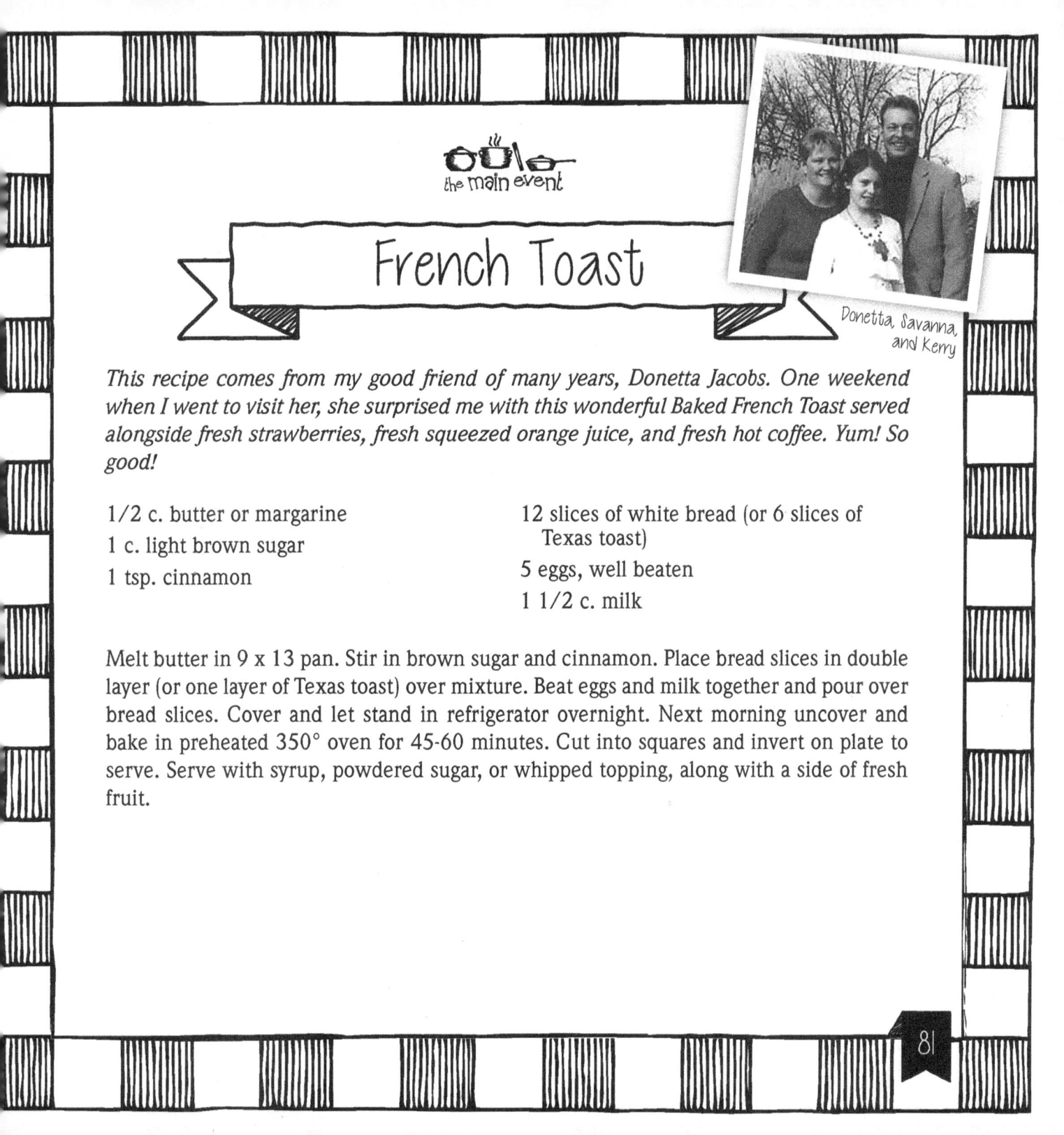

French Toast

Donetta, Savanna, and Kerry

This recipe comes from my good friend of many years, Donetta Jacobs. One weekend when I went to visit her, she surprised me with this wonderful Baked French Toast served alongside fresh strawberries, fresh squeezed orange juice, and fresh hot coffee. Yum! So good!

1/2 c. butter or margarine
1 c. light brown sugar
1 tsp. cinnamon

12 slices of white bread (or 6 slices of Texas toast)
5 eggs, well beaten
1 1/2 c. milk

Melt butter in 9 x 13 pan. Stir in brown sugar and cinnamon. Place bread slices in double layer (or one layer of Texas toast) over mixture. Beat eggs and milk together and pour over bread slices. Cover and let stand in refrigerator overnight. Next morning uncover and bake in preheated 350° oven for 45-60 minutes. Cut into squares and invert on plate to serve. Serve with syrup, powdered sugar, or whipped topping, along with a side of fresh fruit.

the main event

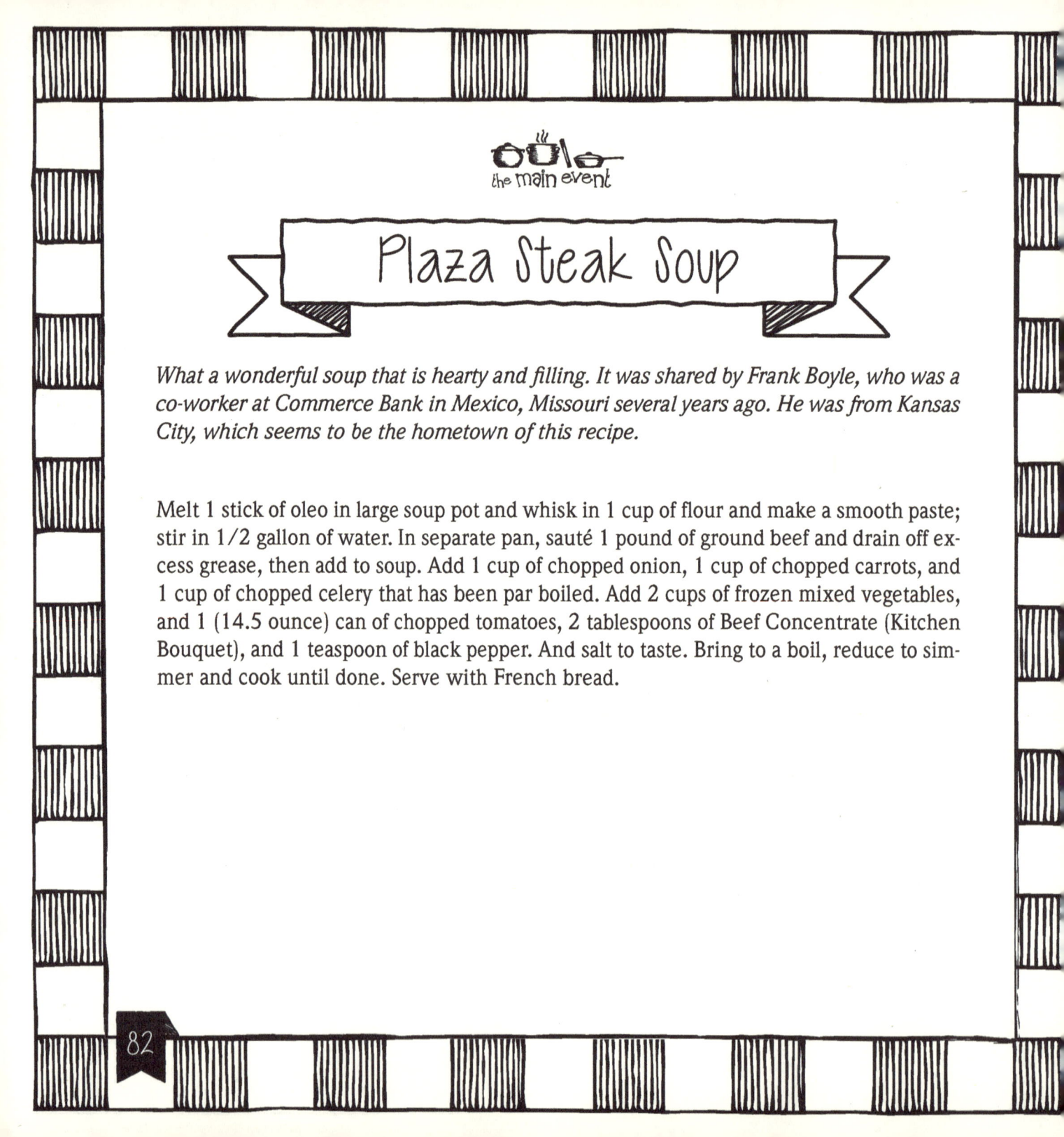

Plaza Steak Soup

What a wonderful soup that is hearty and filling. It was shared by Frank Boyle, who was a co-worker at Commerce Bank in Mexico, Missouri several years ago. He was from Kansas City, which seems to be the hometown of this recipe.

Melt 1 stick of oleo in large soup pot and whisk in 1 cup of flour and make a smooth paste; stir in 1/2 gallon of water. In separate pan, sauté 1 pound of ground beef and drain off excess grease, then add to soup. Add 1 cup of chopped onion, 1 cup of chopped carrots, and 1 cup of chopped celery that has been par boiled. Add 2 cups of frozen mixed vegetables, and 1 (14.5 ounce) can of chopped tomatoes, 2 tablespoons of Beef Concentrate (Kitchen Bouquet), and 1 teaspoon of black pepper. And salt to taste. Bring to a boil, reduce to simmer and cook until done. Serve with French bread.

the main event

Herbed Vegetable Beef Soup

Bo Gordon

My friend Jeane Gordon's husband, Bo, is a very good cook. He is always trying something new. He works with the recipes by changing, adding, and subtracting until he has the perfect flavor. So this is one of his best.

- 2 lbs. stew meat
- 2 Tbsp. cooking oil
- 1 lg. can tomato juice
- 1 med. onion, chopped
- 2 tsp. black pepper
- 2 tsp. salt
- 2 tsp. garlic powder
- 1 tsp. crushed rosemary
- 1 tsp. dried oregano
- 1 tsp. dried basil
- 1 tsp. ground marjoram
- 2 bay leaves
- 2 c. cubed potatoes
- 2 cans sliced carrots
- 2 cans whole green beans
- 2 cans corn
- 2 cans peas

Add beef broth as necessary to your desired thickness.

Brown stew meat in oil in large pot, add can of tomato juice and all spices; cook on range top covered and on low simmer for 2 hours or until meat is tender. Add potatoes and all vegetables (undrained) and continue cooking until potatoes are fork tender. Always taste and add more of the herbs that you like.

the main event

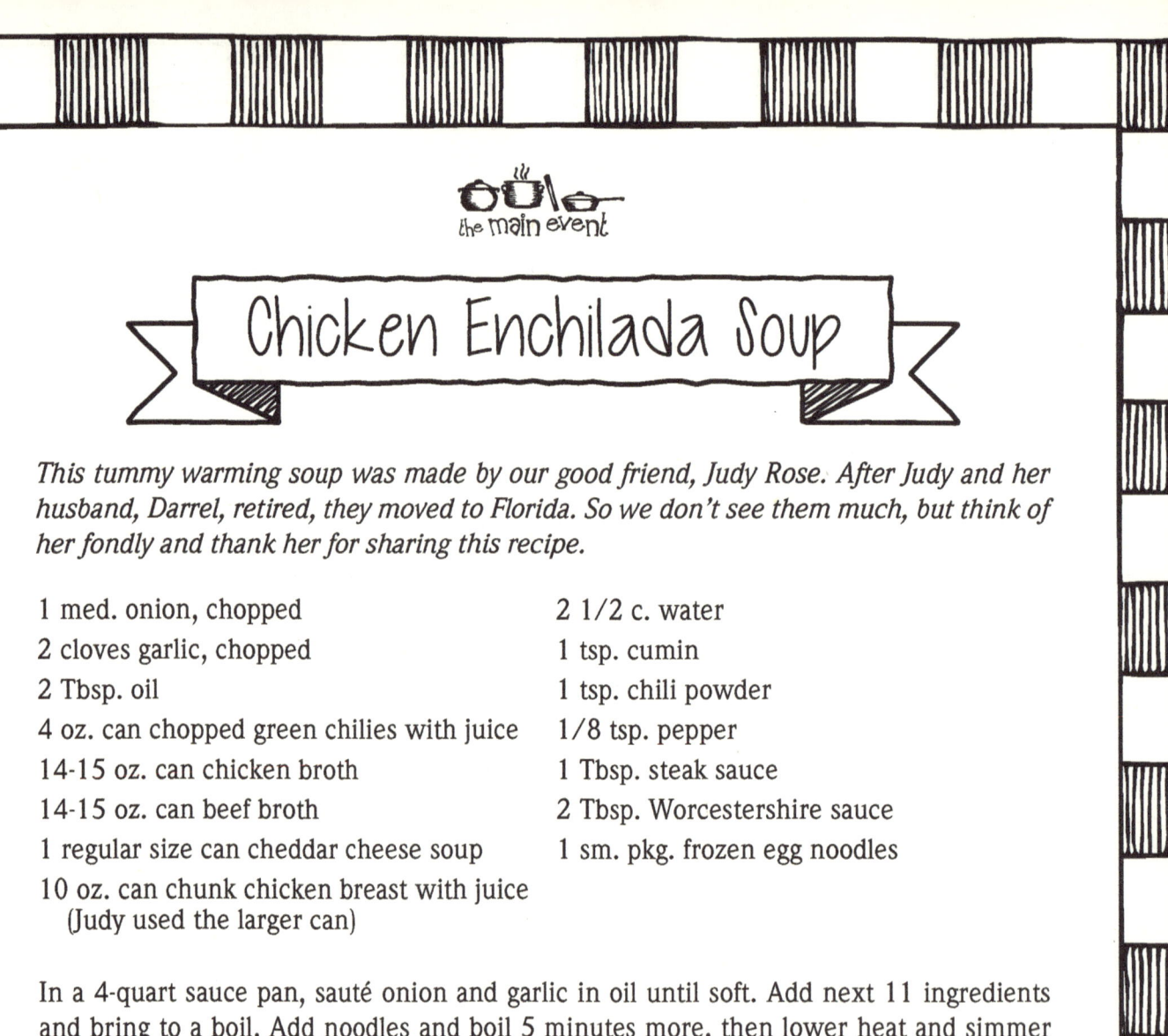

Chicken Enchilada Soup

This tummy warming soup was made by our good friend, Judy Rose. After Judy and her husband, Darrel, retired, they moved to Florida. So we don't see them much, but think of her fondly and thank her for sharing this recipe.

1 med. onion, chopped
2 cloves garlic, chopped
2 Tbsp. oil
4 oz. can chopped green chilies with juice
14-15 oz. can chicken broth
14-15 oz. can beef broth
1 regular size can cheddar cheese soup
10 oz. can chunk chicken breast with juice
   (Judy used the larger can)

2 1/2 c. water
1 tsp. cumin
1 tsp. chili powder
1/8 tsp. pepper
1 Tbsp. steak sauce
2 Tbsp. Worcestershire sauce
1 sm. pkg. frozen egg noodles

In a 4-quart sauce pan, sauté onion and garlic in oil until soft. Add next 11 ingredients and bring to a boil. Add noodles and boil 5 minutes more, then lower heat and simmer 25 minutes.

the main event

Broccoli Cheese Soup

My good friend Jan, also has the best recipe for Broccoli Cheese Soup, so here is the recipe. Jan said it had been passed on to her by our co-worker, Art Porter.

1/2 stick butter	4 c. noodles or potatoes
1 med. onion	2 – 10 oz. pkg. chopped broccoli
Sauté chopped onion in butter until clear.	1/8 tsp. garlic powder
6 c. water	1 lb. Velveeta cheese
6 tsp. chicken bouillon	1 1/2 qts. Half and Half

Combine water and bouillon, add to sautéed onions, add and cook the potatoes approximately 3 minutes, add broccoli and cook approximately 3 more minutes, or until tender, turn down heat, add chunks of cheese slowly, stir, until melted, add Half and Half, and heat through; do not boil.

the main event

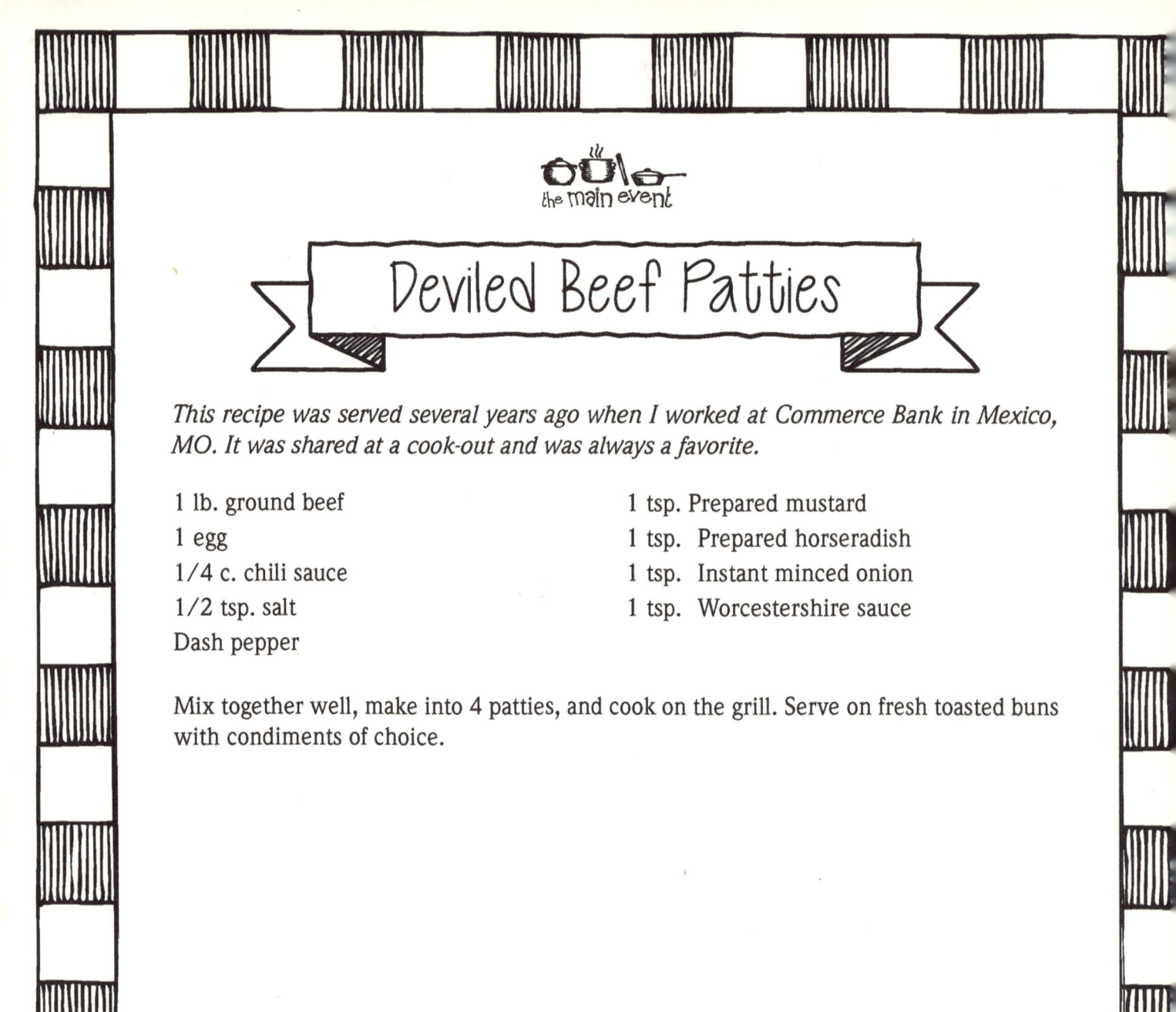

Deviled Beef Patties

This recipe was served several years ago when I worked at Commerce Bank in Mexico, MO. It was shared at a cook-out and was always a favorite.

1 lb. ground beef
1 egg
1/4 c. chili sauce
1/2 tsp. salt
Dash pepper

1 tsp. Prepared mustard
1 tsp. Prepared horseradish
1 tsp. Instant minced onion
1 tsp. Worcestershire sauce

Mix together well, make into 4 patties, and cook on the grill. Serve on fresh toasted buns with condiments of choice.

the main event

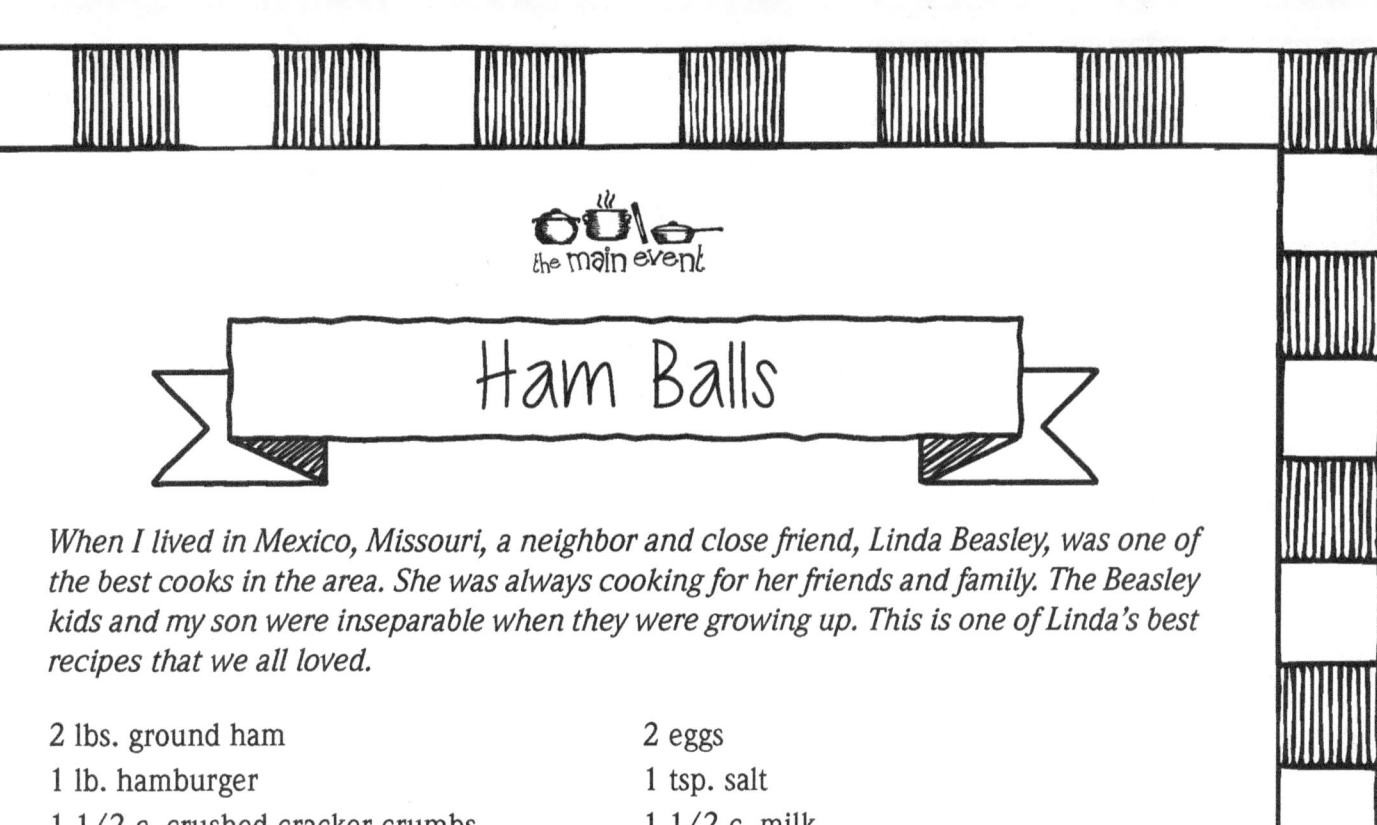

Ham Balls

When I lived in Mexico, Missouri, a neighbor and close friend, Linda Beasley, was one of the best cooks in the area. She was always cooking for her friends and family. The Beasley kids and my son were inseparable when they were growing up. This is one of Linda's best recipes that we all loved.

2 lbs. ground ham	2 eggs
1 lb. hamburger	1 tsp. salt
1 1/2 c. crushed cracker crumbs	1 1/2 c. milk

Mix together and shape into large balls. Place close together in a deep pan and mix the following ingredients together and pour over the ham balls, then bake 2 hours in the deep covered pan at 350°.

2 cans of tomato soup	1 c. brown sugar
1/2 c. vinegar	1/2 c. smoky barbecue sauce

It is delicious served with mashed potatoes!

the main event

Cheesy Zucchini Lasagna

This is a healthy addition to your summer menu that was once again given to me by Joyce Rader. It is always good use for the proliferate zucchini and is a delicious meatless meal.

- 2 c. shredded fat-free or low fat mozzarella cheese (8 oz.)
- 2 c. shredded zucchini
- 1 c. nonfat or low fat ricotta cheese
- 1/2 tsp. Italian Seasoning
- 1/4 c. grated Parmesan cheese
- 2 3/4 c. meatless spaghetti sauce
- 9 uncooked lasagna noodles

Heat oven to 350°. Reserve 1/2 cup of mozzarella cheese. Mix remaining mozzarella cheese, zucchini, ricotta cheese, Italian Seasoning and Parmesan cheese. Spread 3/4 cup of the spaghetti sauce in ungreased rectangular baking dish, (11 x 7 x 1 ½ or 12 x 7 ½ x 1 ½) and top with 3 of the noodles. Spread half of the cheese mixture over noodles in dish; top with 3/4 cup of the spaghetti sauce. Repeat with 3 noodles, remaining cheese mixture and 3/4 cup of the spaghetti sauce. Top with remaining noodles and spaghetti sauce.

Cover with foil and bake about 1 hour or until noodles are tender. Remove from oven; sprinkle with reserved mozzarella cheese. Let stand 15 minutes before cutting to serve.

8 servings

the main event

Roasted Veggie Lasagna

The following is a variation that I made up on this recipe that turned out very well!

Roasted vegetables
2 c. shredded fat-free or part skim mozzarella cheese (8 oz)
1 c. nonfat or low-fat ricotta cheese
1/4 c. grated Parmesan cheese
2 3/4 c. meatless spaghetti sauce
9 uncooked lasagna noodles
Fresh basil chopped—approximately 1/4 – 1/3 c.

Roast vegetables (I used zucchini, yellow squash, red pepper and sliced mushrooms). Dice in bite-size pieces, spray cookie sheet, put veggies on sheet, drizzle with olive oil, and then add salt, pepper, garlic powder, and Italian seasoning to taste. Roast in 425° oven about 30 minutes, stirring about every 10 minutes, or until desired doneness.

Heat oven to 350°. Reserve 1/2 cup of mozzarella cheese. Mix remaining mozzarella cheese, ricotta cheese, and Parmesan cheese. Spread 3/4 cup of the spaghetti sauce in ungreased rectangular baking dish, (11 x 7 x 1.5 or 12 x 7.5 x 1.5). Top with 3 of the noodles. Spread half of the cheese mixture over noodles in dish and 1/2 the vegetables; top with 3/4 cup of the spaghetti sauce and the fresh basil. Repeat with 3 noodles, remaining cheese mixture, roasted veggies and 3/4 cup of the spaghetti sauce. Top with remaining noodles and spaghetti sauce.

Cover with aluminum foil and bake about 1 hour or until noodles are tender. Remove from oven; sprinkle with reserved mozzarella cheese. Let stand 15 minutes before cutting. 8 servings

the main event

South of the Border Lasagna

While visiting in South Carolina with Steve's brother, Ken and wife Marilyn, Marilyn cooked this delicious variation of lasagna one evening for dinner. What a treat it was.

2 lbs. ground beef
1 onion, chopped
1 clove garlic, minced
2 Tbsp. chili powder
3 c. tomato sauce
1 tsp. sugar
Salt (to taste)
1/2 c. sliced black olives
4 oz. can chopped green chilies
12 corn tortillas
vegetable oil
2 c. sm. curd cottage cheese
1 egg, beaten
8 oz. Monterey Jack cheese, grated
4 oz. cheddar cheese grated

Brown meat and drain. Add onion and garlic and cook until soft. Sprinkle chili powder over meat and mix well. Add tomato sauce, sugar, salt, black olives, and green chilies. Simmer 15 minutes. Soften tortillas in hot oil and drain on paper towels. Beat cottage cheese and egg together and set aside. Layer in 9 x 13 casserole: 1/3 of meat sauce, 1/2 of jack cheese, 1/2 of cottage cheese mixture, 1/2 of tortillas. Repeat layering one more time, topping with last 1/3 of meat sauce. Cover with grated cheddar cheese and bake in 350° oven for 30 minutes.

the main event

Lobster House Flounder Parmesan

This is another recipe from Marge Winters.

2 lbs. flounder fillets
1 c. sour cream
1/4 c. parmesan cheese
1 Tbsp. lemon juice

1 Tbsp. grated onion
Dash hot pepper sauce
Paprika and parsley for seasoning

Arrange fish in single layer; cover with dressing made from sour cream, parmesan cheese, lemon juice, onion, and hot pepper sauce. Sprinkle with paprika and parsley. Bake in 350° oven for 25-30 minutes.

the main event

Crustless Crab Quiche

Within the last few weeks I was blessed to be in a Bible study/small group with some wonderful ladies. We met at Sue Westenhaver's lovely Bed and Breakfast in Osage Beach, The Inn at Harbour Ridge. Our group liked to cook and share recipes. We would meet, have the study, and then we would take turns at providing a great lunch to share and spend some time visiting. This recipe is from Ruth Fowler and was one of the favorites that we were lucky enough to have been given.

- 8 oz. fresh sliced mushroom
- 1/4 c. chopped yellow onion
- 1/4 c. chopped sweet red pepper
- 2 Tbsp. butter
- 4 lg. eggs
- 1 c. sour cream
- 1 c. sm. curd cottage cheese
- 1/2 c. grated parmesan cheese
- 1/2 c. flour
- 1/2 tsp. salt
- 4 drops Tabasco sauce
- 2 c. shredded Monterey Jack Cheese
- 2 sm. cans crab meat

Sauté mushrooms, onion, and red pepper in 2 Tablespoons butter until tender. Remove from pan and drain on paper towels.

Blend eggs, sour cream, cottage cheese, Parmesan cheese, flour, salt, and Tabasco. Fold in mushroom mixture, Jack cheese, and crabmeat. Pour into a prepared 10-inch quiche dish. Bake at 350° for 45 minutes or until knife inserted comes out clean. It should be puffed and golden brown. Let stand 5 minutes before serving.

the main event

Ham and Beans (cooked in the oven)

I was blessed to work at Bagnell Dam during my career with Ameren. The guys in the control room would sometimes cook up a meal to be shared with all, so there had to be lots of it and easy to do. One of the good cooks that shared this interesting and somewhat easy recipe was Keith Mentel.

2 lbs. great northern beans
1 lb. pinto beans
1 med. onion

1 lg. ham bone or smoked hocks
22-24 c. water

Cook covered in large roaster in oven for 2 1/2 to 3 hours at 375°. Serve with cornbread for quite a tasty meal.

the main event

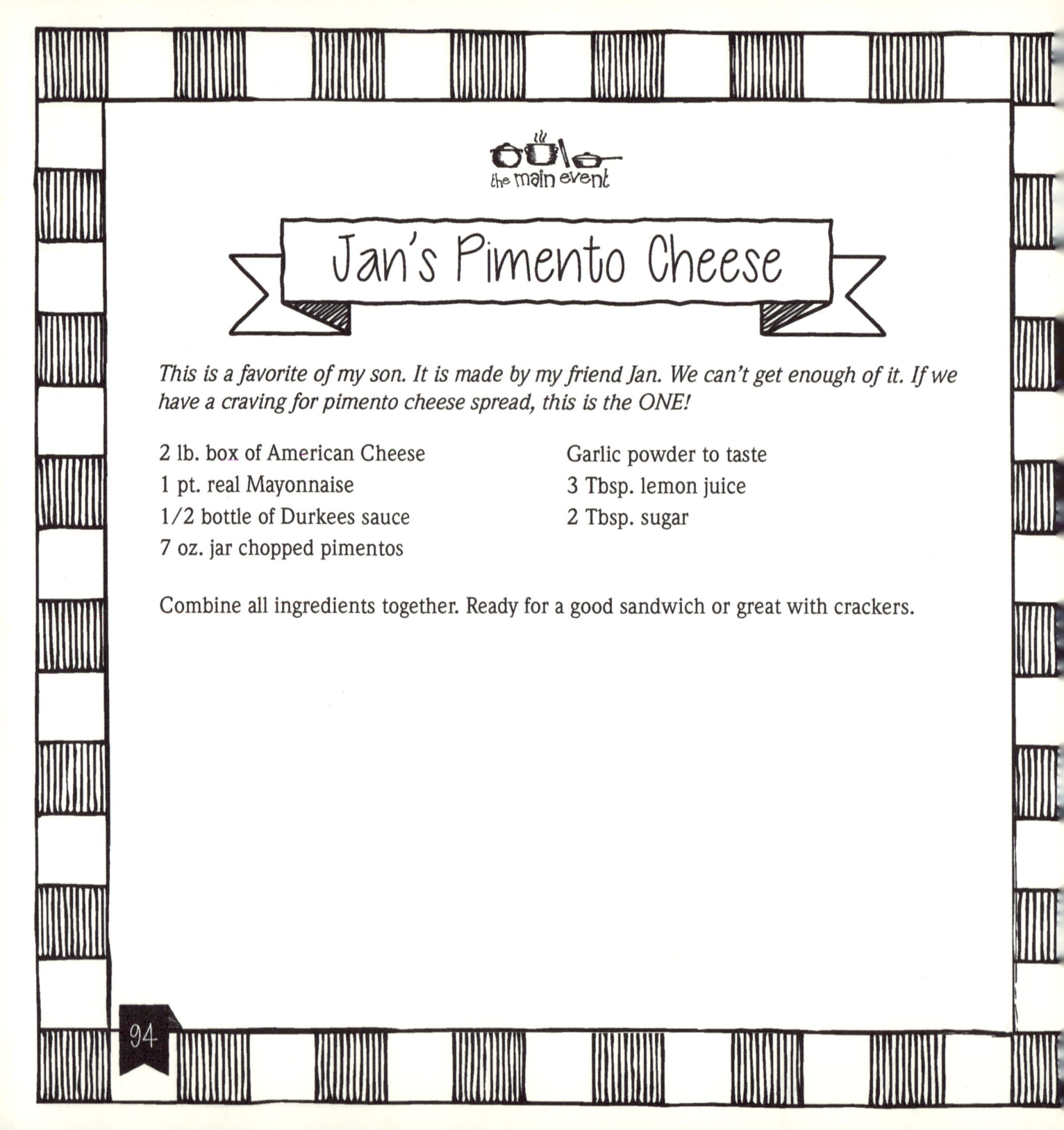

Jan's Pimento Cheese

This is a favorite of my son. It is made by my friend Jan. We can't get enough of it. If we have a craving for pimento cheese spread, this is the ONE!

2 lb. box of American Cheese
1 pt. real Mayonnaise
1/2 bottle of Durkees sauce
7 oz. jar chopped pimentos

Garlic powder to taste
3 Tbsp. lemon juice
2 Tbsp. sugar

Combine all ingredients together. Ready for a good sandwich or great with crackers.

the main event

Spicy Pimento Cheese

This is another variation on pimento cheese that has become a family favorite. Very quick and easy.

- 1 c. grated mild cheddar cheese
- 1 c. grated pepper jack cheese
- 4 oz. cream cheese (softened)
- 2 oz. jar of pimentos, chopped
- Salt and pepper to taste
- 1/4 c. mayonnaise (may need a little more depending on consistency wanted)

Beat the cream cheese in bowl until smooth; add the cheddar and pepper jack cheese, pimentos, salt/pepper, and mayo. Continue to beat with hand mixer until well combined. Serve with crackers or on toast, can also add extra mayo to serve as chip dip or with veggies.

the main event

Smoky Salmon Fillets

This recipe is a favorite that has been shared by many and has been tweaked to taste.

Fruitwood or hickory chips (we use Mesquite)
1 tsp. onion powder
1 tsp. garlic powder
1/4 tsp. salt
1/4 tsp. pepper
1 salmon fillet with skin (approximately 1 1/2 lbs. is a good size)

Soak the wood chips in water at least 30 minutes. Combine onion powder, garlic powder, salt, and pepper; rub fillet with mixture. Cover and refrigerate for 30 minutes. Prepare charcoal fire in smoker; let it burn 15 to 20 minutes. Drain the wood chips and place them on the hot coals. Place water pan in smoker; add water to pan to depth of fill line. Place fillet, skin side down on upper food rack; cover with smoker lid. Cook for approximately 1 1/2 hours until the fish flakes easily when tested with a fork. This will make 4 dinner servings, but I like to serve with crackers as an appetizer.

Some people like to use all onion powder, 2 teaspoons, instead of the 1:1 split of onion and garlic powder. So season to taste.

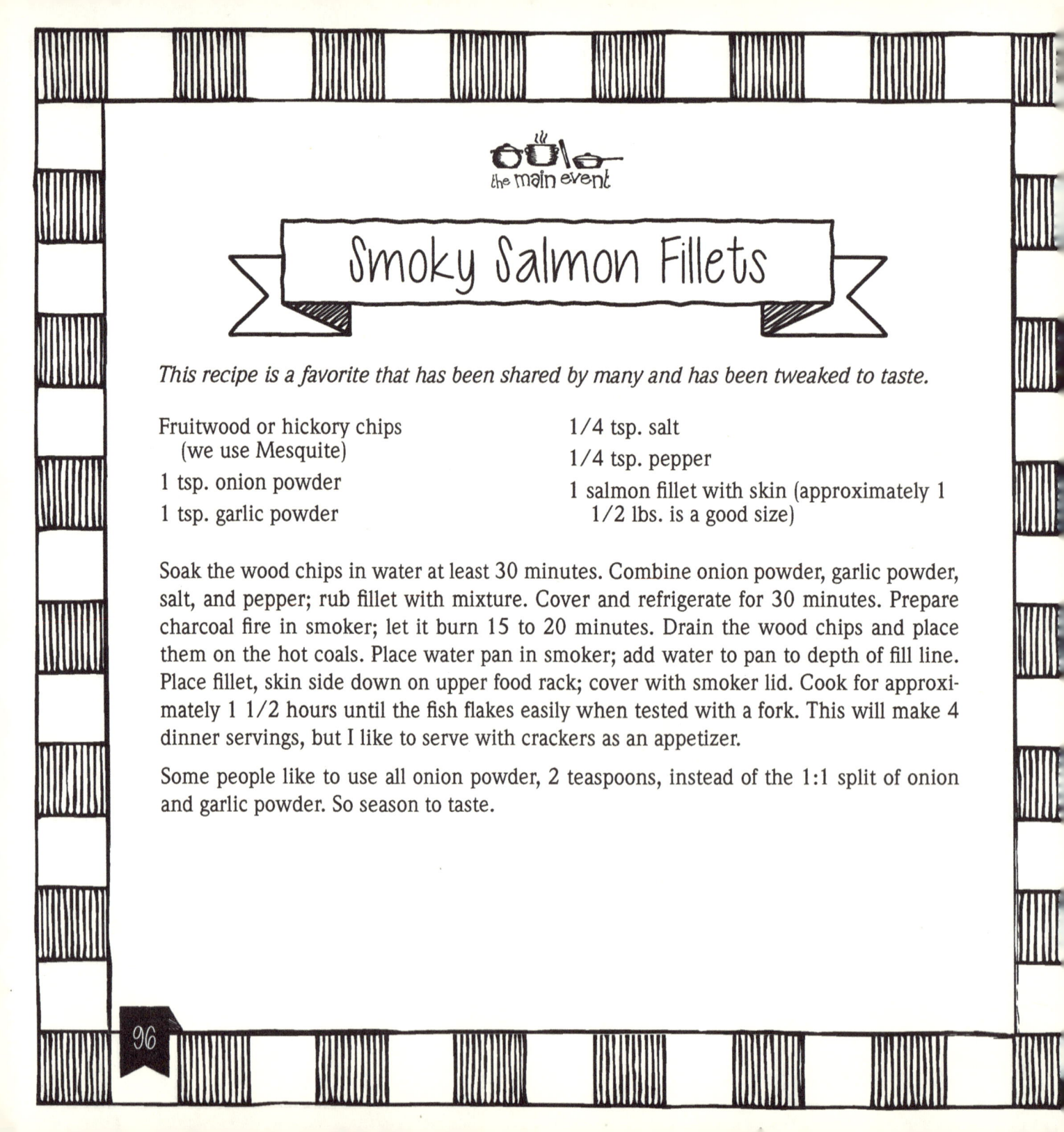

the main event

Leo's Clam Chowder

This is another recipe that my friend, Leo, was famous for, his Clam Chowder that he liked to make and share with the office in the cold winter.

1 can clams
2 cans of New England style Clam Chowder

2 cans Cream of Potato Soup
1 1/2 c. Half and Half

Mix together and heat slowly over low heat or heat on low in slow cooker. Ready to serve.

the main event

Beef Brisket

Another co-worker that I met when I first moved to the Lake was Katie Mathews, and she was well known for her office favorite, beef brisket.

1 can beef consommé
1/3 bottle of liquid smoke
1/3 bottle soy sauce

Combine and pour over brisket, cover with foil, and marinate overnight. Cook approximately 4 hours at 300°. Cool and slice across the grain, put back in juice to reheat.

the main event

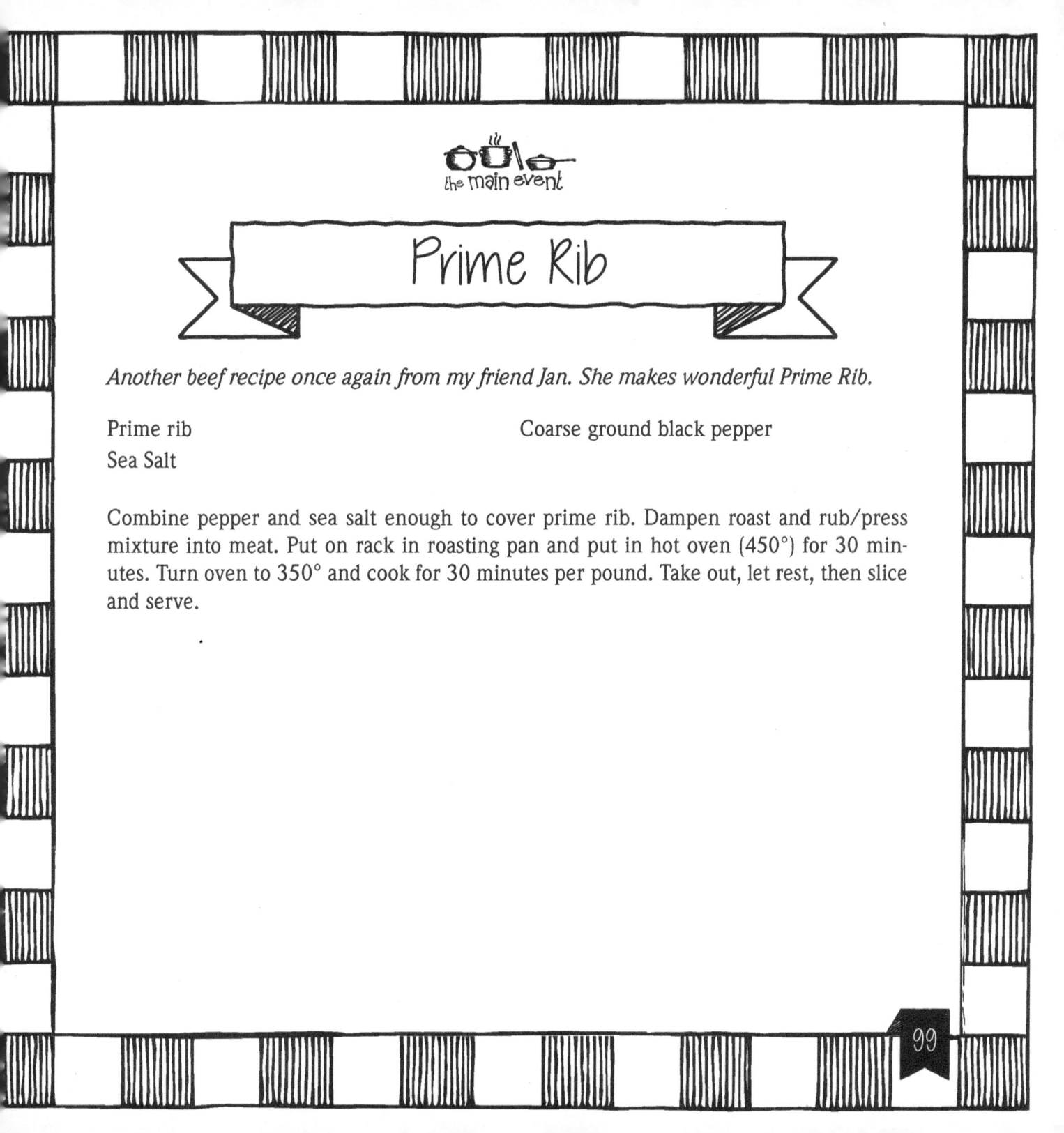

Prime Rib

Another beef recipe once again from my friend Jan. She makes wonderful Prime Rib.

Prime rib
Sea Salt

Coarse ground black pepper

Combine pepper and sea salt enough to cover prime rib. Dampen roast and rub/press mixture into meat. Put on rack in roasting pan and put in hot oven (450°) for 30 minutes. Turn oven to 350° and cook for 30 minutes per pound. Take out, let rest, then slice and serve.

the main event

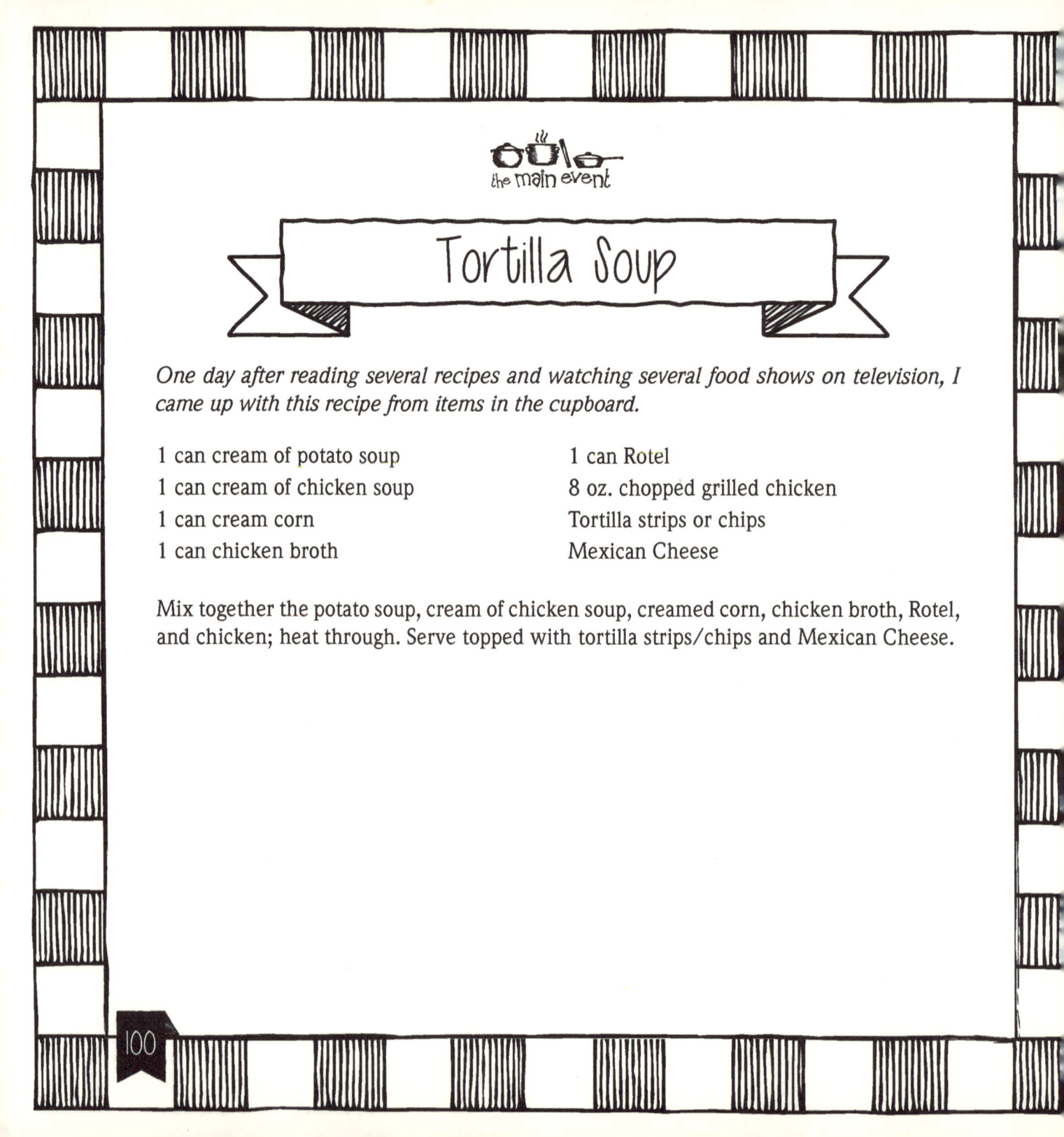

Tortilla Soup

One day after reading several recipes and watching several food shows on television, I came up with this recipe from items in the cupboard.

1 can cream of potato soup
1 can cream of chicken soup
1 can cream corn
1 can chicken broth
1 can Rotel
8 oz. chopped grilled chicken
Tortilla strips or chips
Mexican Cheese

Mix together the potato soup, cream of chicken soup, creamed corn, chicken broth, Rotel, and chicken; heat through. Serve topped with tortilla strips/chips and Mexican Cheese.

the main event

Steve and Linda's Chicken Noodle Soup

I love a good pot of chicken noodle soup, so after many tries, we have come up with our favorite version of this yummy delight. It will warm your tummy, and it always soothes your head when you might have that tough cold.

- 3 c. diced chicken (we use one de-boned rotisserie chicken)
- 2 Tbsp. butter
- 1/2 tsp. Black Kettle Seasoning (or similar season salt)
- 8 oz. box sliced white mushrooms
- 2 carrots, diced
- 1 stalk celery, diced
- 32 oz. box chicken stock
- 32 oz. box chicken broth (reserve 1/4 c. and stir in 2 Tbsp. of corn starch and add at end to thicken soup)
- 1 bouillon cube or 3/4 tsp. of chicken soup base
- 16 oz. pkg. frozen Home-style egg noodles

Melt butter in large pan; add seasoning, sauté mushrooms, carrots, and celery until soft. Add chicken, broth, bouillon, and stock and bring to a boil, add the noodles and cook 20-25 minutes (according to directions on noodle package) until done, stir in the broth/corn starch mixture and thicken. Serve with crusty bread.

Steve and Linda

the main event

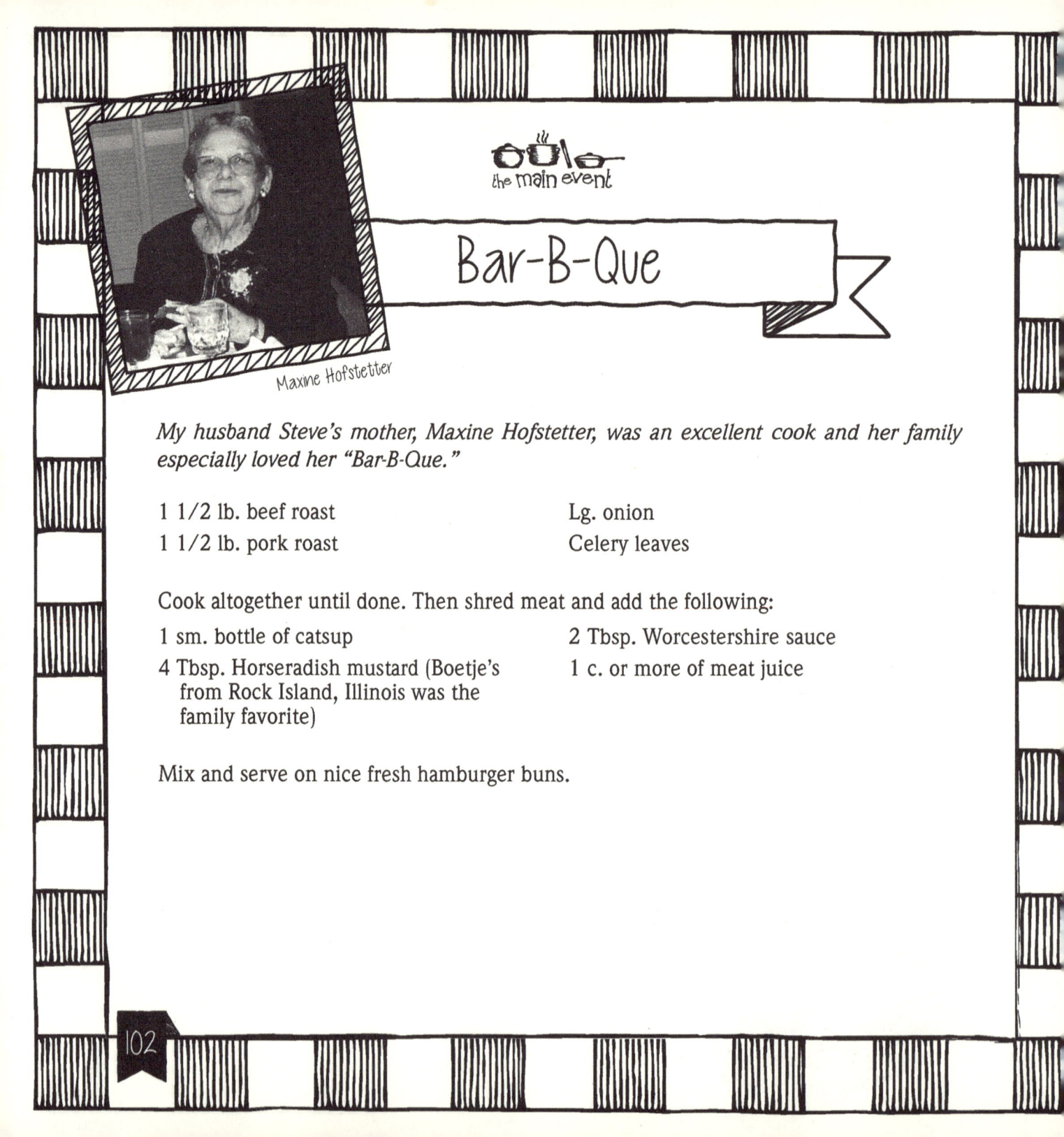

Bar-B-Que

Maxine Hofstetter

My husband Steve's mother, Maxine Hofstetter, was an excellent cook and her family especially loved her "Bar-B-Que."

1 1/2 lb. beef roast
1 1/2 lb. pork roast
Lg. onion
Celery leaves

Cook altogether until done. Then shred meat and add the following:

1 sm. bottle of catsup
4 Tbsp. Horseradish mustard (Boetje's from Rock Island, Illinois was the family favorite)
2 Tbsp. Worcestershire sauce
1 c. or more of meat juice

Mix and serve on nice fresh hamburger buns.

the main event

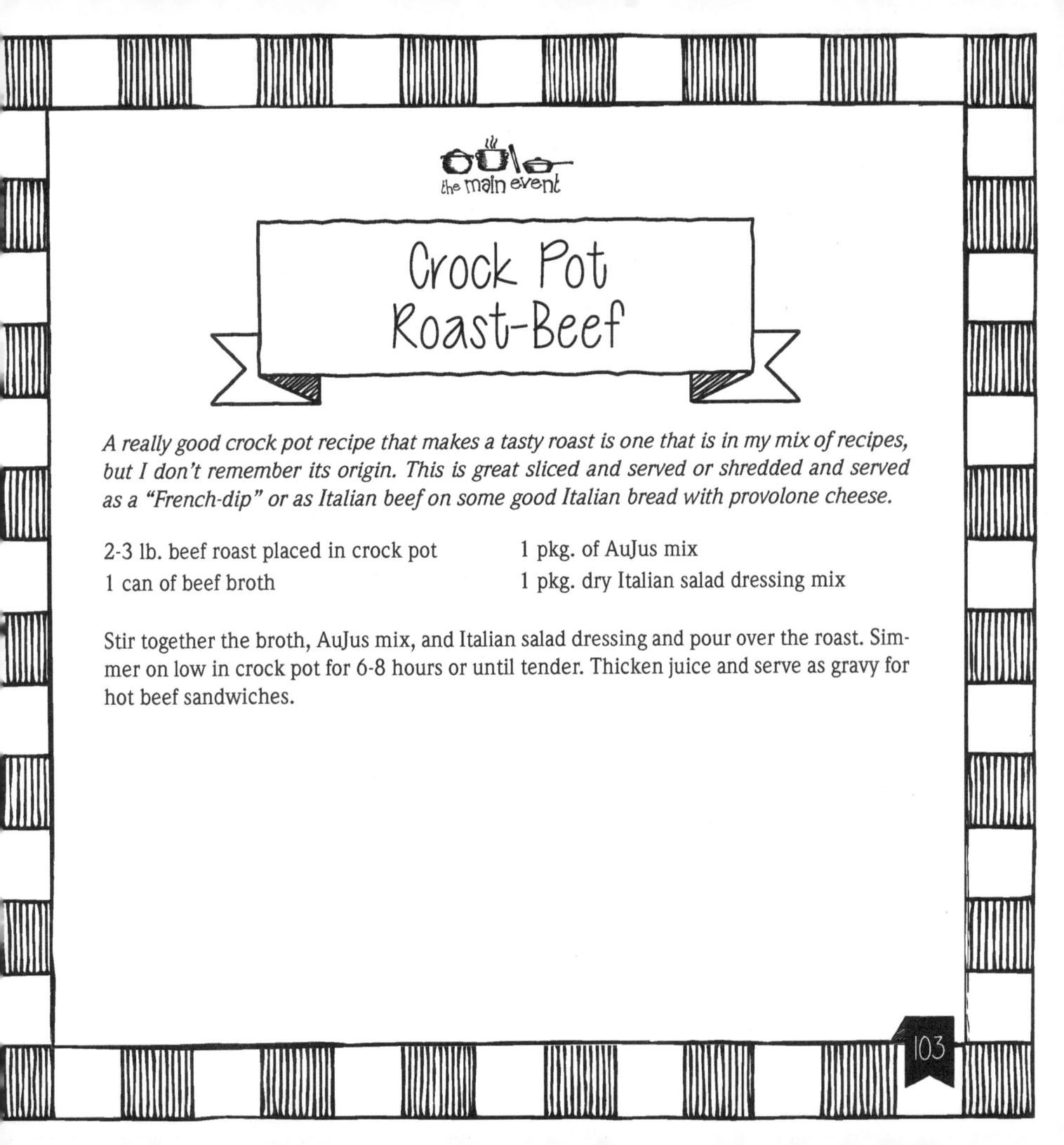

Crock Pot Roast-Beef

A really good crock pot recipe that makes a tasty roast is one that is in my mix of recipes, but I don't remember its origin. This is great sliced and served or shredded and served as a "French-dip" or as Italian beef on some good Italian bread with provolone cheese.

2-3 lb. beef roast placed in crock pot
1 can of beef broth
1 pkg. of AuJus mix
1 pkg. dry Italian salad dressing mix

Stir together the broth, AuJus mix, and Italian salad dressing and pour over the roast. Simmer on low in crock pot for 6-8 hours or until tender. Thicken juice and serve as gravy for hot beef sandwiches.

the main event

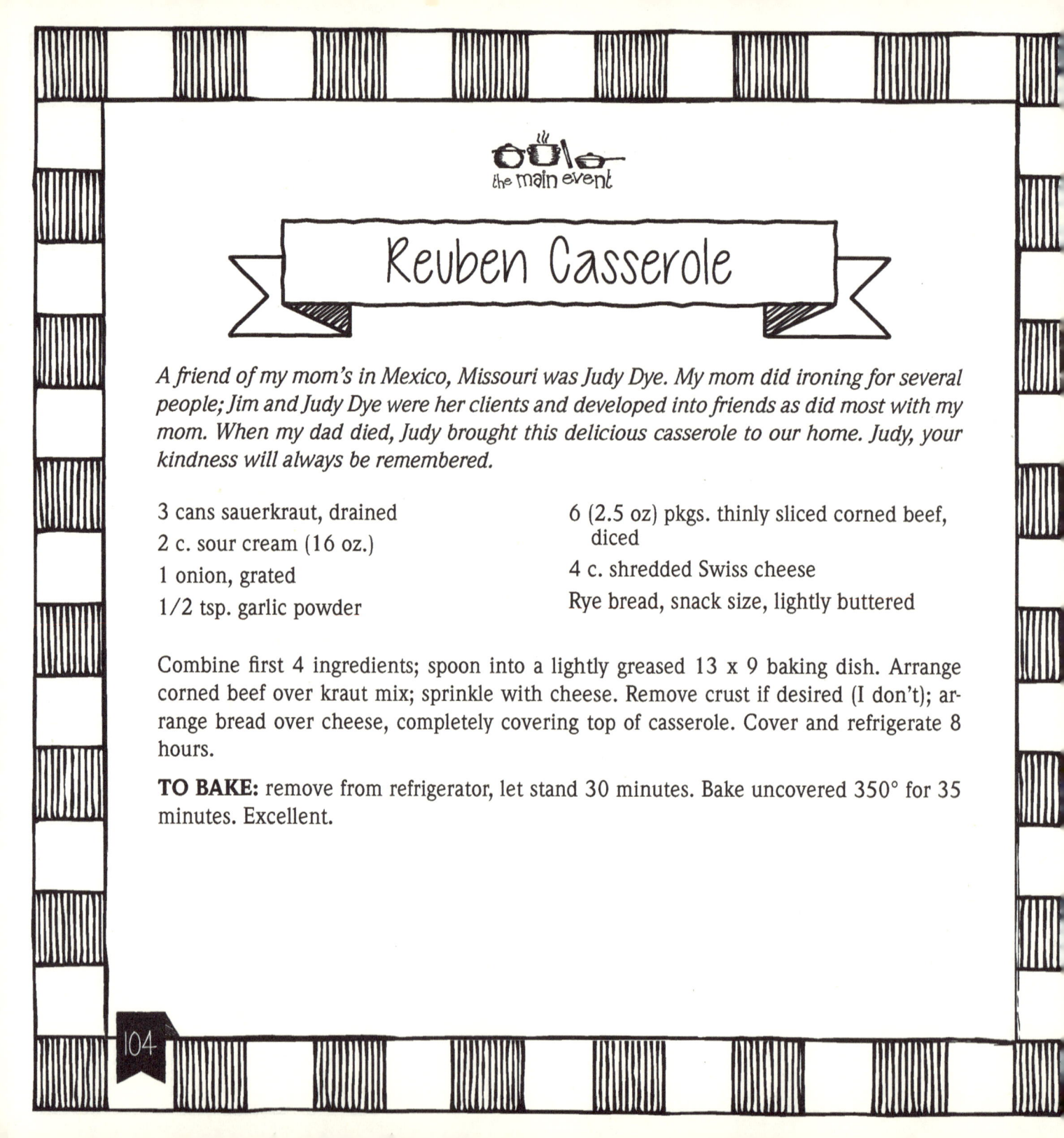

Reuben Casserole

A friend of my mom's in Mexico, Missouri was Judy Dye. My mom did ironing for several people; Jim and Judy Dye were her clients and developed into friends as did most with my mom. When my dad died, Judy brought this delicious casserole to our home. Judy, your kindness will always be remembered.

- 3 cans sauerkraut, drained
- 2 c. sour cream (16 oz.)
- 1 onion, grated
- 1/2 tsp. garlic powder
- 6 (2.5 oz) pkgs. thinly sliced corned beef, diced
- 4 c. shredded Swiss cheese
- Rye bread, snack size, lightly buttered

Combine first 4 ingredients; spoon into a lightly greased 13 x 9 baking dish. Arrange corned beef over kraut mix; sprinkle with cheese. Remove crust if desired (I don't); arrange bread over cheese, completely covering top of casserole. Cover and refrigerate 8 hours.

TO BAKE: remove from refrigerator, let stand 30 minutes. Bake uncovered 350° for 35 minutes. Excellent.

the main event

Creamy Fettuccine Alfredo

Misty Horn

This is another great recipe from Misty Horn, one of her family's favorites.

8 oz. pkg. cream cheese (I use 1/3 less fat)
3/4 c. grated parmesan cheese
1/2 c. margarine (I use Smart Balance)
1/2 c. milk (I use skim)
8 oz. Fettuccine; cooked
(This is just an estimate)

In large saucepan, combine all ingredients except the cooked fettuccine. Stir on low until heated and smooth. Add fettuccine, toss lightly.

*Even with the low-fat ingredients, it's still really creamy!

the main event

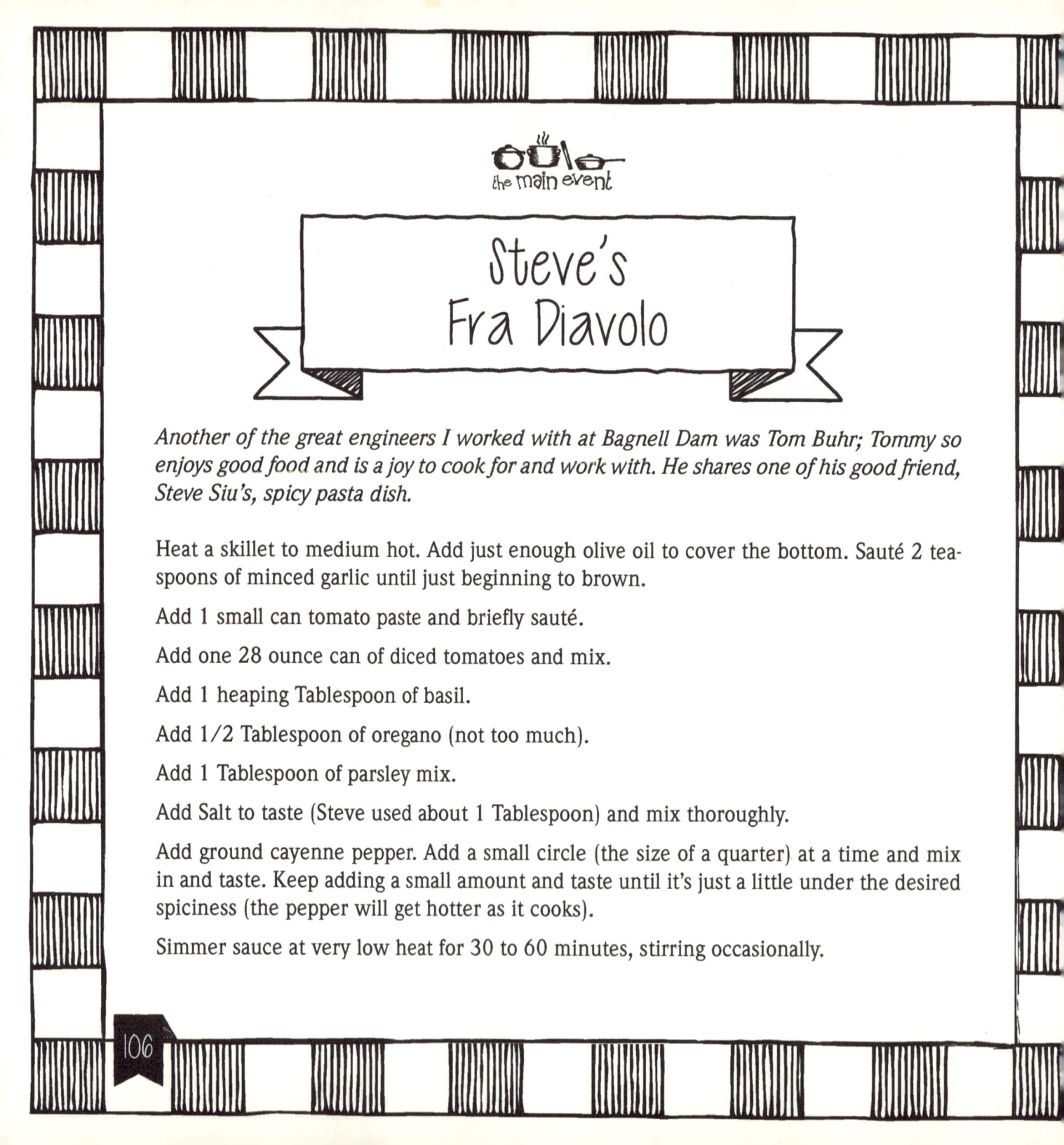

Steve's Fra Diavolo

Another of the great engineers I worked with at Bagnell Dam was Tom Buhr; Tommy so enjoys good food and is a joy to cook for and work with. He shares one of his good friend, Steve Siu's, spicy pasta dish.

Heat a skillet to medium hot. Add just enough olive oil to cover the bottom. Sauté 2 teaspoons of minced garlic until just beginning to brown.

Add 1 small can tomato paste and briefly sauté.

Add one 28 ounce can of diced tomatoes and mix.

Add 1 heaping Tablespoon of basil.

Add 1/2 Tablespoon of oregano (not too much).

Add 1 Tablespoon of parsley mix.

Add Salt to taste (Steve used about 1 Tablespoon) and mix thoroughly.

Add ground cayenne pepper. Add a small circle (the size of a quarter) at a time and mix in and taste. Keep adding a small amount and taste until it's just a little under the desired spiciness (the pepper will get hotter as it cooks).

Simmer sauce at very low heat for 30 to 60 minutes, stirring occasionally.

the main event

Tom and Mary Buhr

Cook one pound of pasta. Drain and place on platter.

At the same time sauté 1 to 2 pounds of shrimp (halved if jumbo, peeled if medium or large) with 1 teaspoon of minced garlic and just a little olive oil in a hot pan. This will cook very quickly. As soon as the shrimp is done, add the sauce. Add 1/4 to 1/2 cup white wine, mix, and heat through until the mixture starts to bubble (boil).

Pour shrimp and sauce over the pasta. Sprinkle with Parmesan or Romano cheese and serve.

the main event

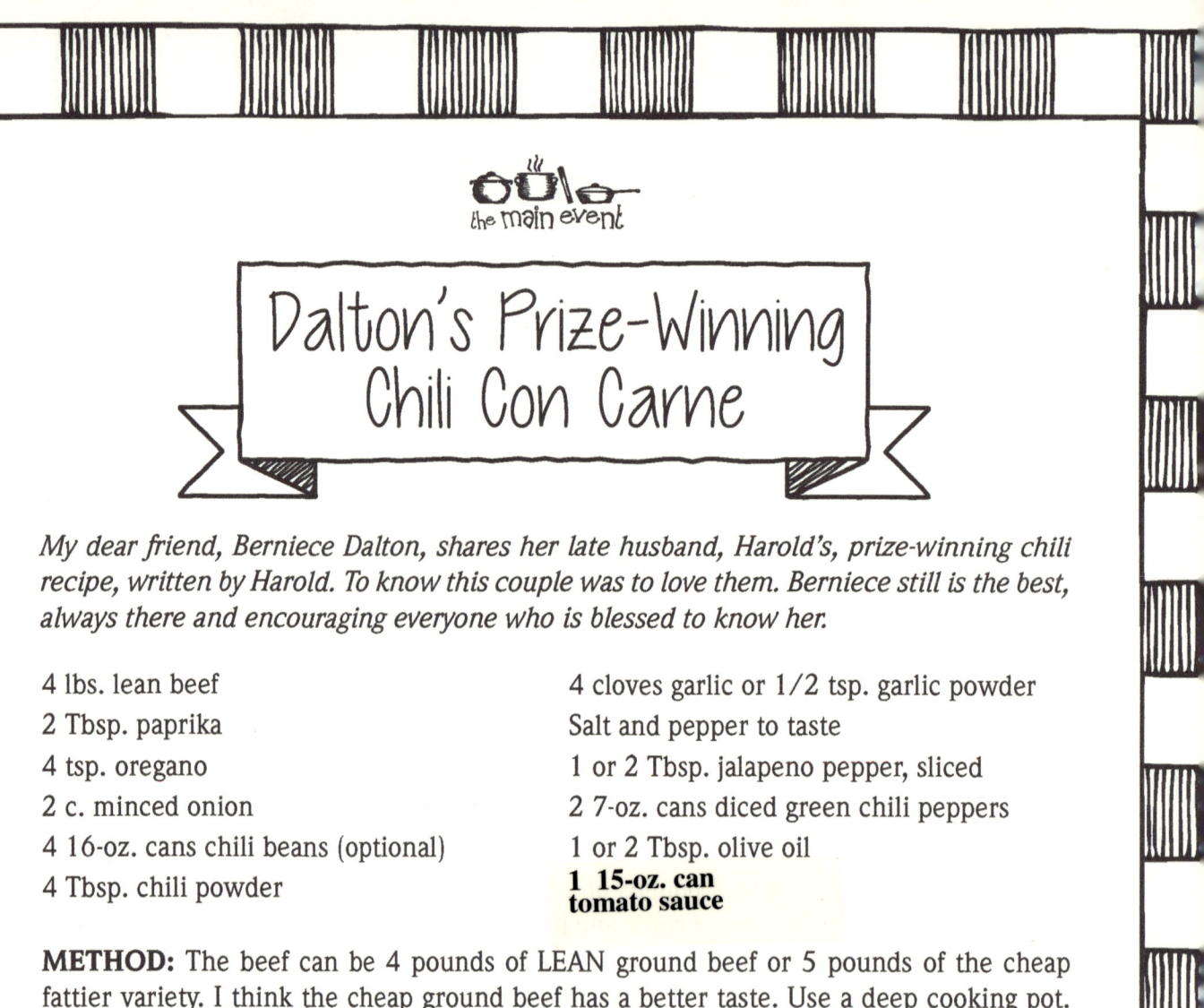

Dalton's Prize-Winning Chili Con Carne

My dear friend, Berniece Dalton, shares her late husband, Harold's, prize-winning chili recipe, written by Harold. To know this couple was to love them. Berniece still is the best, always there and encouraging everyone who is blessed to know her.

- 4 lbs. lean beef
- 2 Tbsp. paprika
- 4 tsp. oregano
- 2 c. minced onion
- 4 16-oz. cans chili beans (optional)
- 4 Tbsp. chili powder
- 4 cloves garlic or 1/2 tsp. garlic powder
- Salt and pepper to taste
- 1 or 2 Tbsp. jalapeno pepper, sliced
- 2 7-oz. cans diced green chili peppers
- 1 or 2 Tbsp. olive oil
- **1 15-oz. can tomato sauce**

METHOD: The beef can be 4 pounds of LEAN ground beef or 5 pounds of the cheap fattier variety. I think the cheap ground beef has a better taste. Use a deep cooking pot. Cover the bottom with the olive oil or a good other oil. Heat the oil and cook the meat to a light brown. Then pour off all the fat and water that surface.

While the meat is cooking, use a blender to combine the following: Pour in one cup of water. Add onion cut in chunks and use the "chopper mode" on the blender to chop onion fairly fine. Check cup measurements on blender container to see if you now have 3 cups of onion and water in it. Then add paprika, oregano, chili powder, garlic (minced if

the main event

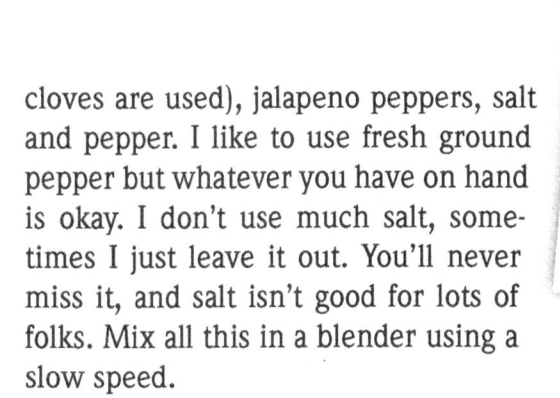

cloves are used), jalapeno peppers, salt and pepper. I like to use fresh ground pepper but whatever you have on hand is okay. I don't use much salt, sometimes I just leave it out. You'll never miss it, and salt isn't good for lots of folks. Mix all this in a blender using a slow speed.

Harold and Berniece Dalton

After the meat has browned and you have poured off all the liquid fat and water, pour in the blender mixture and stir. Use some hot faucet water to get all the blender mixture rinsed out and poured into the pot. Add the diced green chili peppers and the chili beans. The beans are optional, but if you leave them out, you're missing something great. Pour in the tomato sauce.

Use low heat to bring mixture to a simmer. After simmer begins, lower heat to allow a very slow simmer and cook for one hour. Stir once in a while with large spoon or even use an egg turner.

When it's done, it's ready to eat, but all chili tastes better the next day after letting it sit in a cool place such as outside on a cold winter night or in the refrigerator otherwise.

We freeze this in meal size containers for future use. Enjoy!

the main event

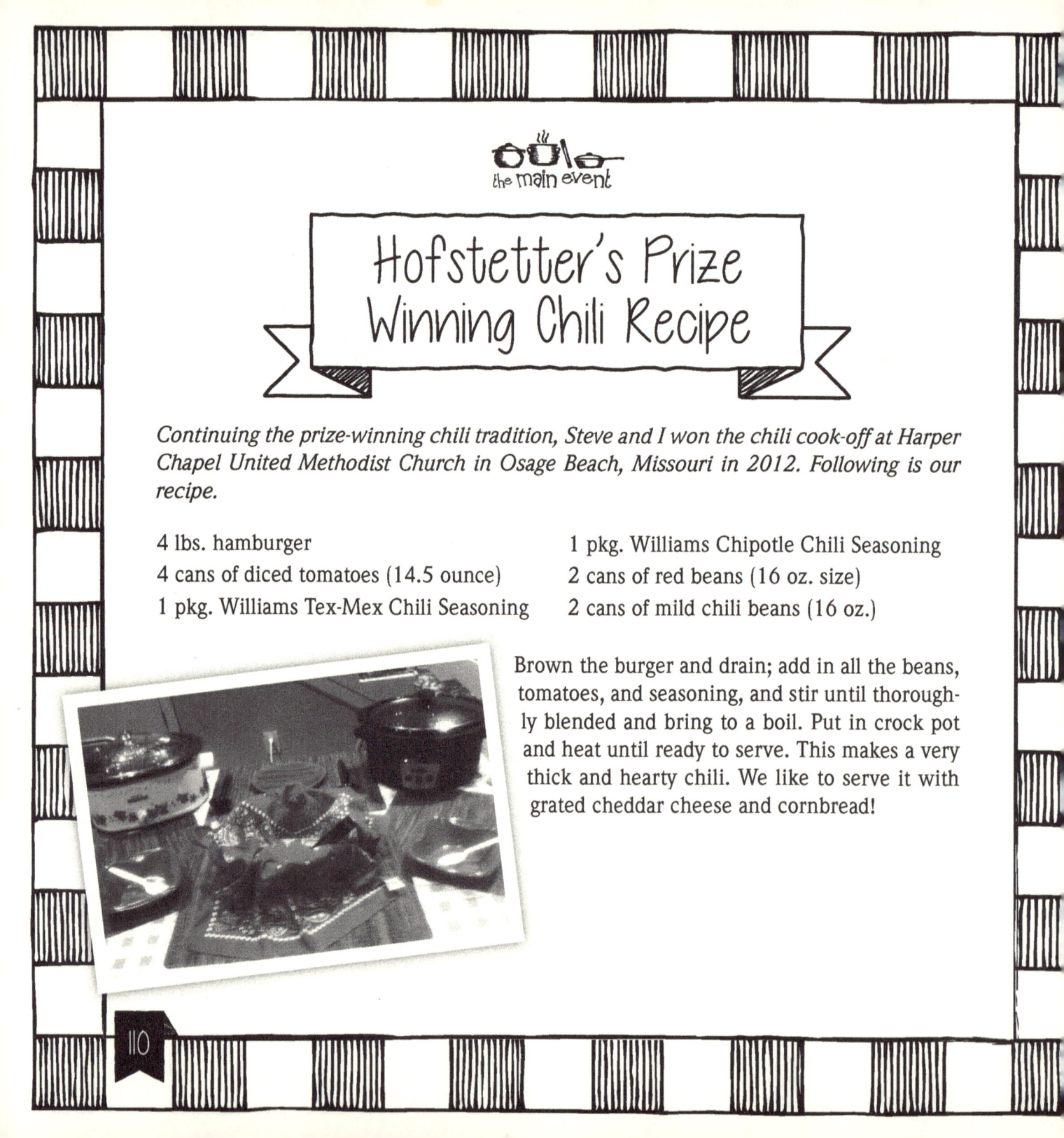

Hofstetter's Prize Winning Chili Recipe

Continuing the prize-winning chili tradition, Steve and I won the chili cook-off at Harper Chapel United Methodist Church in Osage Beach, Missouri in 2012. Following is our recipe.

4 lbs. hamburger
4 cans of diced tomatoes (14.5 ounce)
1 pkg. Williams Tex-Mex Chili Seasoning

1 pkg. Williams Chipotle Chili Seasoning
2 cans of red beans (16 oz. size)
2 cans of mild chili beans (16 oz.)

Brown the burger and drain; add in all the beans, tomatoes, and seasoning, and stir until thoroughly blended and bring to a boil. Put in crock pot and heat until ready to serve. This makes a very thick and hearty chili. We like to serve it with grated cheddar cheese and cornbread!

the main event

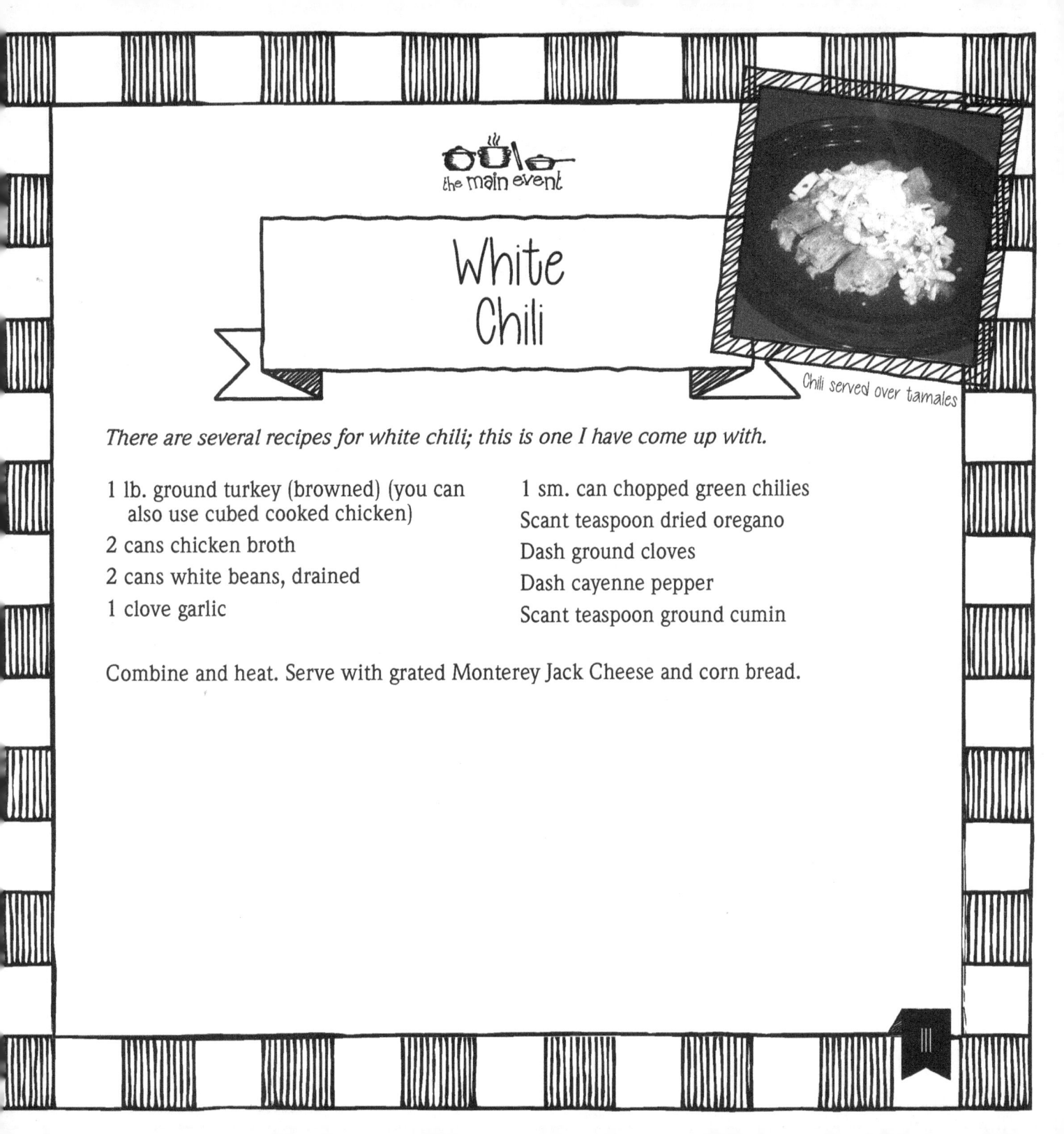

White Chili

Chili served over tamales

There are several recipes for white chili; this is one I have come up with.

- 1 lb. ground turkey (browned) (you can also use cubed cooked chicken)
- 2 cans chicken broth
- 2 cans white beans, drained
- 1 clove garlic
- 1 sm. can chopped green chilies
- Scant teaspoon dried oregano
- Dash ground cloves
- Dash cayenne pepper
- Scant teaspoon ground cumin

Combine and heat. Serve with grated Monterey Jack Cheese and corn bread.

the main event

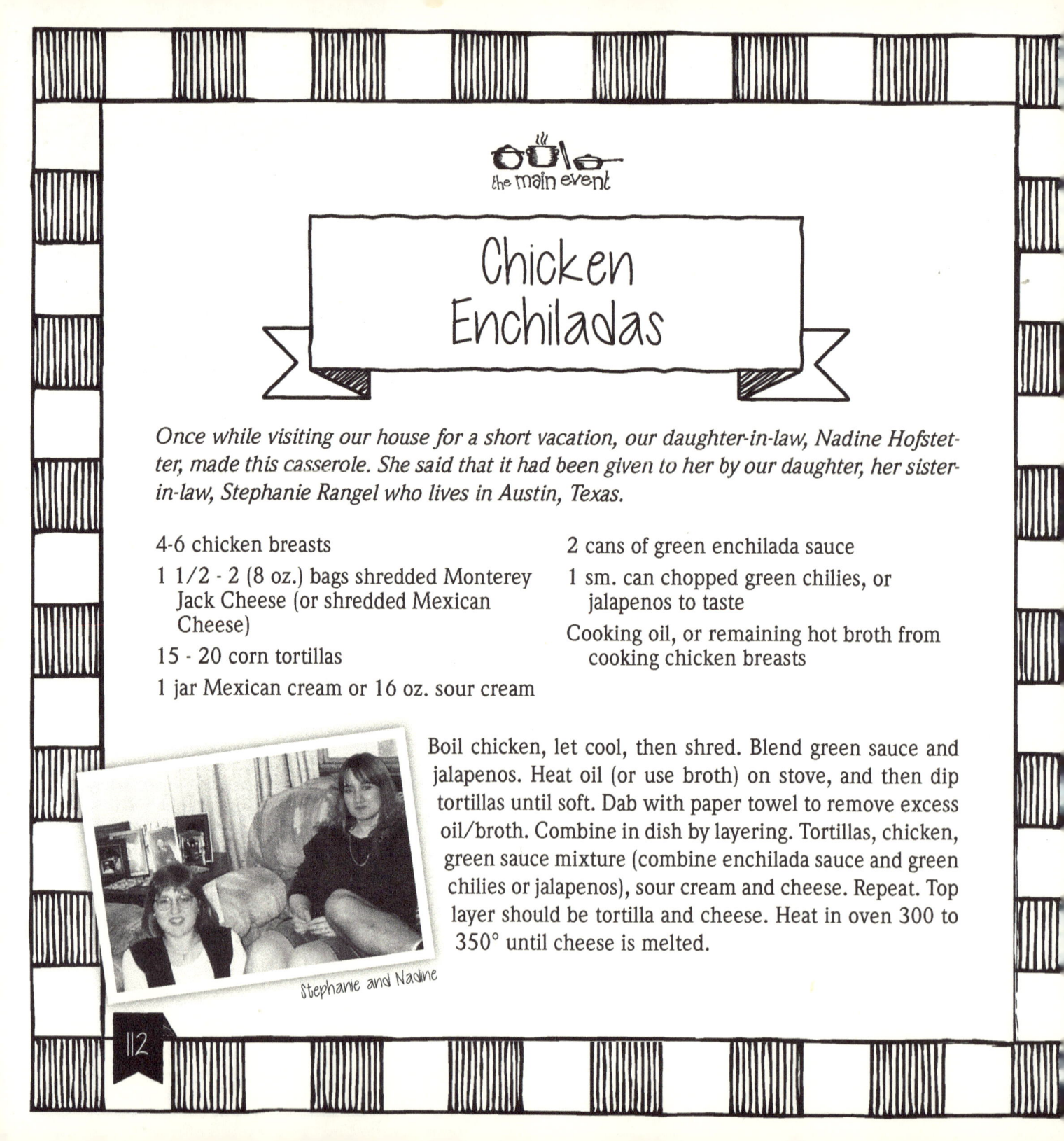

Chicken Enchiladas

Once while visiting our house for a short vacation, our daughter-in-law, Nadine Hofstetter, made this casserole. She said that it had been given to her by our daughter, her sister-in-law, Stephanie Rangel who lives in Austin, Texas.

- 4-6 chicken breasts
- 1 1/2 - 2 (8 oz.) bags shredded Monterey Jack Cheese (or shredded Mexican Cheese)
- 15 - 20 corn tortillas
- 1 jar Mexican cream or 16 oz. sour cream
- 2 cans of green enchilada sauce
- 1 sm. can chopped green chilies, or jalapenos to taste
- Cooking oil, or remaining hot broth from cooking chicken breasts

Boil chicken, let cool, then shred. Blend green sauce and jalapenos. Heat oil (or use broth) on stove, and then dip tortillas until soft. Dab with paper towel to remove excess oil/broth. Combine in dish by layering. Tortillas, chicken, green sauce mixture (combine enchilada sauce and green chilies or jalapenos), sour cream and cheese. Repeat. Top layer should be tortilla and cheese. Heat in oven 300 to 350° until cheese is melted.

Stephanie and Nadine

the main event

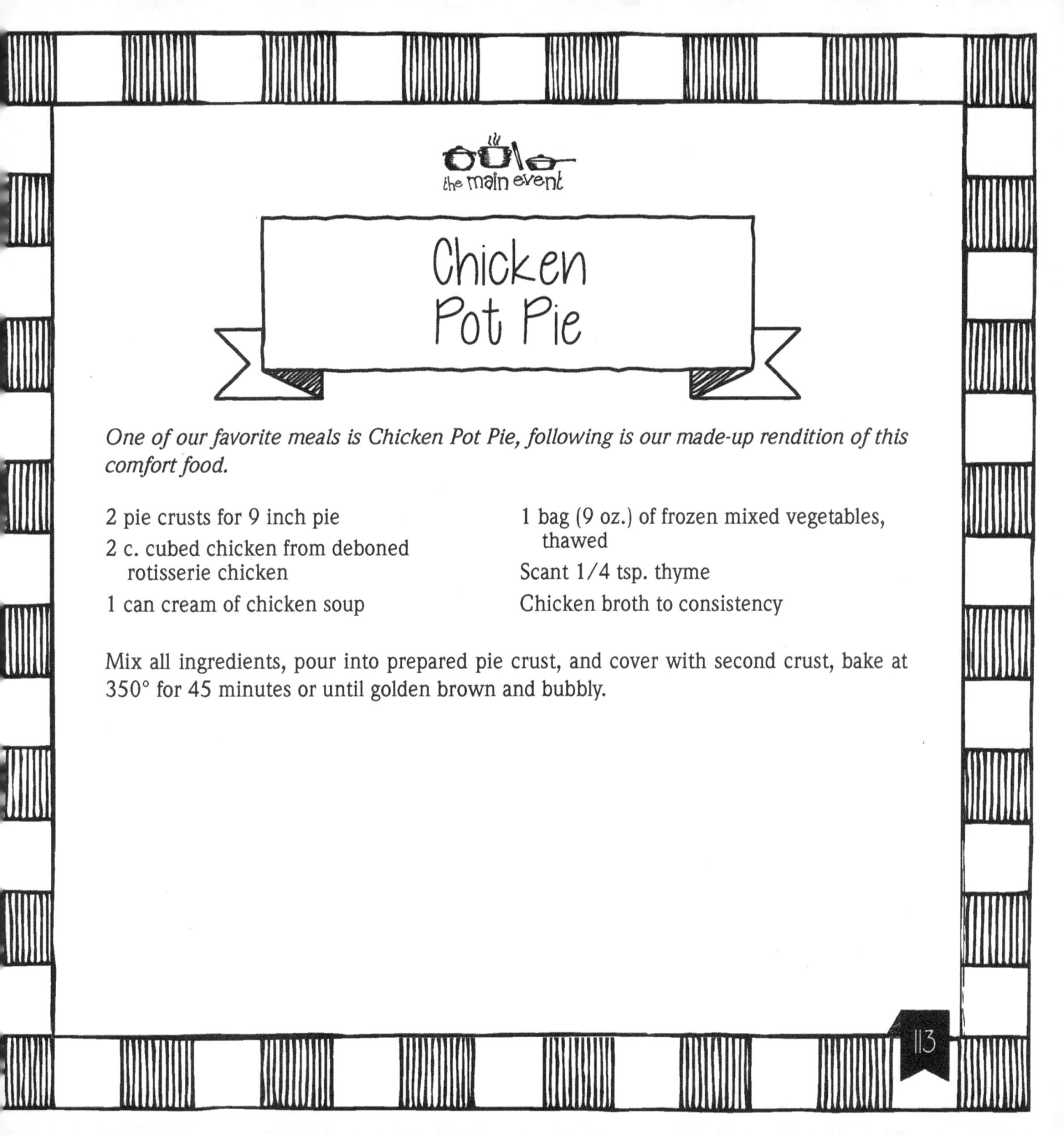

Chicken Pot Pie

One of our favorite meals is Chicken Pot Pie, following is our made-up rendition of this comfort food.

- 2 pie crusts for 9 inch pie
- 2 c. cubed chicken from deboned rotisserie chicken
- 1 can cream of chicken soup
- 1 bag (9 oz.) of frozen mixed vegetables, thawed
- Scant 1/4 tsp. thyme
- Chicken broth to consistency

Mix all ingredients, pour into prepared pie crust, and cover with second crust, bake at 350° for 45 minutes or until golden brown and bubbly.

the main event

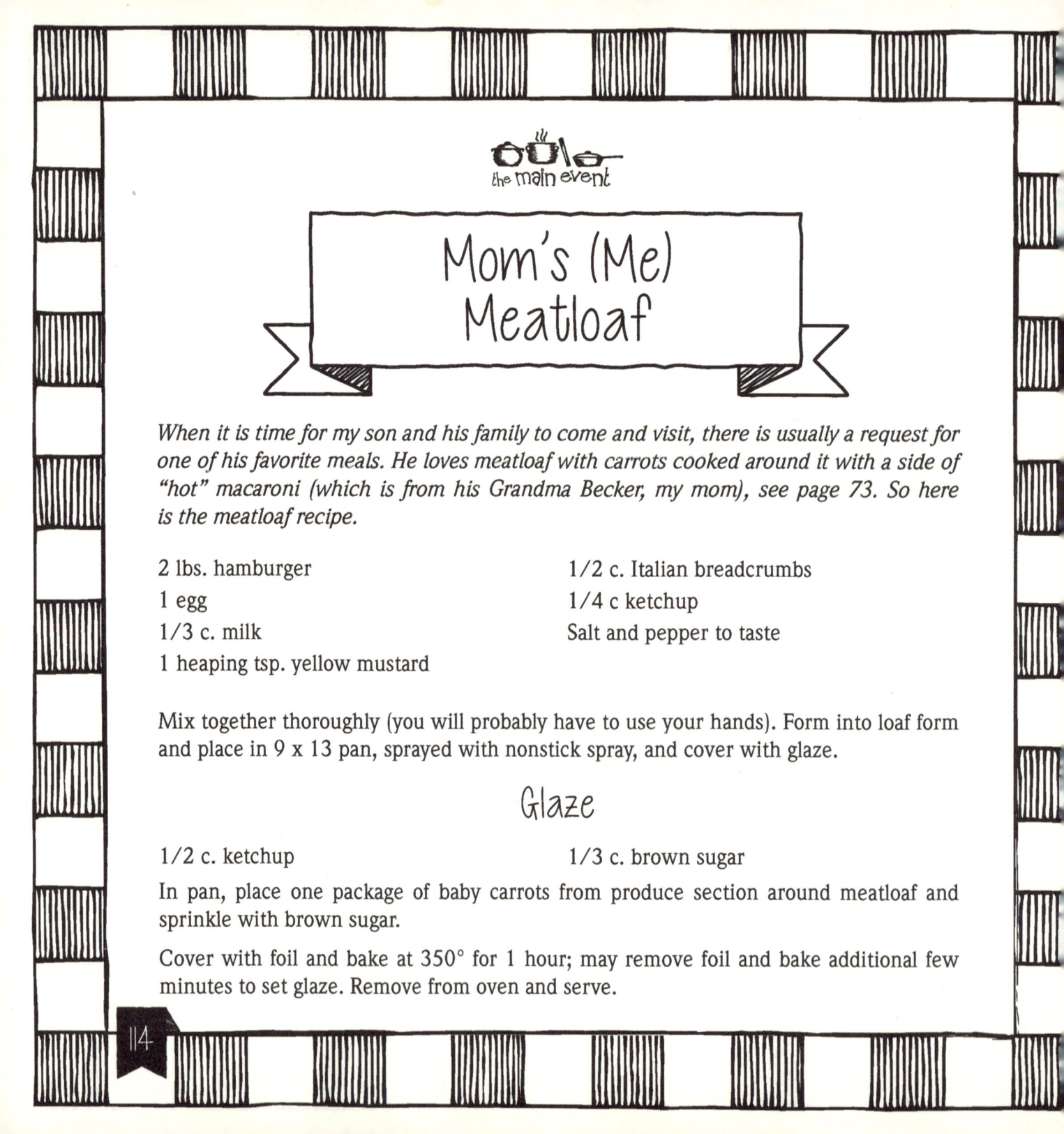

Mom's (Me) Meatloaf

When it is time for my son and his family to come and visit, there is usually a request for one of his favorite meals. He loves meatloaf with carrots cooked around it with a side of "hot" macaroni (which is from his Grandma Becker, my mom), see page 73. So here is the meatloaf recipe.

2 lbs. hamburger
1 egg
1/3 c. milk
1 heaping tsp. yellow mustard

1/2 c. Italian breadcrumbs
1/4 c ketchup
Salt and pepper to taste

Mix together thoroughly (you will probably have to use your hands). Form into loaf form and place in 9 x 13 pan, sprayed with nonstick spray, and cover with glaze.

Glaze

1/2 c. ketchup   1/3 c. brown sugar

In pan, place one package of baby carrots from produce section around meatloaf and sprinkle with brown sugar.

Cover with foil and bake at 350° for 1 hour; may remove foil and bake additional few minutes to set glaze. Remove from oven and serve.

Lost Snickerdoodles {page 152}

desserts &
other sweet treats

115

desserts & other sweet treats

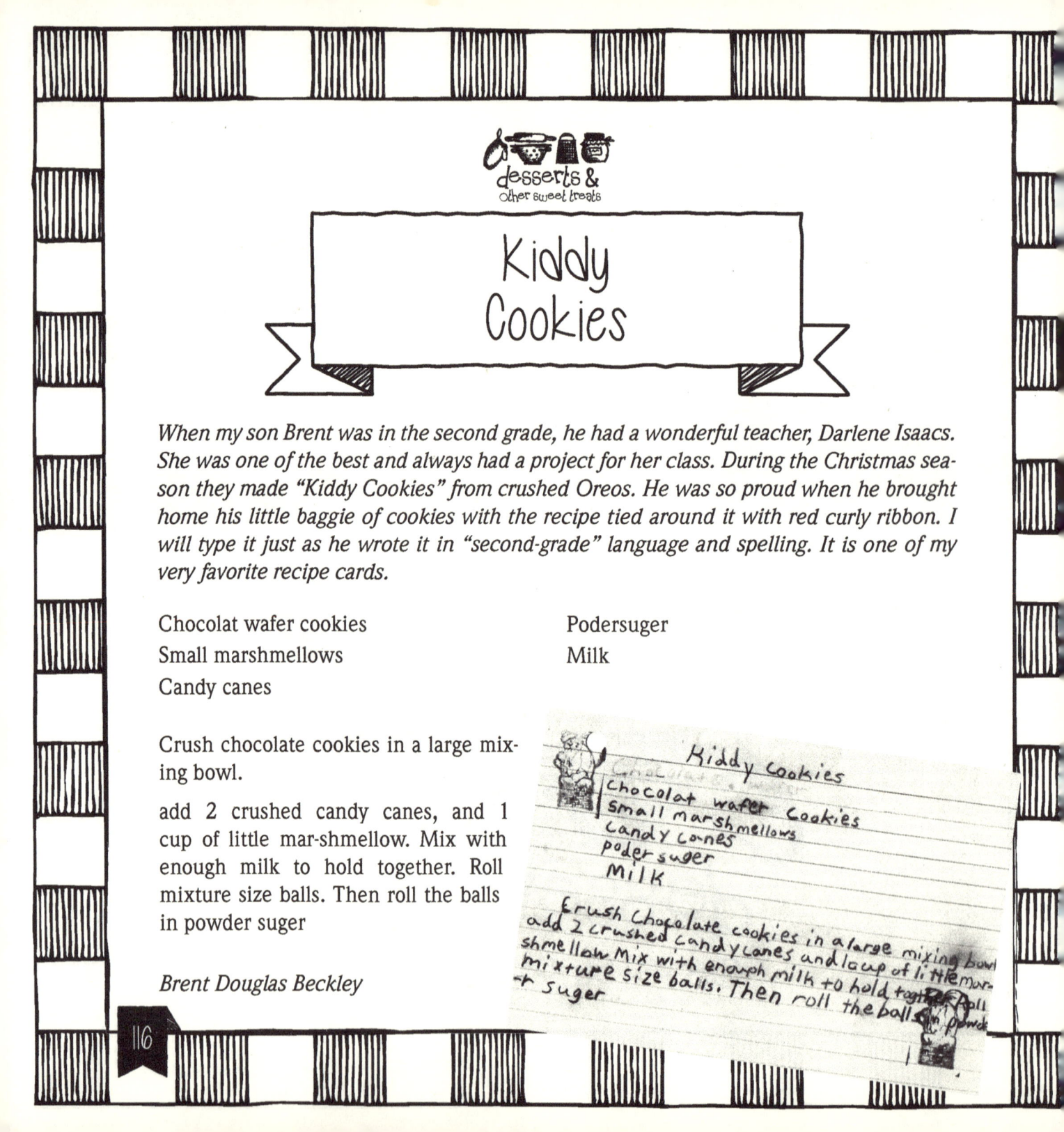

Kiddy Cookies

When my son Brent was in the second grade, he had a wonderful teacher, Darlene Isaacs. She was one of the best and always had a project for her class. During the Christmas season they made "Kiddy Cookies" from crushed Oreos. He was so proud when he brought home his little baggie of cookies with the recipe tied around it with red curly ribbon. I will type it just as he wrote it in "second-grade" language and spelling. It is one of my very favorite recipe cards.

Chocolat wafer cookies
Small marshmellows
Candy canes
Podersuger
Milk

Crush chocolate cookies in a large mixing bowl.

add 2 crushed candy canes, and 1 cup of little mar-shmellow. Mix with enough milk to hold together. Roll mixture size balls. Then roll the balls in powder suger

Brent Douglas Beckley

desserts & other sweet treats

Rhubarb Custard Pie

This recipe is my husband, Steve's, favorite pie. It is from his mother, Maxine Hofstetter. It is made by the family with her smile in mind.

For a 9" pie (pie crust for double pie crust—recipe follows)

- 3 eggs
- 1 2/3 Tbsp. milk
- 2 c. sugar
- 1/4 c. Flour
- 3/4 tsp. Nutmeg (I use fresh grated)
- 4 c. Rhubarb
- 1 Tbsp. butter

Add beaten egg to milk, sugar, flour, and nutmeg. Mix the sliced rhubarb into above mixture. Pour into prepared pie crust and dot with butter. Make a lattice top out of pie crust. Bake at 400° for 50-60 minutes. Be prepared, there could be a spill in the oven!

Pie Crust:

- 2 c. sifted flour
- 1 tsp. salt
- 2/3 c. vegetable shortening
- 5-7 Tbsp. ice cold water

Chill flour and shortening. Sift flour and salt. Cut in shortening till pieces are the size of small peas. Sprinkle water over, 1 Tablespoon at a time, tossing after each addition. Form into ball. Flatten on lightly floured surface. Divide in half and roll to desired thickness.

desserts & other sweet treats

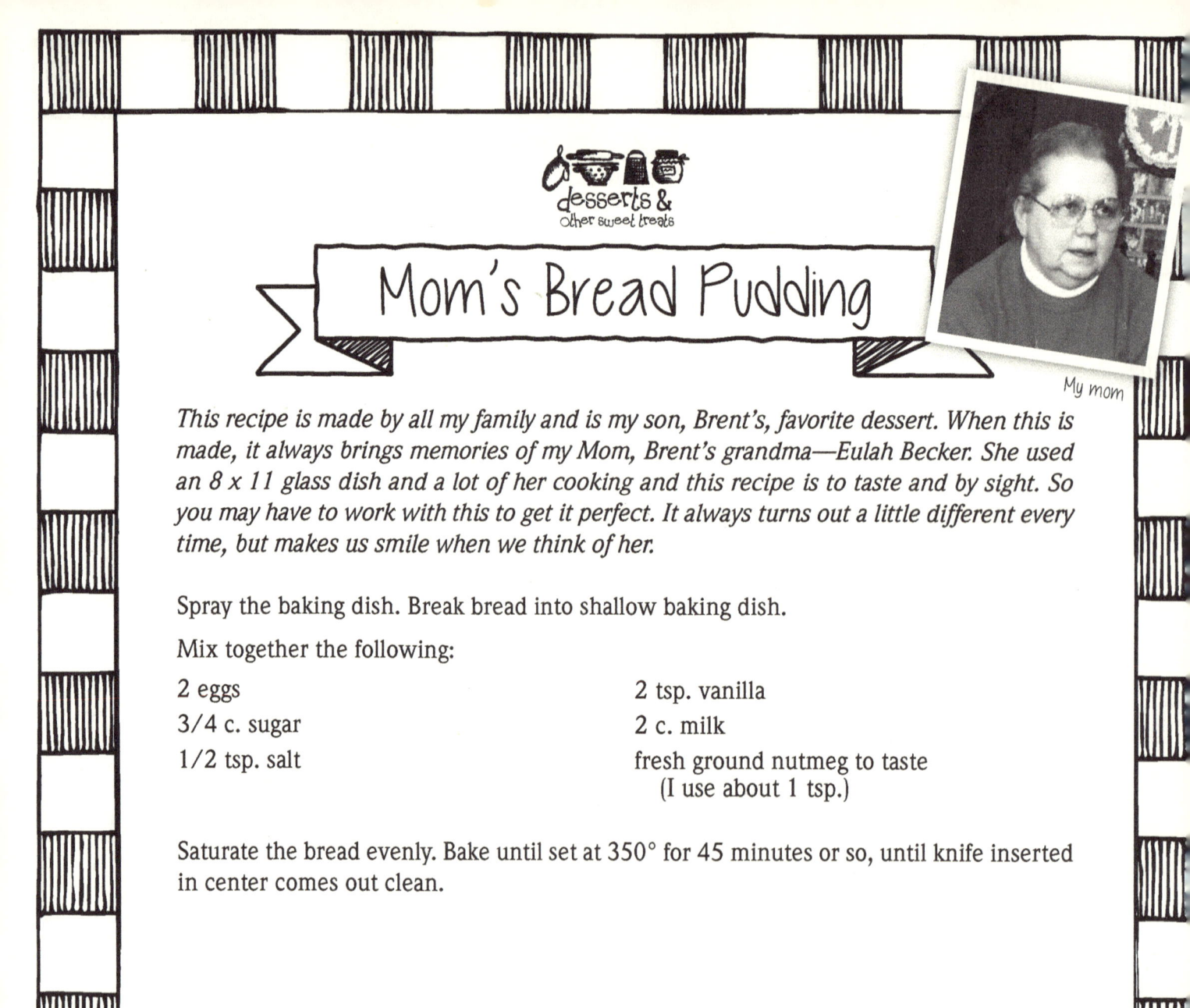

Mom's Bread Pudding

My mom

This recipe is made by all my family and is my son, Brent's, favorite dessert. When this is made, it always brings memories of my Mom, Brent's grandma—Eulah Becker. She used an 8 x 11 glass dish and a lot of her cooking and this recipe is to taste and by sight. So you may have to work with this to get it perfect. It always turns out a little different every time, but makes us smile when we think of her.

Spray the baking dish. Break bread into shallow baking dish.

Mix together the following:

- 2 eggs
- 3/4 c. sugar
- 1/2 tsp. salt
- 2 tsp. vanilla
- 2 c. milk
- fresh ground nutmeg to taste (I use about 1 tsp.)

Saturate the bread evenly. Bake until set at 350° for 45 minutes or so, until knife inserted in center comes out clean.

desserts & other sweet treats

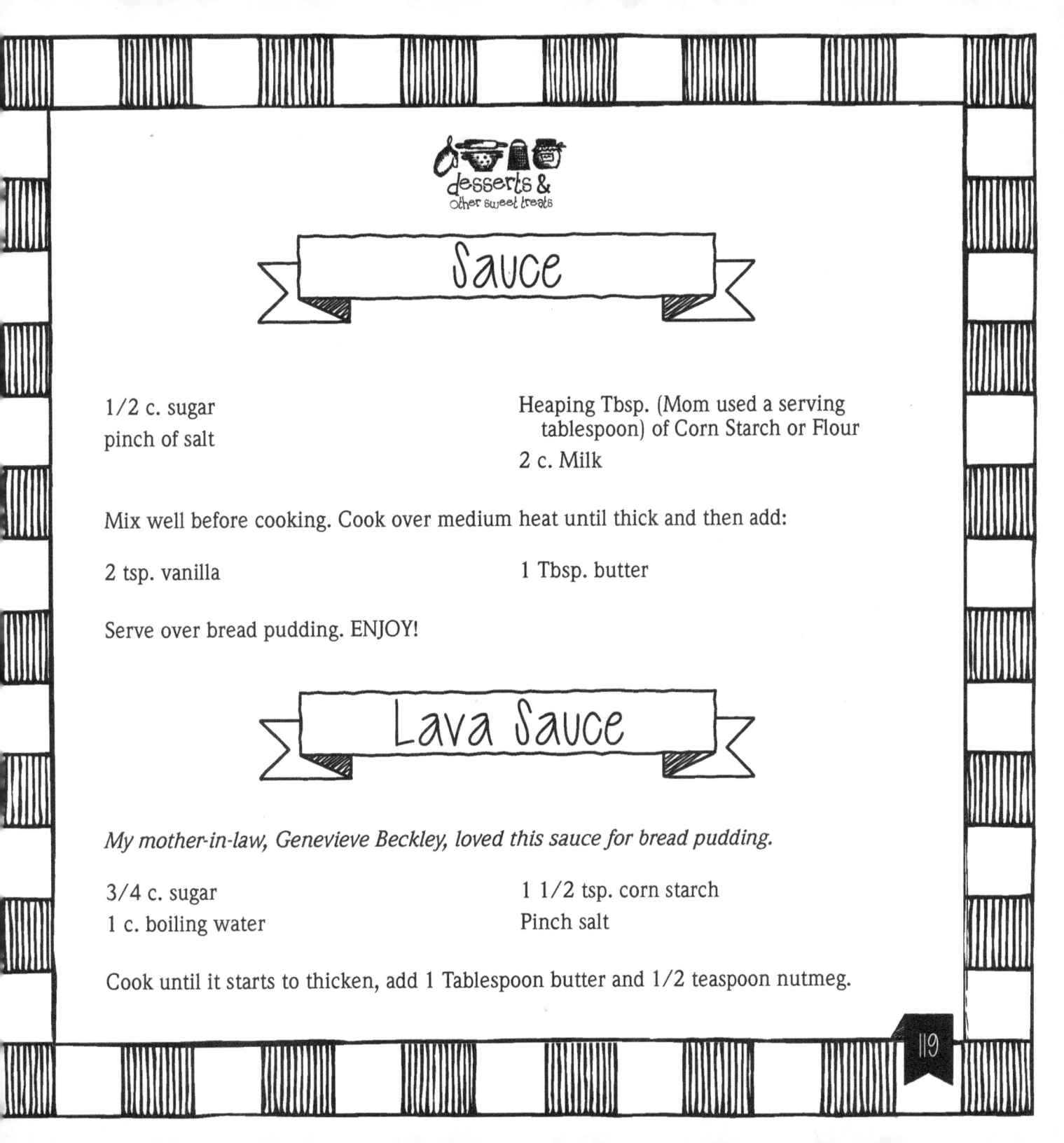

Sauce

1/2 c. sugar
pinch of salt

Heaping Tbsp. (Mom used a serving tablespoon) of Corn Starch or Flour
2 c. Milk

Mix well before cooking. Cook over medium heat until thick and then add:

2 tsp. vanilla

1 Tbsp. butter

Serve over bread pudding. ENJOY!

Lava Sauce

My mother-in-law, Genevieve Beckley, loved this sauce for bread pudding.

3/4 c. sugar
1 c. boiling water

1 1/2 tsp. corn starch
Pinch salt

Cook until it starts to thicken, add 1 Tablespoon butter and 1/2 teaspoon nutmeg.

desserts & other sweet treats

Bread Pudding

This is another variation of bread pudding, from another co-worker, Barb Farris's family that is very good and the sauce is poured over the cake like pudding to serve.

16 oz. loaf white bread
2 1/4 c. sugar
4 eggs
4 c. milk
2 tsp. vanilla

Beat eggs, add sugar, milk and vanilla and sprinkle with cinnamon. Grease 13 x 9 pan with butter. Break up bread in pan and pour egg mixture over it. Push bread into milk. Sprinkle with a little more cinnamon and put 6 pats of butter on top. Bake for 50 minutes at 350°.

Vanilla Sauce

1 cup sugar and 2 Tablespoons corn starch—mix together in sauce pan.

Gradually add 1 cup boiling water. Cook until thick. Remove from stove and add 1 stick of butter (cut up) and 2 Tablespoons vanilla. Stir well and pour over baked bread pudding. Ready to serve.

desserts & other sweet treats

Russian Tea Cakes

Another of Steve's mom's recipes that is his family's favorite is her Russian Tea Cakes, which she always had to make plenty of during the holidays.

- 1 c. butter, room temperature
- 1/2 c. powdered sugar (sifted)
- 1 tsp. vanilla
- 2 1/2 c. sifted flour
- 1/4 tsp. salt
- 3/4 c. chopped nuts

Mix together well and chill dough, roll into 1 inch balls, bake 2 1/2 inches apart on ungreased pan. Bake 10-12 minutes in 400° oven. Roll in powdered sugar while warm, then again when cool. Makes approximately 4 dozen.

desserts & other sweet treats

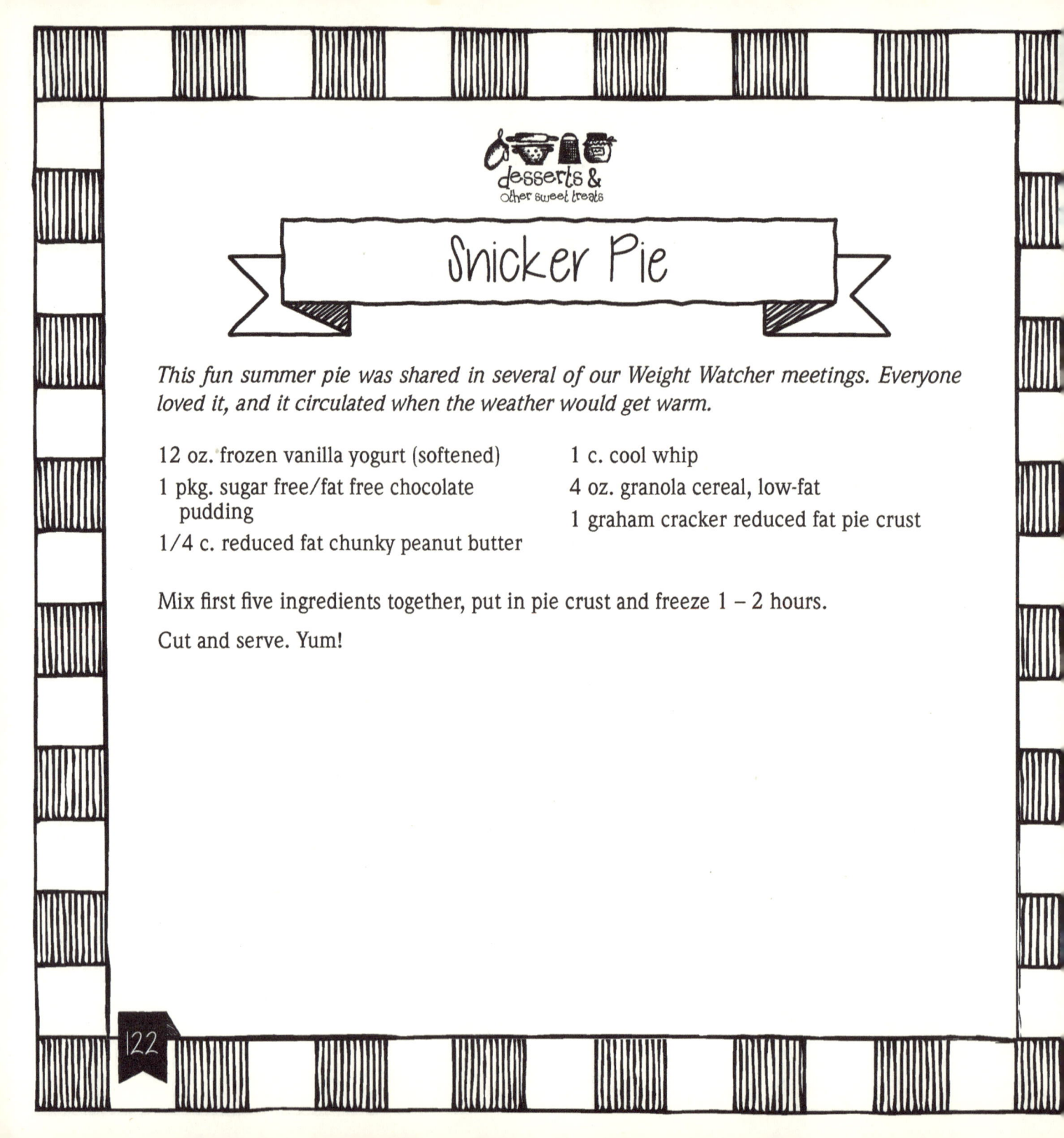

Snicker Pie

This fun summer pie was shared in several of our Weight Watcher meetings. Everyone loved it, and it circulated when the weather would get warm.

- 12 oz. frozen vanilla yogurt (softened)
- 1 pkg. sugar free/fat free chocolate pudding
- 1/4 c. reduced fat chunky peanut butter
- 1 c. cool whip
- 4 oz. granola cereal, low-fat
- 1 graham cracker reduced fat pie crust

Mix first five ingredients together, put in pie crust and freeze 1 – 2 hours.

Cut and serve. Yum!

desserts & other sweet treats

Low-Fat Key Lime Pie

A very good friend of mine, Deb Jones, who now lives in Republic, Missouri, made this refreshing dessert one summer afternoon while visiting with us. It was an immediate hit, and we like to serve it on a hot summer evening to cool our palate.

1 reduced fat graham cracker crust
1 (1/16 oz) pkg. sugar-free lime gelatin
1/4 c. boiling water

8 oz. container fat-free whipped topping, thawed
2 (6 oz.) containers low-fat key lime pie yogurt

In a large heat-resistant bowl, dissolve gelatin in boiling water. Stir in yogurt with wire whisk. Fold in whipped topping with wooden spoon. Pour into crust and refrigerate for at least 2 hours. Cut and serve. 8 servings.

desserts & other sweet treats

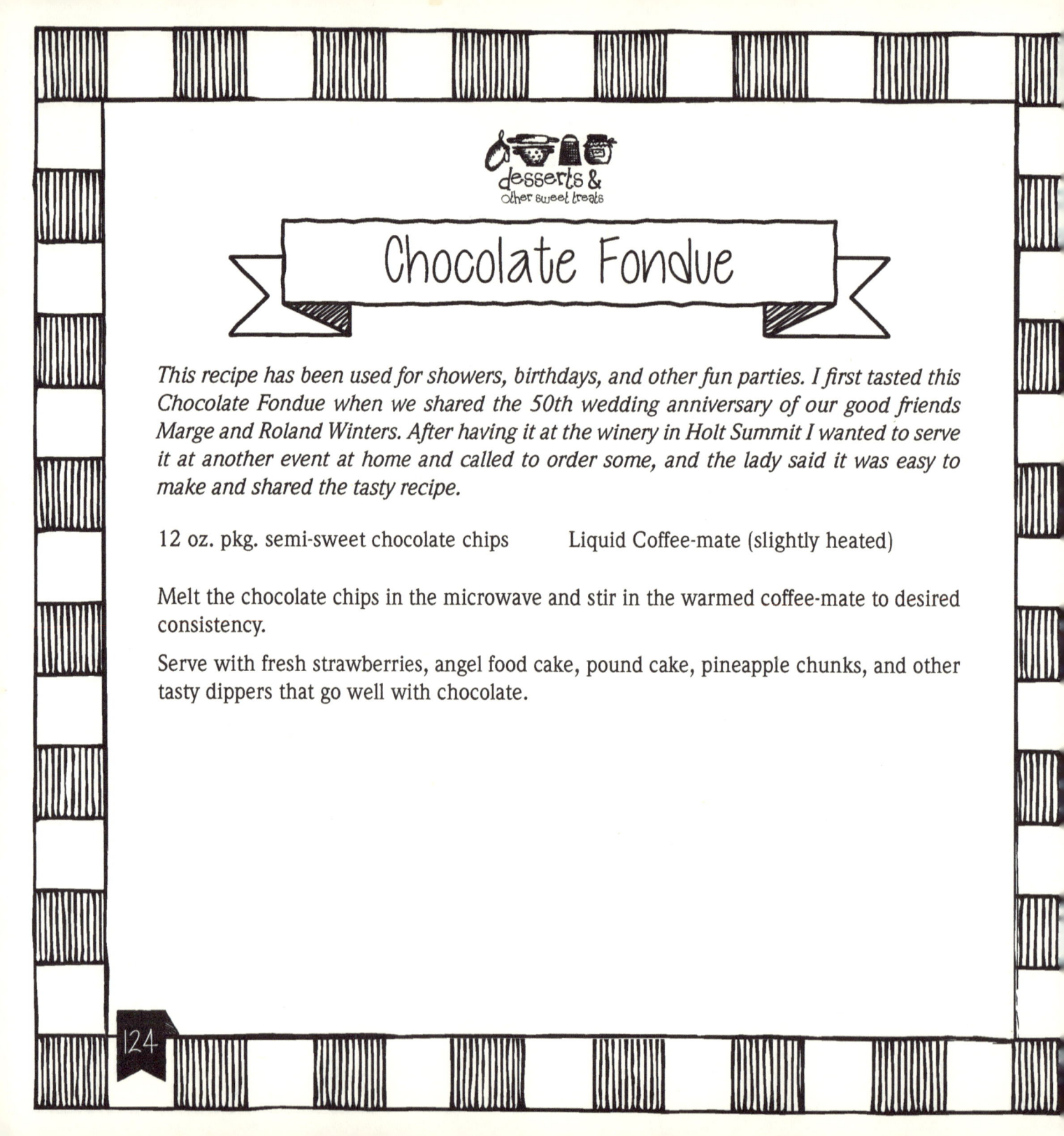

Chocolate Fondue

This recipe has been used for showers, birthdays, and other fun parties. I first tasted this Chocolate Fondue when we shared the 50th wedding anniversary of our good friends Marge and Roland Winters. After having it at the winery in Holt Summit I wanted to serve it at another event at home and called to order some, and the lady said it was easy to make and shared the tasty recipe.

12 oz. pkg. semi-sweet chocolate chips   Liquid Coffee-mate (slightly heated)

Melt the chocolate chips in the microwave and stir in the warmed coffee-mate to desired consistency.

Serve with fresh strawberries, angel food cake, pound cake, pineapple chunks, and other tasty dippers that go well with chocolate.

desserts & other sweet treats

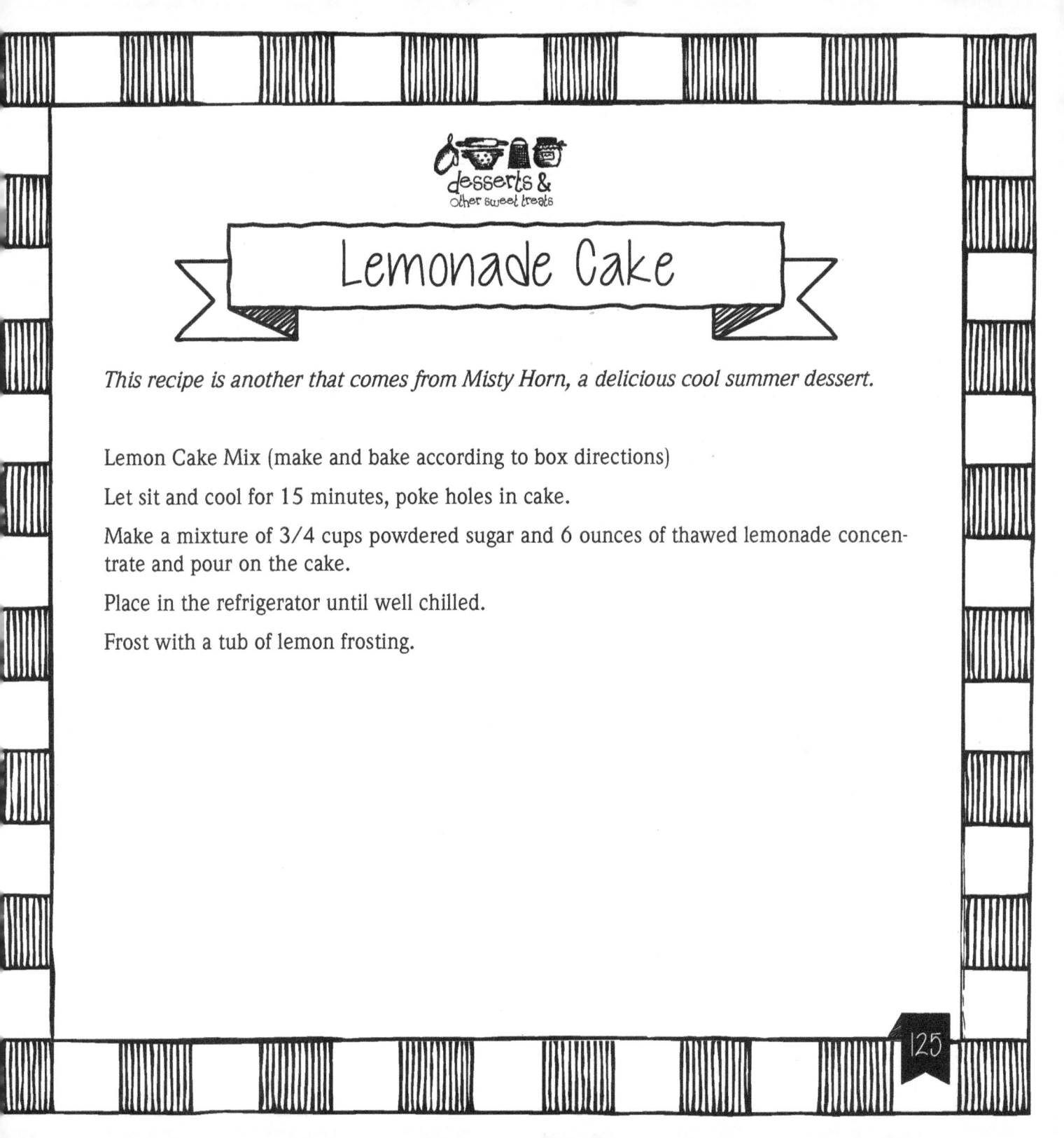

Lemonade Cake

This recipe is another that comes from Misty Horn, a delicious cool summer dessert.

Lemon Cake Mix (make and bake according to box directions)

Let sit and cool for 15 minutes, poke holes in cake.

Make a mixture of 3/4 cups powdered sugar and 6 ounces of thawed lemonade concentrate and pour on the cake.

Place in the refrigerator until well chilled.

Frost with a tub of lemon frosting.

desserts & other sweet treats

Grandma Linda's Baseball Cookies

This recipe is a combination of several that has turned into a favorite for my grandson, Brendan's, baseball team. It came from our daughter, Stephanie, in Texas, and we have changed this and that and have come up with the following recipe. It makes a lot of large cookies, which is ideal for the crowd.

4 c. flour
4 eggs
2 tsp. baking soda
3 tsp. vanilla
1 tsp. salt
2 c. semi-sweet choc chips (12 oz. pkg)
1 c. softened salted butter
2 c. white chocolate chips
1 c. Crisco (white)
1 1/2 c. white sugar
1 1/2 c. brown sugar

Sift flour, soda and salt together. Put aside.

In a large mixing bowl, place butter, shortening, sugars, eggs, and vanilla; mix on low until blended, about 30 seconds. Then on high for 3 minutes. Stir flour mixture in by hand with a wooden spoon. When well mixed, add the mixed chocolate chips. (If you do not want the white chocolate chips, you can use 2 cups of nut pieces, but the boys did not want the nuts and preferred the white chocolate chips.)

Chill the dough overnight, covered, in the mixing bowl. Then on ungreased cookie sheet

Nixa Rookies Nevada Tourney Winners July 2012

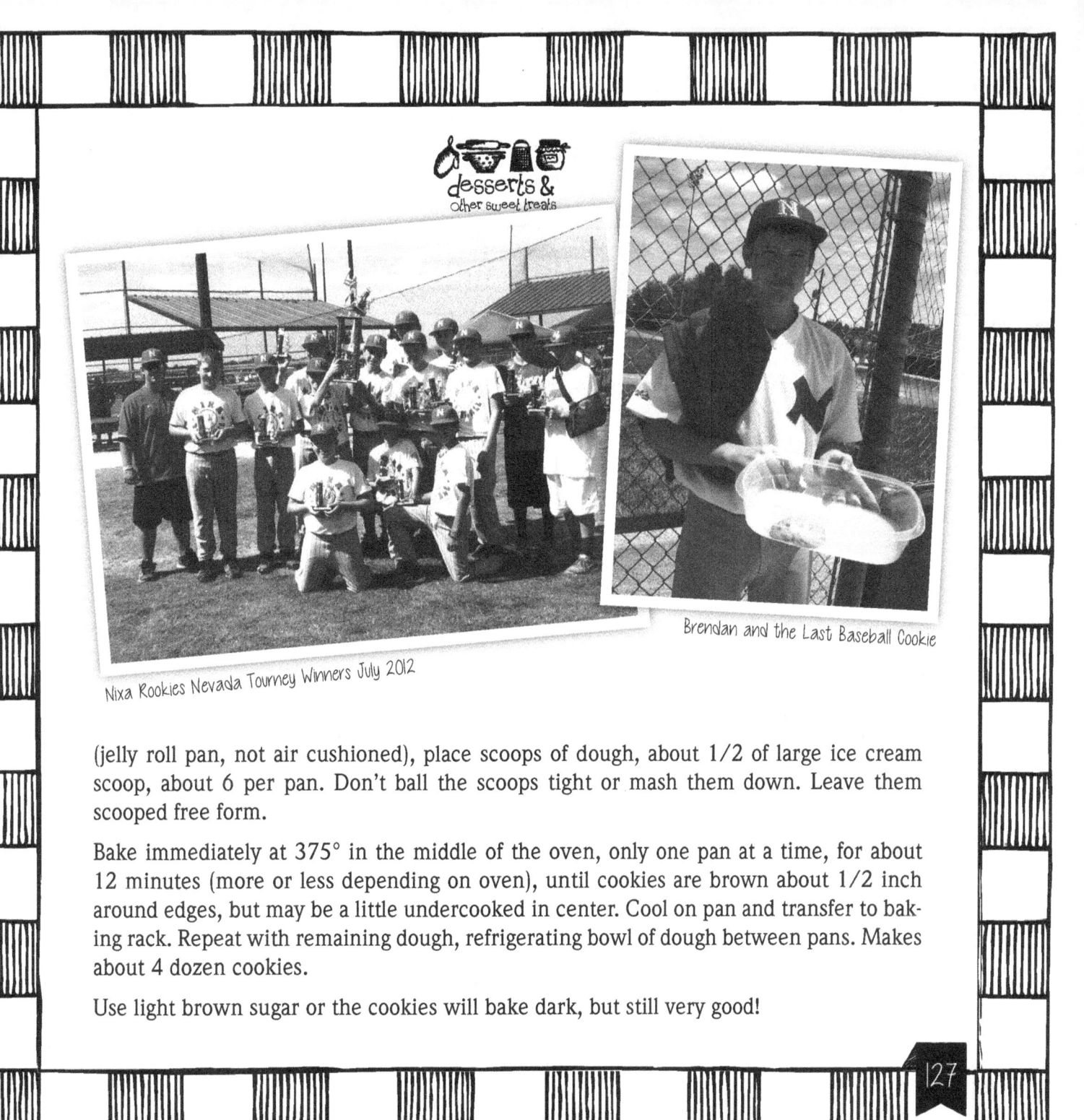

Brendan and the Last Baseball Cookie

(jelly roll pan, not air cushioned), place scoops of dough, about 1/2 of large ice cream scoop, about 6 per pan. Don't ball the scoops tight or mash them down. Leave them scooped free form.

Bake immediately at 375° in the middle of the oven, only one pan at a time, for about 12 minutes (more or less depending on oven), until cookies are brown about 1/2 inch around edges, but may be a little undercooked in center. Cool on pan and transfer to baking rack. Repeat with remaining dough, refrigerating bowl of dough between pans. Makes about 4 dozen cookies.

Use light brown sugar or the cookies will bake dark, but still very good!

desserts & other sweet treats

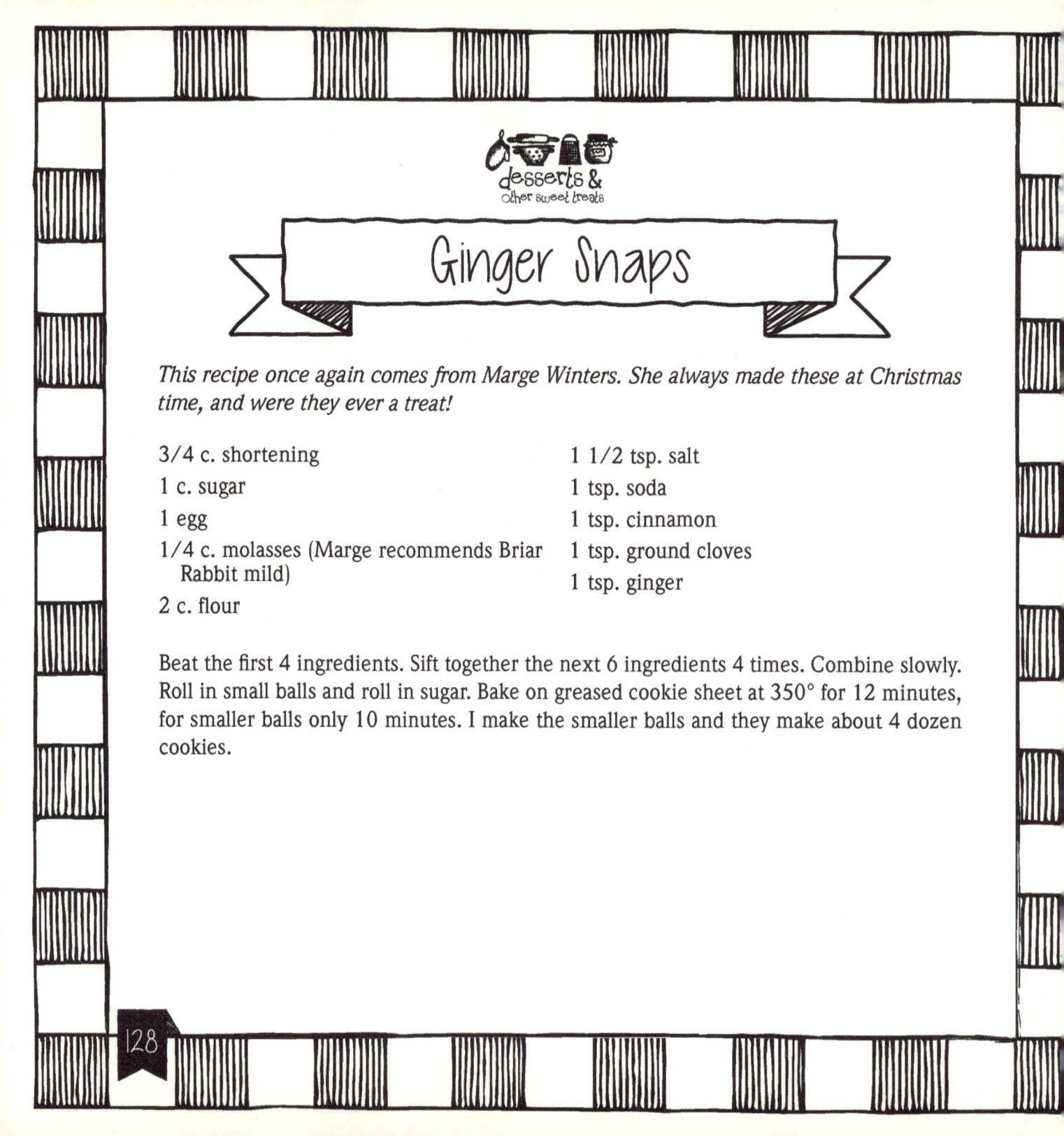

Ginger Snaps

This recipe once again comes from Marge Winters. She always made these at Christmas time, and were they ever a treat!

- 3/4 c. shortening
- 1 c. sugar
- 1 egg
- 1/4 c. molasses (Marge recommends Briar Rabbit mild)
- 2 c. flour
- 1 1/2 tsp. salt
- 1 tsp. soda
- 1 tsp. cinnamon
- 1 tsp. ground cloves
- 1 tsp. ginger

Beat the first 4 ingredients. Sift together the next 6 ingredients 4 times. Combine slowly. Roll in small balls and roll in sugar. Bake on greased cookie sheet at 350° for 12 minutes, for smaller balls only 10 minutes. I make the smaller balls and they make about 4 dozen cookies.

desserts & other sweet treats

Cherry Crunch

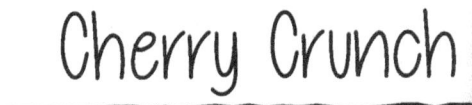

A wonderful dessert from my mom that is loved by my sister Karen and is a yummy cherry crunch.

Crust:
- 40 graham crackers, rolled fine (two packages)
- 3/4 c. sugar
- 1 tsp. cinnamon
- 1 1/2 sticks margarine or butter

Filling:
- 1 qt. cherries
- 1 1/2 c. sugar
- 5 Tbsp. cornstarch

Topping
- 4 or 5 egg whites, stiffly beaten
- 1 c. sugar

Melt butter; mix with cracker crumbs, sugar and cinnamon. Pat 3/4 of mixture in bottom and sides of large buttered pan (9 x 13). Mix cornstarch and sugar together (dry), then add to cherries. Cook until thickened and clear, stirring constantly. Pour over crumb mixture in pan. Beat egg whites until stiff; add sugar. Spread this mixture over cherries and cover with remaining crumbs. Bake 35 minutes at 275° oven.

I have used 2 large cans (21 oz.) of cherry pie filling to replace cooked cherries, if in a hurry.

desserts & other sweet treats

Raisin Pie

Grandma Belcher

This raisin pie was one of my Grandma Belcher's (my Mom's Mom) best. There was never a bite left over.

Put 1 large box of raisins in a saucepan and cover with water about 1/2 inch above raisins. Add 1 Tablespoon of vinegar. Cook raisins until plump.

Mix together and add to raisins:
1 1/4 c. sugar   1/4 tsp. salt
1 heaping Tbsp. flour

Cook until thickened, and then add 1 rounded Tablespoon of butter.

Makes two, double crust pies. Bake until light brown, 400-425° about 25 to 30 minutes.

Icing

Mix light cream, vanilla, and powdered sugar to make a thin glaze. Spread over warm pies.

desserts & other sweet treats

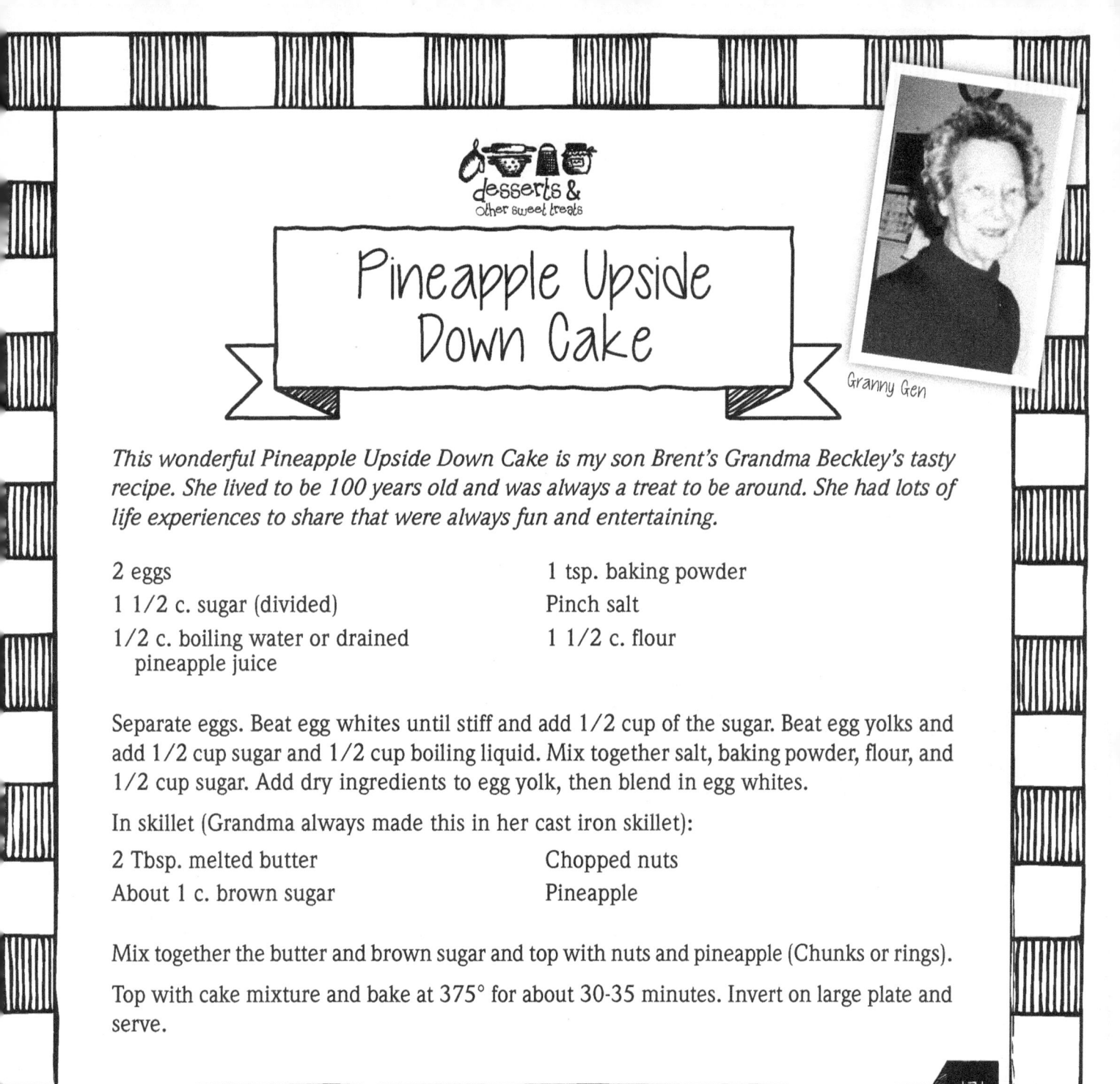

Pineapple Upside Down Cake

Granny Gen

This wonderful Pineapple Upside Down Cake is my son Brent's Grandma Beckley's tasty recipe. She lived to be 100 years old and was always a treat to be around. She had lots of life experiences to share that were always fun and entertaining.

- 2 eggs
- 1 1/2 c. sugar (divided)
- 1/2 c. boiling water or drained pineapple juice
- 1 tsp. baking powder
- Pinch salt
- 1 1/2 c. flour

Separate eggs. Beat egg whites until stiff and add 1/2 cup of the sugar. Beat egg yolks and add 1/2 cup sugar and 1/2 cup boiling liquid. Mix together salt, baking powder, flour, and 1/2 cup sugar. Add dry ingredients to egg yolk, then blend in egg whites.

In skillet (Grandma always made this in her cast iron skillet):

- 2 Tbsp. melted butter
- About 1 c. brown sugar
- Chopped nuts
- Pineapple

Mix together the butter and brown sugar and top with nuts and pineapple (Chunks or rings).

Top with cake mixture and bake at 375° for about 30-35 minutes. Invert on large plate and serve.

desserts & other sweet treats

White Wedding Cake Cupcakes

This is a requested recipe for the now popular cupcakes that everyone is making and sharing. This cupcake tastes like the best white wedding cake!

1 (18.25) oz. box white cake mix
1 1/3 c. water
3 lg. egg whites
2 Tbsp. unsalted butter, melted
2 tsp. almond extract
2 tsp. vanilla extract

Makes 18 cupcakes. Line muffin cups with muffin papers and preheat oven to 350°. With electric mixer, beat the cake mix, water, eggs whites, melted butter and extracts in a large bowl for 2 to 2 1/2 minutes until well blended. Using about 1/3 cup batter (I use an ice cream scoop), spoon the batter into the prepared tins. Bake the cupcakes until they are very pale golden brown on top, about 15 minutes. Cool cupcakes on cooling rack and frost with Buttercream Frosting.

Buttercream Frosting for Wedding Cake Cupcakes (and variations)

4 c. powdered sugar
6 Tbsp. butter (room temperature)
1 tsp vanilla extract
1/2 tsp. almond extract
1/4 c. milk
dash salt

Cream butter in bowl, add about 1/2 the powdered sugar, beating well. Beat in milk and extracts. Gradually beat in remaining powdered sugar; may need to add additional milk (small amount at a time) to make frosting of spreadable consistency.

Variations:

Plain Butter Cream by adding 1 1/2 teaspoons of vanilla extract—no almond extract.

Chocolate Buttercream Frosting by adding 2 Tablespoons of powdered cocoa with just vanilla extract, once again no almond.

desserts & other sweet treats

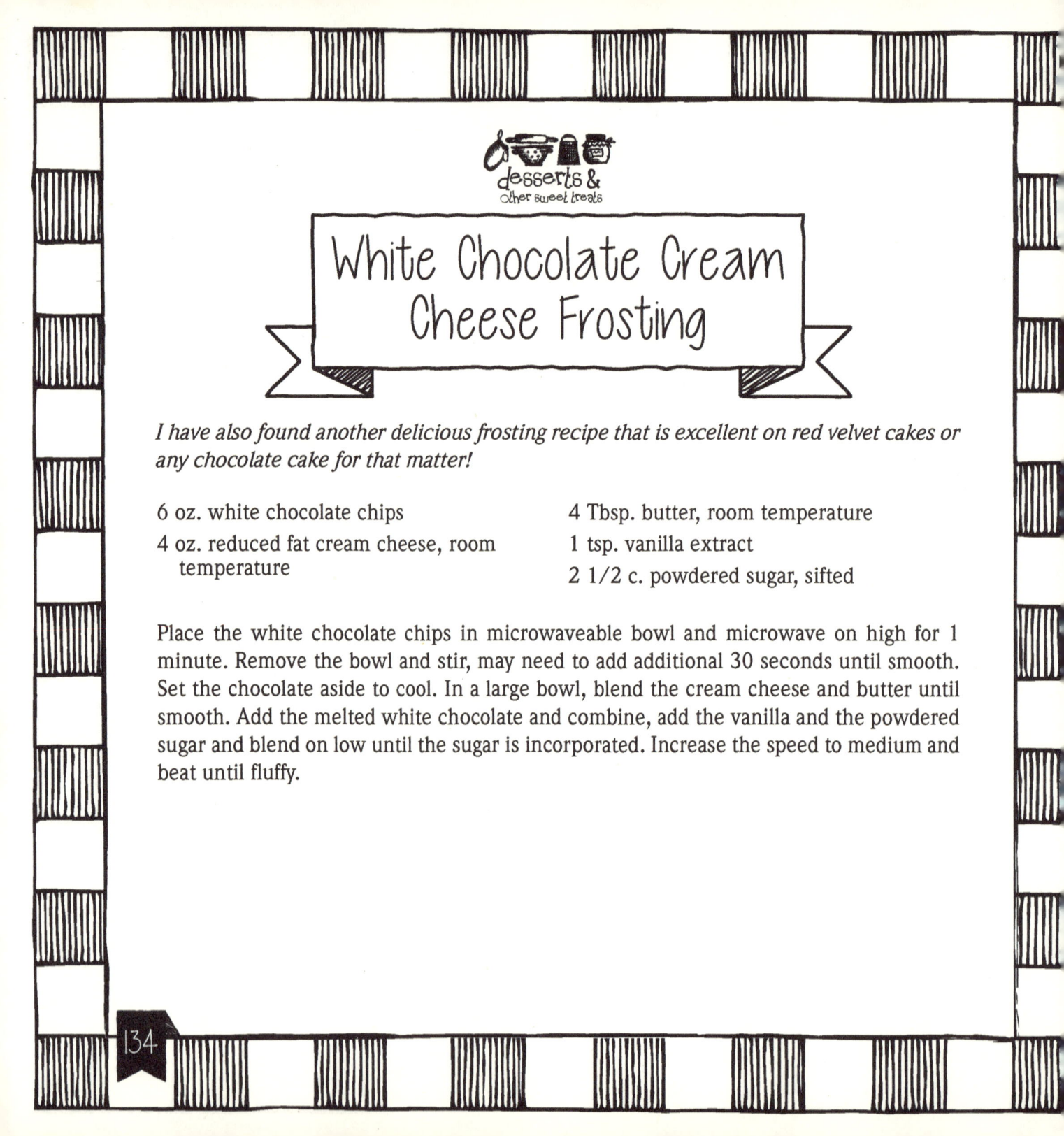

White Chocolate Cream Cheese Frosting

I have also found another delicious frosting recipe that is excellent on red velvet cakes or any chocolate cake for that matter!

- 6 oz. white chocolate chips
- 4 oz. reduced fat cream cheese, room temperature
- 4 Tbsp. butter, room temperature
- 1 tsp. vanilla extract
- 2 1/2 c. powdered sugar, sifted

Place the white chocolate chips in microwaveable bowl and microwave on high for 1 minute. Remove the bowl and stir, may need to add additional 30 seconds until smooth. Set the chocolate aside to cool. In a large bowl, blend the cream cheese and butter until smooth. Add the melted white chocolate and combine, add the vanilla and the powdered sugar and blend on low until the sugar is incorporated. Increase the speed to medium and beat until fluffy.

desserts & other sweet treats

German Apple Cake

One of the engineers that I worked with at Bagnell Dam was also a wonderful baker. So, I will have some of Jim Diederich's recipes in my book. This one is his moist apple cake. Jim and his wife, Sharon, are wonderful friends who are always willing to share good food.

2 lg. eggs (or 3 sm.)

1 c. cooking oil

Beat eggs – add oil – beat until foamy

2 c. sugar

2 c. flour

2 tsp. cinnamon

1 tsp. baking soda

1 tsp. vanilla

1/2 tsp. salt

4 c. thinly sliced apples (peeled)

1/2 c. chopped pecans

Mix all ingredients together (batter will be very stiff) and put in 11 x 7 pan. Bake in 350° oven for 40-50 minutes.

Icing

1 sm. pkg. cream cheese (3 or 4 oz.)

2 Tbsp. margarine

1 tsp. vanilla

1 1/2 c. powdered sugar

Mix together and ice cooled cake.

desserts & other sweet treats

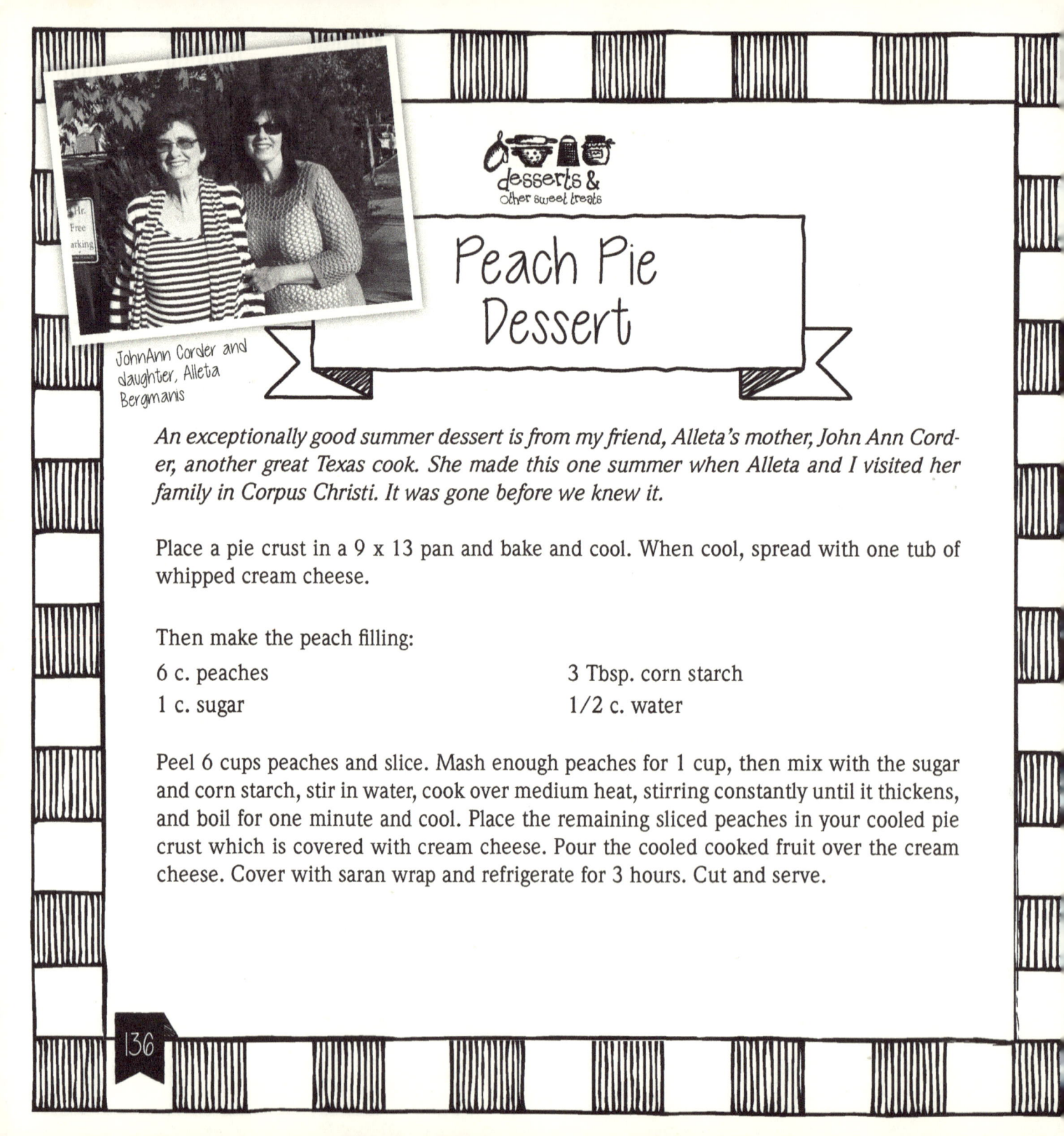

Peach Pie Dessert

JohnAnn Corder and daughter, Alleta Bergmanis

An exceptionally good summer dessert is from my friend, Alleta's mother, John Ann Corder, another great Texas cook. She made this one summer when Alleta and I visited her family in Corpus Christi. It was gone before we knew it.

Place a pie crust in a 9 x 13 pan and bake and cool. When cool, spread with one tub of whipped cream cheese.

Then make the peach filling:

6 c. peaches
1 c. sugar
3 Tbsp. corn starch
1/2 c. water

Peel 6 cups peaches and slice. Mash enough peaches for 1 cup, then mix with the sugar and corn starch, stir in water, cook over medium heat, stirring constantly until it thickens, and boil for one minute and cool. Place the remaining sliced peaches in your cooled pie crust which is covered with cream cheese. Pour the cooled cooked fruit over the cream cheese. Cover with saran wrap and refrigerate for 3 hours. Cut and serve.

desserts & other sweet treats

Carrot Cake

My good friend Jan Parish, makes the best Carrot Cake around. When I sponsored several blood drives in the Lake area, Jan would always bring this cake to serve at the refreshment table. It was said that some people came to donate blood just to have Jan's cake.

2 c. sugar
1 1/2 c. Wesson oil
4 eggs
2 c. flour
3 c. grated carrots

1/2 to 1 c. chopped nuts
2 tsp. cinnamon
1 tsp. soda
1 tsp. salt
1/4 tsp. nutmeg, 1/4 tsp. ginger, 1/4 tsp. cloves (these 3 spices are optional)

Mix together, put in 9 x 13 pan, bake at 350° for approximately 50-60 minutes.

Jan's Cream Cheese Frosting

1 stick softened butter
8 oz. cream cheese, room temperature
1 lb. box powdered sugar

2 tsp. vanilla
Dash of salt – squeeze of lemon juice

Cream together and spread on cooled cake.

desserts & other sweet treats

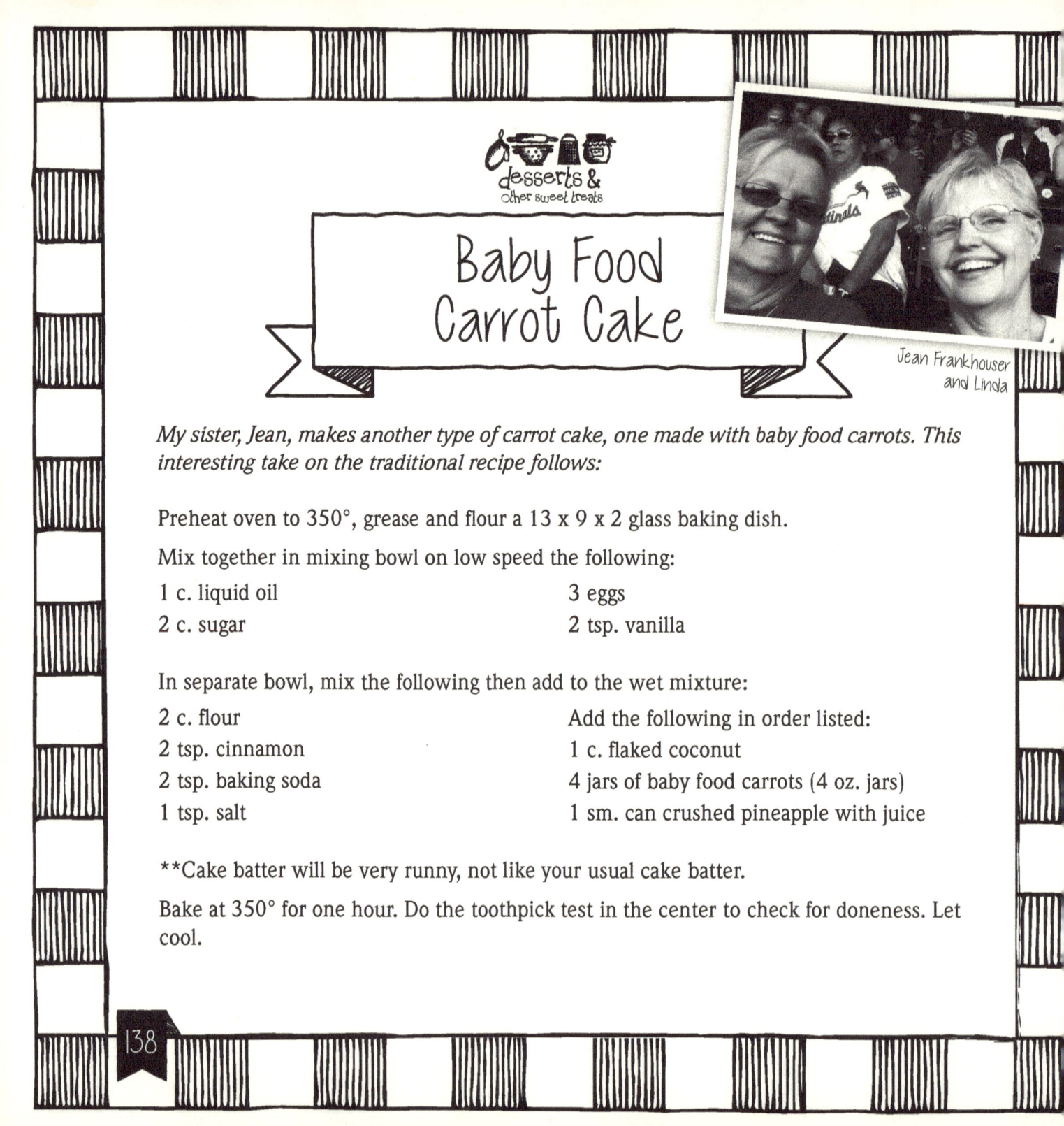

Baby Food Carrot Cake

Jean Frankhouser and Linda

My sister, Jean, makes another type of carrot cake, one made with baby food carrots. This interesting take on the traditional recipe follows:

Preheat oven to 350°, grease and flour a 13 x 9 x 2 glass baking dish.

Mix together in mixing bowl on low speed the following:

1 c. liquid oil
2 c. sugar
3 eggs
2 tsp. vanilla

In separate bowl, mix the following then add to the wet mixture:

2 c. flour
2 tsp. cinnamon
2 tsp. baking soda
1 tsp. salt

Add the following in order listed:
1 c. flaked coconut
4 jars of baby food carrots (4 oz. jars)
1 sm. can crushed pineapple with juice

**Cake batter will be very runny, not like your usual cake batter.

Bake at 350° for one hour. Do the toothpick test in the center to check for doneness. Let cool.

desserts & other sweet treats

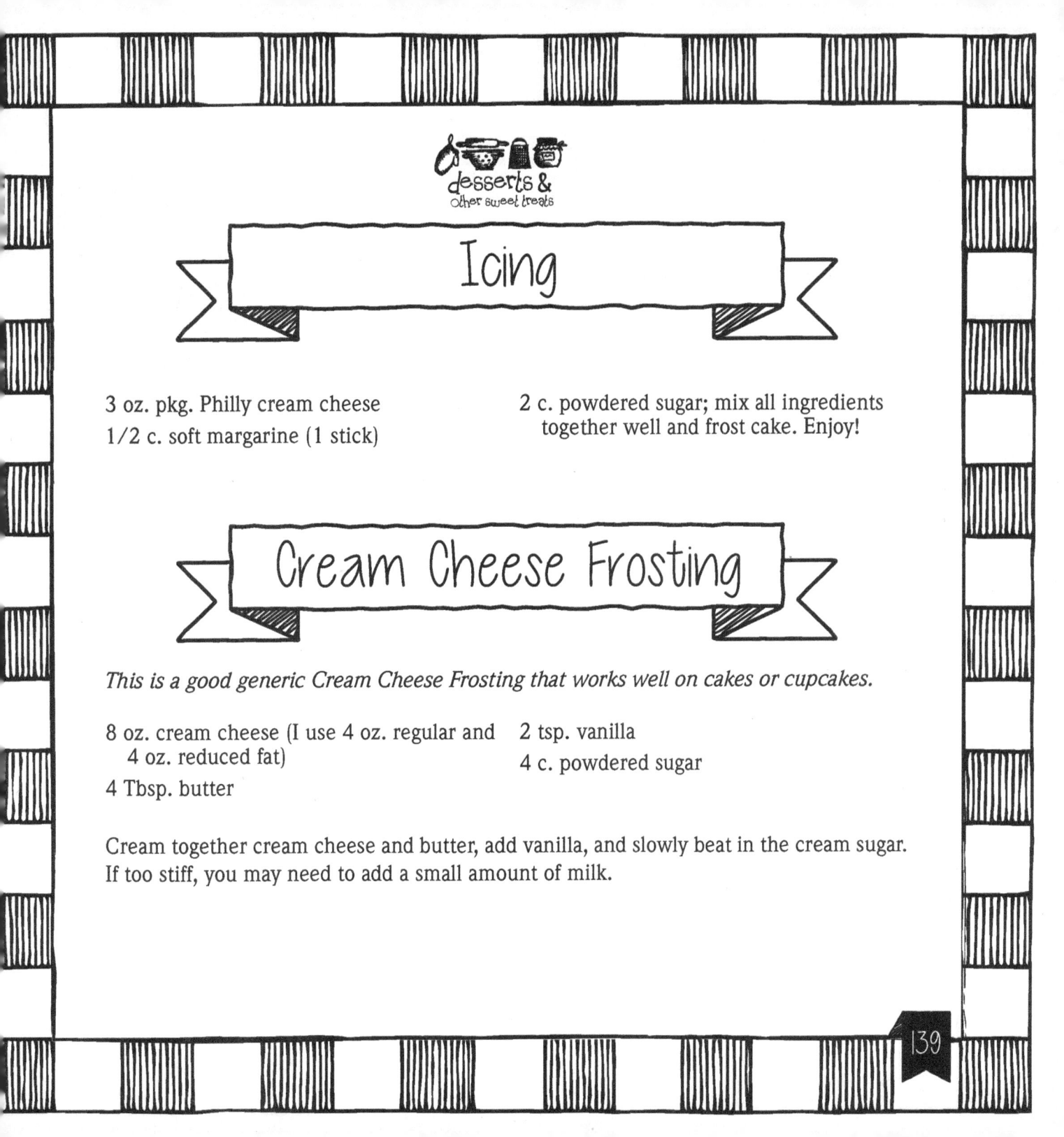

Icing

3 oz. pkg. Philly cream cheese
1/2 c. soft margarine (1 stick)
2 c. powdered sugar; mix all ingredients together well and frost cake. Enjoy!

Cream Cheese Frosting

This is a good generic Cream Cheese Frosting that works well on cakes or cupcakes.

8 oz. cream cheese (I use 4 oz. regular and 4 oz. reduced fat)
4 Tbsp. butter
2 tsp. vanilla
4 c. powdered sugar

Cream together cream cheese and butter, add vanilla, and slowly beat in the cream sugar. If too stiff, you may need to add a small amount of milk.

desserts & other sweet treats

Glorified Brownies

This is an easy and delicious brownie recipe that comes from Judy Blair. Judy is a busy lady who is always fun and has a smile for everyone. Judy and her husband and family own Blair's Landing, a fun shopping area at Lake of the Ozarks.

Judy Blair

2/3 c. flour
1 c. sugar
4 Tbsp. cocoa
1 stick of margarine, softened

2 eggs
1 tsp. vanilla
1/2 c. nuts (optional)

Mix all together with spoon. Spread in greased 11 x 7 pan. Bake at 350° for 20 minutes.

desserts & other sweet treats

Peanut Butter Bars

My grandson, Brendan Beckley, likes to cook, and he loves Reese's peanut butter cups. He enjoys making this recipe to satisfy his cravings.

- 1 c. butter or margarine, melted
- 2 c. graham cracker crumbs
- 2 c. powdered sugar
- 1 c. peanut butter (he uses smooth, but could use crunchy for extra crunch)
- 1 1/2 c. chocolate chips
- 4 Tbsp. peanut butter

In a medium bowl, mix together the butter/margarine, graham cracker crumbs, powdered sugar, and cup of peanut butter until well blended. Press evenly in bottom of 9 x 13 pan. In microwave, melt the chocolate chips with the 4 Tablespoons of peanut butter, stirring until smooth. Spread over the prepared base. Refrigerate for at least one hour before cutting into squares.

Some people like the semi-sweet chocolate chips and others milk chocolate, so it is personal preference.

desserts & other sweet treats

Mother's Soft Pies

Another of the engineers that I worked with at the dam is Ernie Erbschloe. Ernie is a great guy and his wife, Shirley, has shared her mother's soft pie recipe. It is so easy and tasty and can be made in several variations.

One baked pie shell

Filling for Coconut Pie:

- 1 c. sugar
- 2 Tbsp. flour
- 2 Tbsp. corn starch
- 1 pinch salt
- 2 c. milk
- 3 - 4 egg yolks
- 1 c. coconut
- 1 Tbsp. butter
- 1 tsp. vanilla
- (Save the egg whites for meringue)

Mix sugar, corn starch, flour, and salt in separate bowl. Mix egg yolks and milk and put in pan on stove – heat. Slowly whisk in small portions of dry ingredients into yolks and milk until all is mixed. Continue to whisk mixture until cooked and thick. Continual beating will keep lumps from forming. Remove from stove and add vanilla, butter, and coconut. Pour in prebaked pie shell. Add meringue to top, bake at 350° for 10 minutes (sprinkle top lightly with coconut before baking). Cool.

Note: May leave off meringue and use whipped cream.

Shirley Erbschloe and her Mom

Meringue

3-4 egg whites at room temperature   Pinch cream tartar
1 Tbsp. sugar   Pinch salt

With electric mixer, beat in glass bowl until egg whites make peaks; put over pie and bake.

Variations:

Chocolate pie – add 2 rounded Tablespoons of cocoa to dry ingredients. (omit coconut)

Butterscotch – use brown sugar instead of white sugar (1 cup) (omit coconut)

Banana – Leave out coconut and layer bananas and cream filling.

Grandma Witt's Sugar Cookies

My wonderful boss, Warren Witt, was the best. He is always happy, and he and his wife, Joni are always including everyone in their family. Warren loves his Grandma Witt's Sugar Cookie recipe and is sharing it with us. This recipe reminds me of the sugar cookies made at Mr. May's Bakery in my hometown of Mexico, Missouri when I was a kid. Joni's mom has another sugar cookie that is also delicious. Joni's mom made her cookies for her granddaughter; Andrea's wedding, placing one on every plate. If you didn't stake claim to your cookie early at the wedding reception, it surely had disappeared. They were a definite hit! So here are the two family sugar cookie recipes!

- 2 c. sugar
- 1 c. real butter
- 1 c. sour cream
- 3 eggs
- 1 tsp. baking soda
- 2 tsp. baking powder
- 1 tsp. vanilla
- 1/2 tsp. lemon flavoring
- 1/2 tsp. nutmeg
- 4 1/2 c. flour

Mix sugar, butter, and sour cream. Add eggs, baking powder, baking soda, vanilla, lemon, and nutmeg. Mix really well. Start adding flour a little at a time. Cover with wax paper, let sit overnight or 7-8 hours in refrigerator. Roll out, cut, sprinkle with colored sugar on top and bottom. They get real sticky when rolling out so you have to use flour often. You want to keep them thick. After you cut them, wipe the flour off, then sprinkle sugar. Getting the sugar to stick is the hard part. Bake at 375° for 10 minutes. They do not get darker, just bigger. Once done and cool, I recommend layering them with wax paper between layers and a piece of bread in the container to keep the cookies soft.

desserts & other sweet treats

Joni's Mom's Cut-Out Cookies

1 1/2 c. sifted powdered sugar
1 c. butter
1 tsp. vanilla
1/2 tsp. almond flavoring

2 1/2 c. sifted flour
1 tsp. baking soda
1 tsp. cream of tartar
1 egg

Mix sugar and butter, add egg and flavorings. Sift dry ingredients and mix. Refrigerate for several hours. Roll and cut out. Bake at 375° on lightly greased cookie sheet for 7-8 minutes.

Joni, Andrea, Alaina, Joni's mom Kay

desserts & other sweet treats

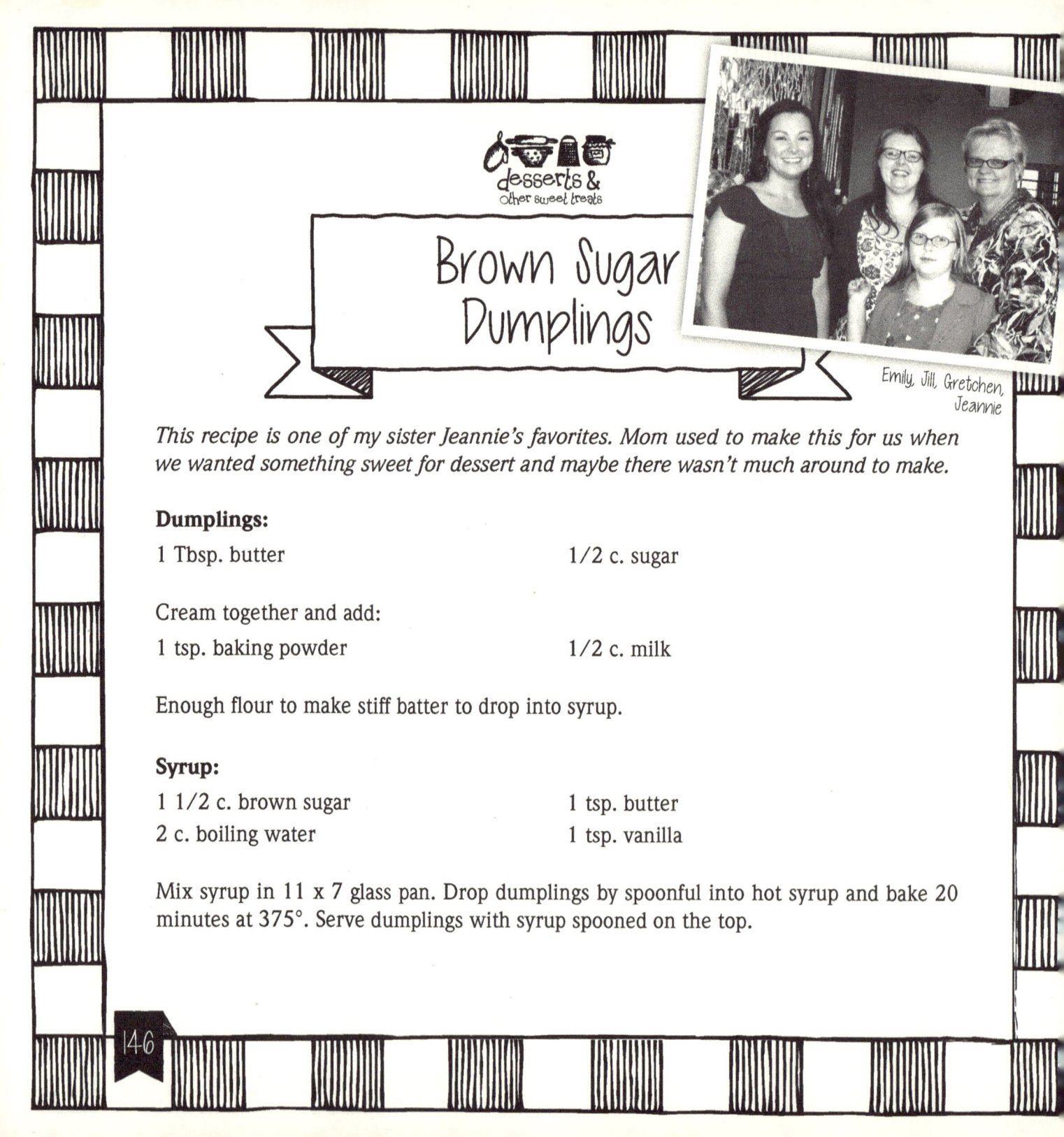

Brown Sugar Dumplings

Emily, Jill, Gretchen, Jeannie

This recipe is one of my sister Jeannie's favorites. Mom used to make this for us when we wanted something sweet for dessert and maybe there wasn't much around to make.

Dumplings:

1 Tbsp. butter   1/2 c. sugar

Cream together and add:

1 tsp. baking powder   1/2 c. milk

Enough flour to make stiff batter to drop into syrup.

Syrup:

1 1/2 c. brown sugar   1 tsp. butter
2 c. boiling water   1 tsp. vanilla

Mix syrup in 11 x 7 glass pan. Drop dumplings by spoonful into hot syrup and bake 20 minutes at 375°. Serve dumplings with syrup spooned on the top.

desserts & other sweet treats

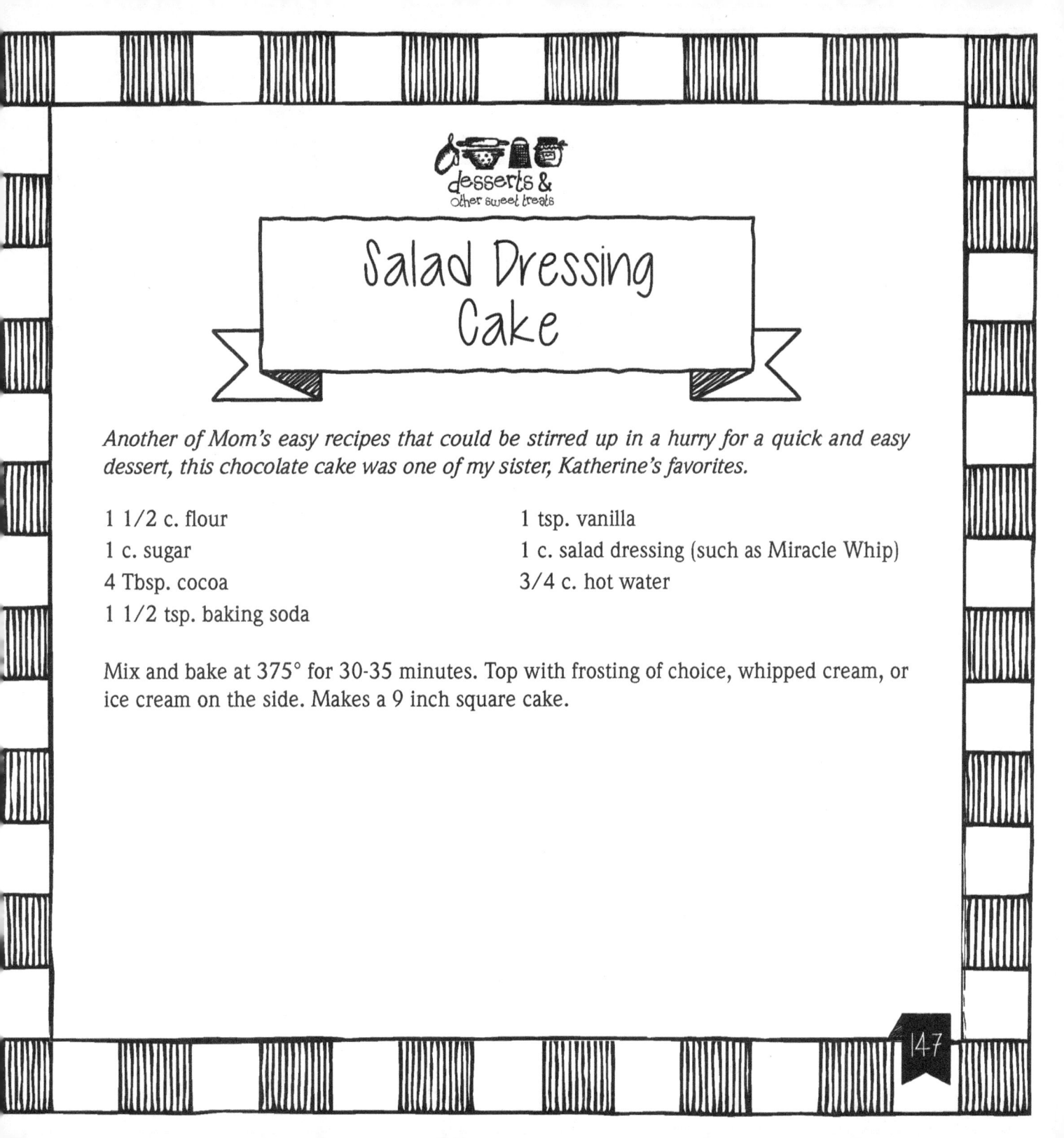

Salad Dressing Cake

Another of Mom's easy recipes that could be stirred up in a hurry for a quick and easy dessert, this chocolate cake was one of my sister, Katherine's favorites.

1 1/2 c. flour
1 c. sugar
4 Tbsp. cocoa
1 1/2 tsp. baking soda
1 tsp. vanilla
1 c. salad dressing (such as Miracle Whip)
3/4 c. hot water

Mix and bake at 375° for 30-35 minutes. Top with frosting of choice, whipped cream, or ice cream on the side. Makes a 9 inch square cake.

desserts & other sweet treats

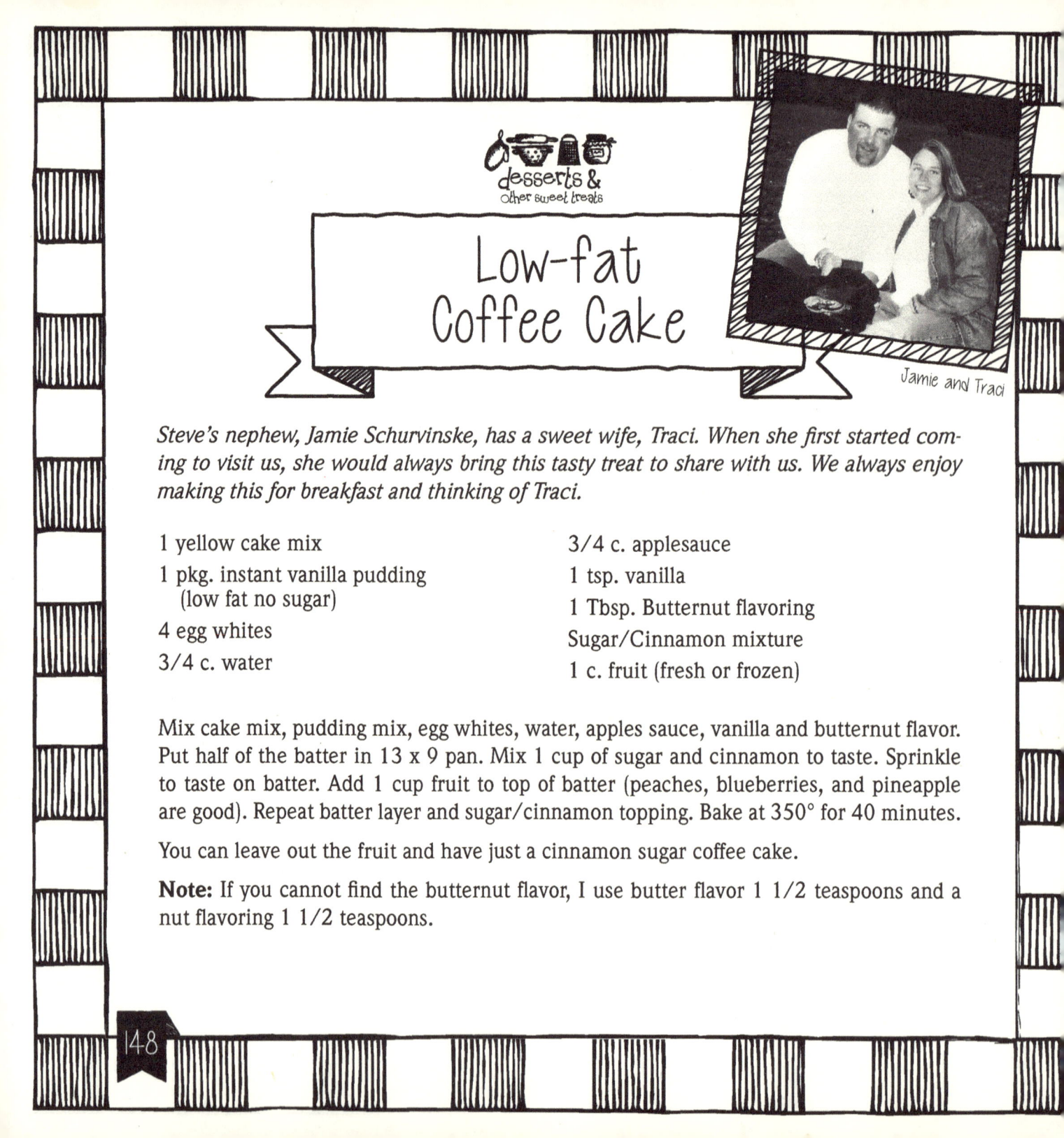

Low-fat Coffee Cake

Jamie and Traci

Steve's nephew, Jamie Schurvinske, has a sweet wife, Traci. When she first started coming to visit us, she would always bring this tasty treat to share with us. We always enjoy making this for breakfast and thinking of Traci.

- 1 yellow cake mix
- 1 pkg. instant vanilla pudding (low fat no sugar)
- 4 egg whites
- 3/4 c. water
- 3/4 c. applesauce
- 1 tsp. vanilla
- 1 Tbsp. Butternut flavoring
- Sugar/Cinnamon mixture
- 1 c. fruit (fresh or frozen)

Mix cake mix, pudding mix, egg whites, water, apples sauce, vanilla and butternut flavor. Put half of the batter in 13 x 9 pan. Mix 1 cup of sugar and cinnamon to taste. Sprinkle to taste on batter. Add 1 cup fruit to top of batter (peaches, blueberries, and pineapple are good). Repeat batter layer and sugar/cinnamon topping. Bake at 350° for 40 minutes.

You can leave out the fruit and have just a cinnamon sugar coffee cake.

Note: If you cannot find the butternut flavor, I use butter flavor 1 1/2 teaspoons and a nut flavoring 1 1/2 teaspoons.

desserts & other sweet treats

Angel Food Cake

This delicious Angel Food Cake recipe comes from Jim Diederich's mother, Carol Marie Diederich; however, Jim bakes it quite often and spoils me with one when it is my birthday. It is the best angel food cake you will ever put in your mouth.

1 c. sifted flour
1 1/2 tsp. cream of tartar
7/8 c. (3/4 c. plus 2 Tbsp.) sugar
1/4 tsp. salt

1 1/2 c. egg whites (about 12 whites)
1 1/2 tsp. vanilla
1/2 tsp. almond extract
3/4 c. sugar

Preheat oven to 375°. Have egg whites at room temperature. Measure and sift together 3 times the flour and sugar. Measure into large mixing bowl egg whites, cream of tartar, salt, vanilla and almond extract. Beat with a wire whip or Mixmaster until foamy throughout. Add gradually 3/4 cup sugar. Beat after each addition. Continue beating after the last addition until meringue is firm and holds stiff straight peaks. Sift flour-sugar mixture in small amounts over the meringue. Fold in each time with wire whip turning the bowl a quarter of a turn with each stroke until mixture is completely blended. This mixture will be very thick. Push the batter carefully, with a scraper, into ungreased tube pan. Cut carefully through the batter going around the tube 5 or 6 times with a knife to break large air bubbles. Bake 30 to 35 minutes. Deep cracks in the top are typical of this cake. Turn pan immediately upside-down. Let cake hang in pan until cold.

desserts & other sweet treats

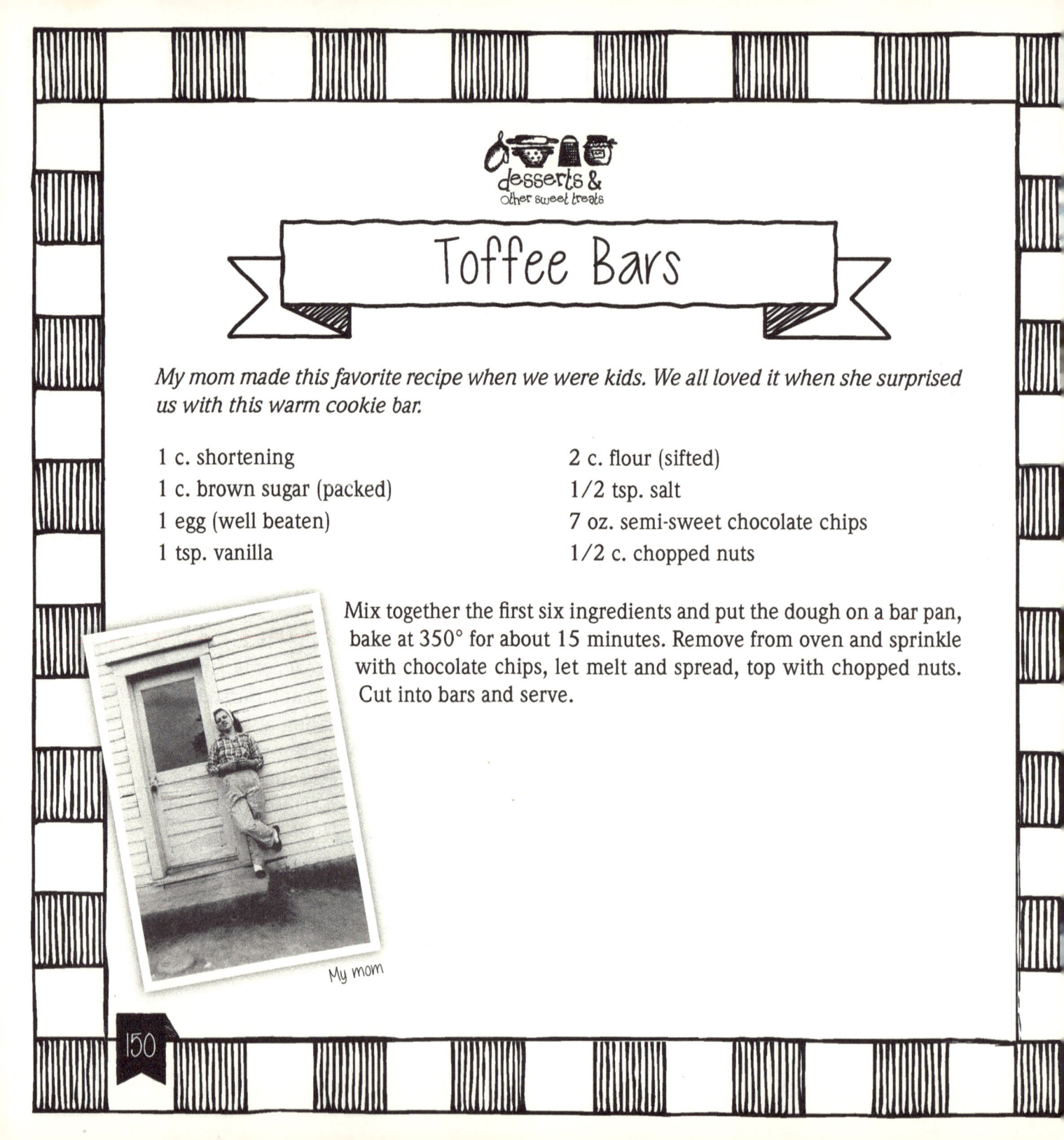

Toffee Bars

My mom made this favorite recipe when we were kids. We all loved it when she surprised us with this warm cookie bar.

1 c. shortening
1 c. brown sugar (packed)
1 egg (well beaten)
1 tsp. vanilla

2 c. flour (sifted)
1/2 tsp. salt
7 oz. semi-sweet chocolate chips
1/2 c. chopped nuts

Mix together the first six ingredients and put the dough on a bar pan, bake at 350° for about 15 minutes. Remove from oven and sprinkle with chocolate chips, let melt and spread, top with chopped nuts. Cut into bars and serve.

My mom

desserts & other sweet treats

Snickerdoodles

I have always loved Snickerdoodle cookies since I was a little girl. My Aunt Augusta made the best, and I always enjoyed them when we went to visit and she had baked the delicious treats. Unfortunately, no one ever thought to get Aunt Augusta's recipe. My good friend Donetta, received this Snickerdoodles cookie recipe from her grandmother. When I tasted them, they so reminded me of my Aunt's cookies, that this is the recipe I now like to use. Whenever I have the opportunity to sample Snickerdoodles at various venues, I never pass up the chance, but so far, none can compare to this recipe from Donetta's grandmother which takes me back to my childhood.

1 c. butter (Grandma used oleo)
1 1/2 c. sugar
2 3/4 c. flour
2 eggs

2 tsp. cream of tartar
1/2 tsp. salt
1 tsp. baking soda

Mix and put in refrigerator for 2 hours. Shape into balls and roll in cinnamon and sugar. Bake at 350-400° approximately 10 minutes or until light golden brown.

desserts & other sweet treats

Lost Snickerdoodle Recipe

Aunt Augusta

Grandma Becker

After continued searching and looking, my sister, Karen, said she had my mom's Snickerdoodle recipe, which had come from my Grandma Becker, thus my Aunt Augusta (her daughter). So here is the lost recipe.

Mix together the following:

1 c. soft shortening	2 eggs
1 1/2 c. sugar	

Sift together:

2 3/4 c. flour	1 tsp. baking soda
2 tsp. cream of tartar	1/2 tsp. salt

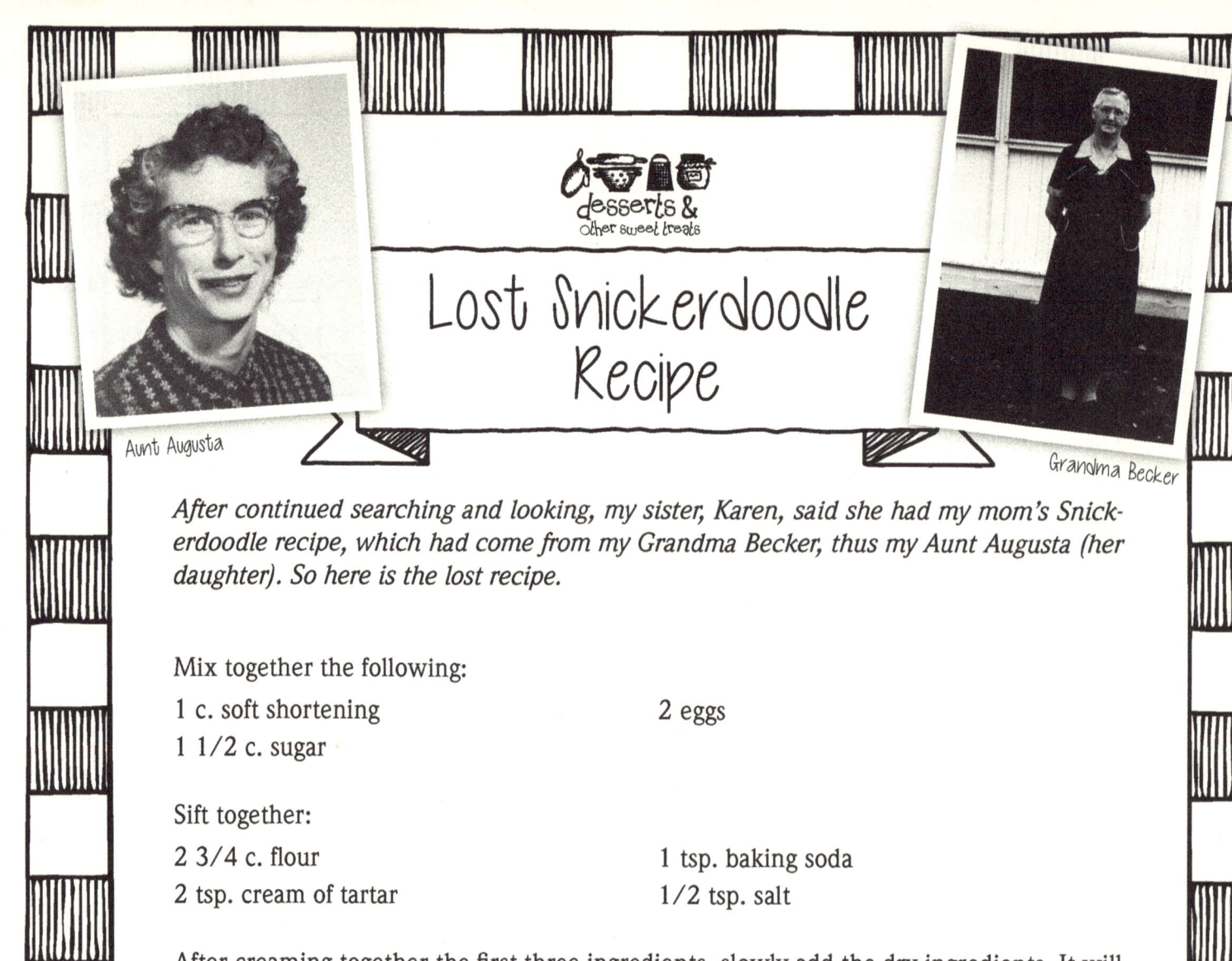

After creaming together the first three ingredients, slowly add the dry ingredients. It will be a dry dough, but will hold together when you roll them into balls. Roll into balls and then roll into the following mixture:

4 Tbsp. sugar	2 tsp. cinnamon

Bake in 400° oven for 8-10 minutes. Makes approximately 5 dozen soft 2-inch cookies.

desserts & other sweet treats

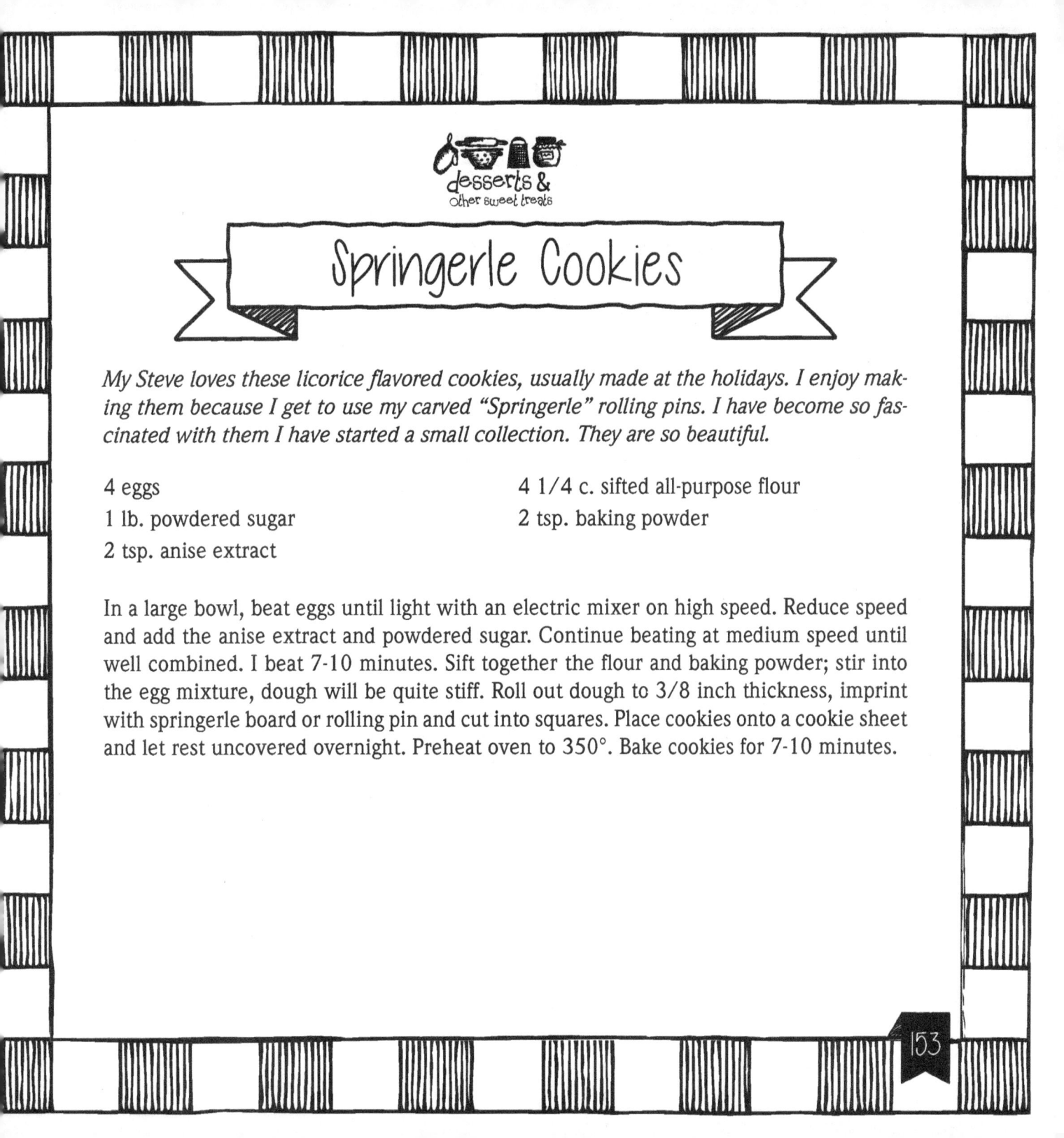

Springerle Cookies

My Steve loves these licorice flavored cookies, usually made at the holidays. I enjoy making them because I get to use my carved "Springerle" rolling pins. I have become so fascinated with them I have started a small collection. They are so beautiful.

4 eggs
1 lb. powdered sugar
2 tsp. anise extract

4 1/4 c. sifted all-purpose flour
2 tsp. baking powder

In a large bowl, beat eggs until light with an electric mixer on high speed. Reduce speed and add the anise extract and powdered sugar. Continue beating at medium speed until well combined. I beat 7-10 minutes. Sift together the flour and baking powder; stir into the egg mixture, dough will be quite stiff. Roll out dough to 3/8 inch thickness, imprint with springerle board or rolling pin and cut into squares. Place cookies onto a cookie sheet and let rest uncovered overnight. Preheat oven to 350°. Bake cookies for 7-10 minutes.

desserts & other sweet treats

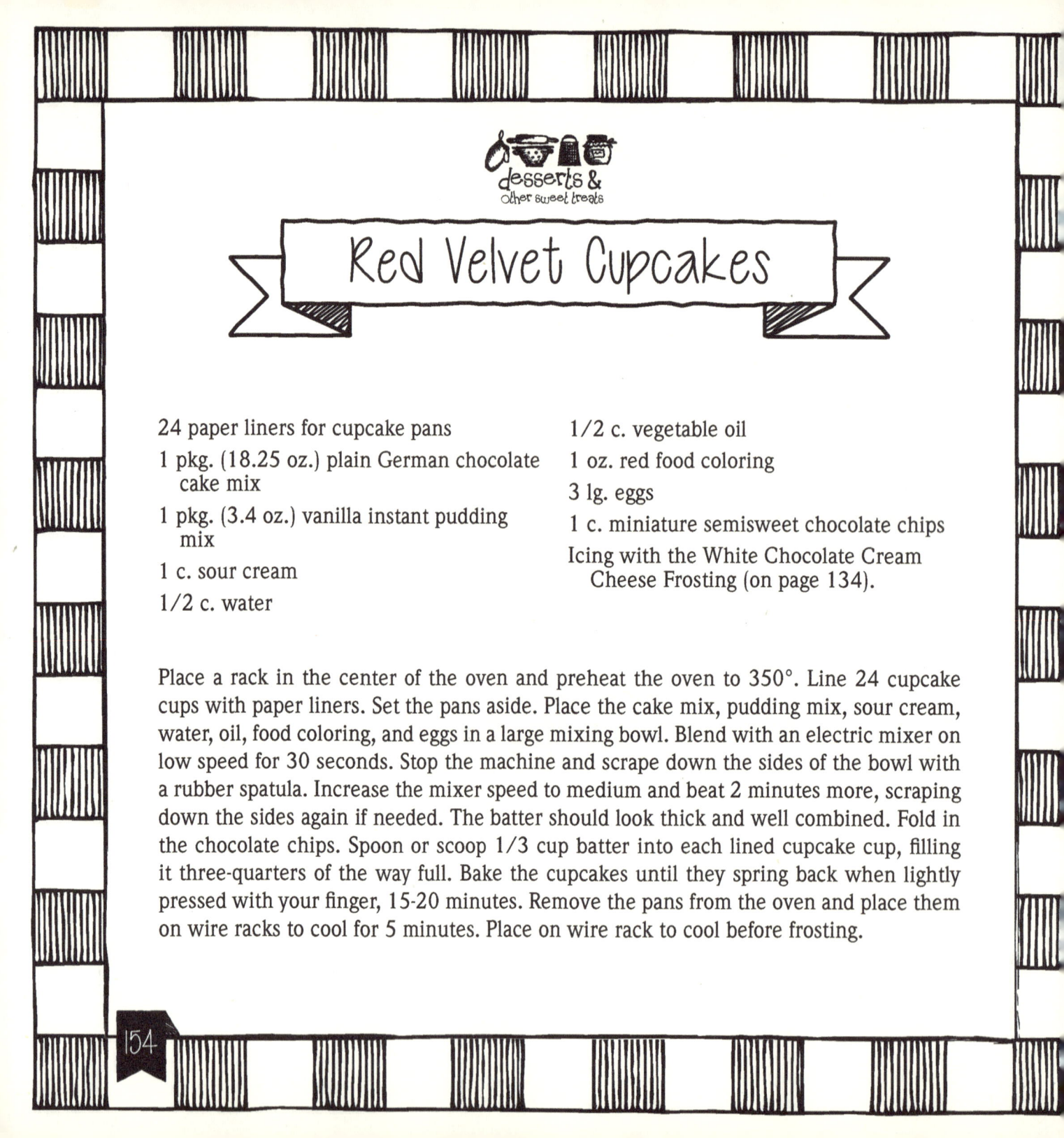

Red Velvet Cupcakes

- 24 paper liners for cupcake pans
- 1 pkg. (18.25 oz.) plain German chocolate cake mix
- 1 pkg. (3.4 oz.) vanilla instant pudding mix
- 1 c. sour cream
- 1/2 c. water
- 1/2 c. vegetable oil
- 1 oz. red food coloring
- 3 lg. eggs
- 1 c. miniature semisweet chocolate chips
- Icing with the White Chocolate Cream Cheese Frosting (on page 134).

Place a rack in the center of the oven and preheat the oven to 350°. Line 24 cupcake cups with paper liners. Set the pans aside. Place the cake mix, pudding mix, sour cream, water, oil, food coloring, and eggs in a large mixing bowl. Blend with an electric mixer on low speed for 30 seconds. Stop the machine and scrape down the sides of the bowl with a rubber spatula. Increase the mixer speed to medium and beat 2 minutes more, scraping down the sides again if needed. The batter should look thick and well combined. Fold in the chocolate chips. Spoon or scoop 1/3 cup batter into each lined cupcake cup, filling it three-quarters of the way full. Bake the cupcakes until they spring back when lightly pressed with your finger, 15-20 minutes. Remove the pans from the oven and place them on wire racks to cool for 5 minutes. Place on wire rack to cool before frosting.

desserts & other sweet treats

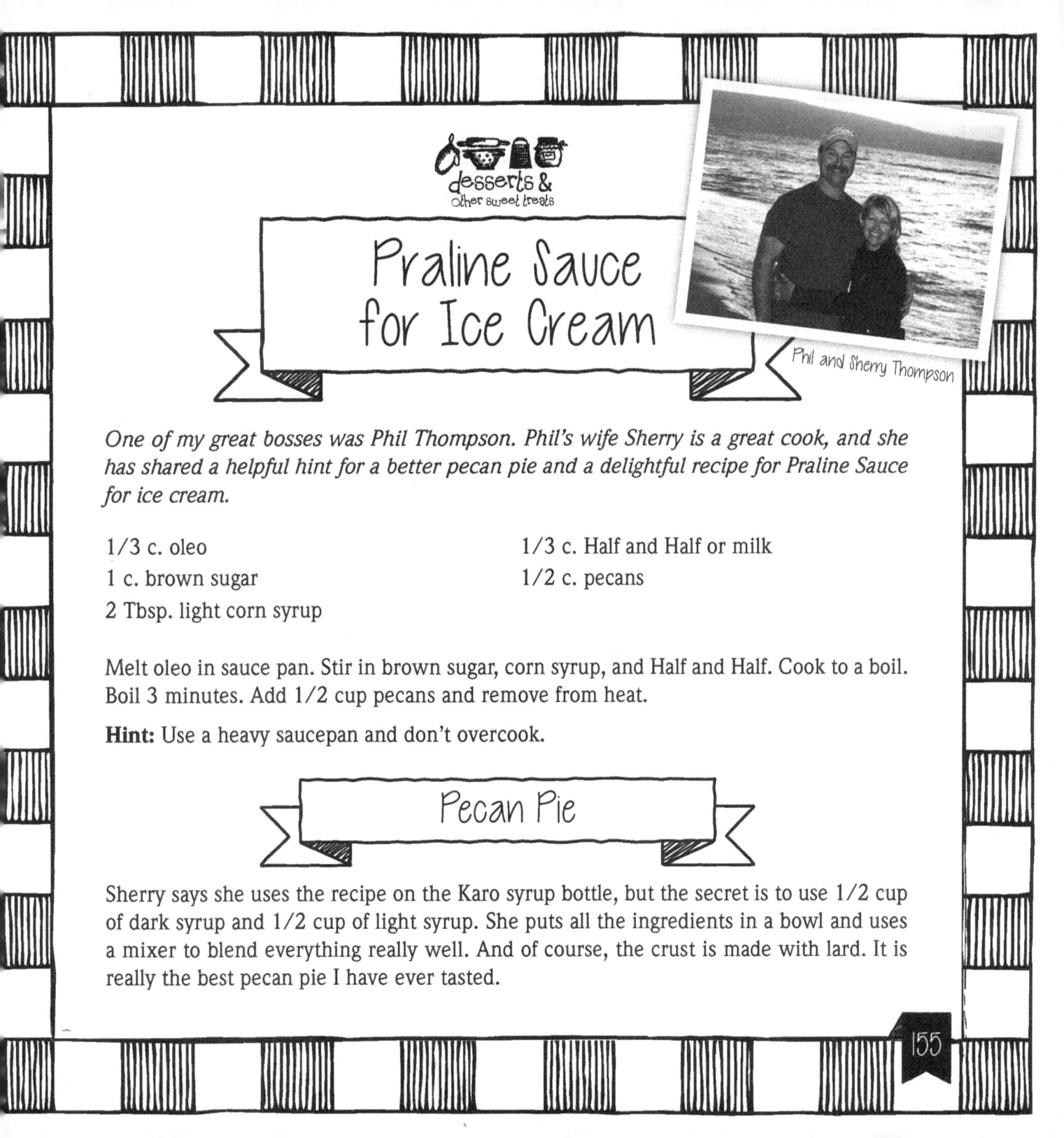

Praline Sauce for Ice Cream

Phil and Sherry Thompson

One of my great bosses was Phil Thompson. Phil's wife Sherry is a great cook, and she has shared a helpful hint for a better pecan pie and a delightful recipe for Praline Sauce for ice cream.

1/3 c. oleo
1 c. brown sugar
2 Tbsp. light corn syrup

1/3 c. Half and Half or milk
1/2 c. pecans

Melt oleo in sauce pan. Stir in brown sugar, corn syrup, and Half and Half. Cook to a boil. Boil 3 minutes. Add 1/2 cup pecans and remove from heat.

Hint: Use a heavy saucepan and don't overcook.

Pecan Pie

Sherry says she uses the recipe on the Karo syrup bottle, but the secret is to use 1/2 cup of dark syrup and 1/2 cup of light syrup. She puts all the ingredients in a bowl and uses a mixer to blend everything really well. And of course, the crust is made with lard. It is really the best pecan pie I have ever tasted.

desserts & other sweet treats

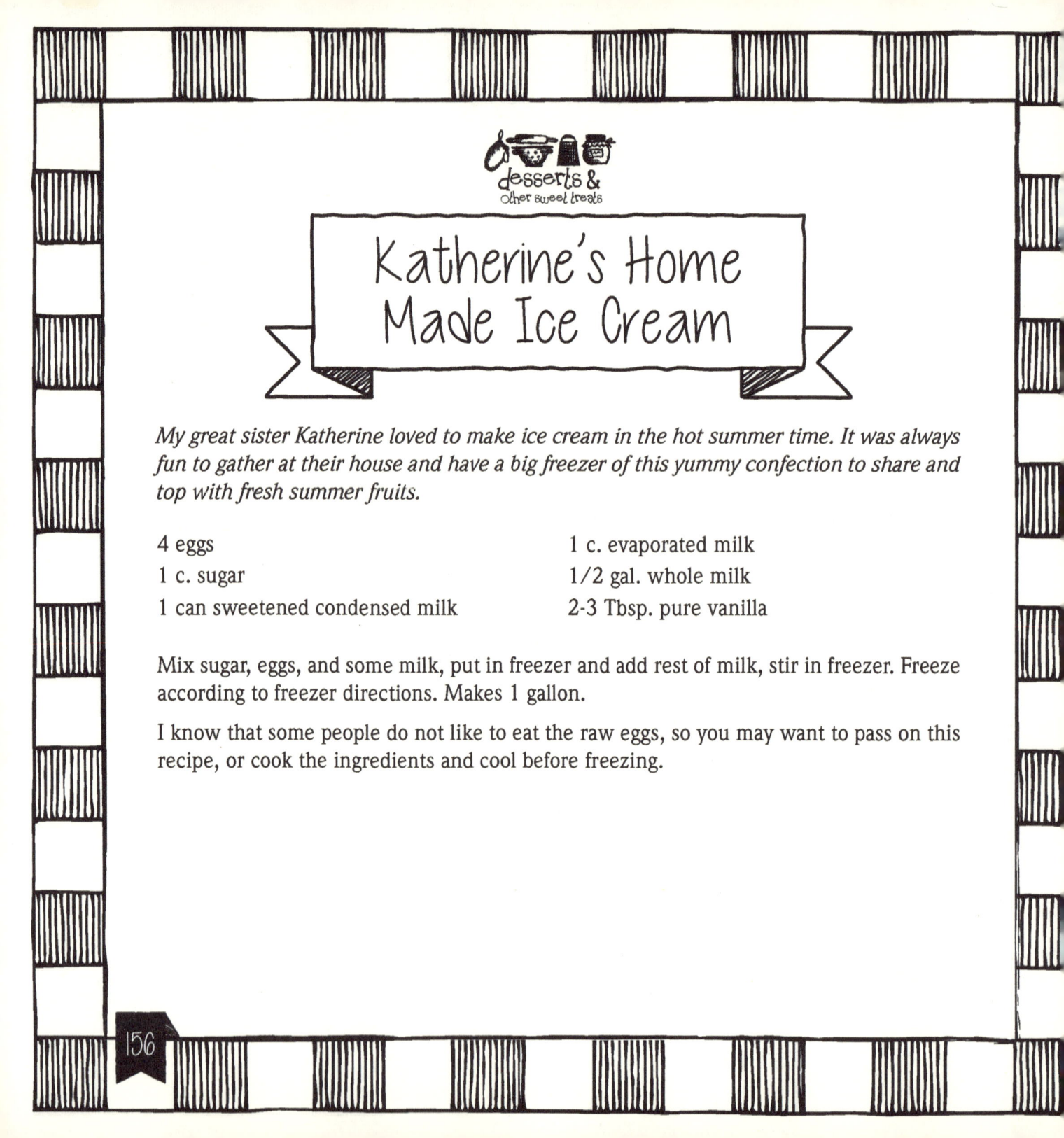

Katherine's Home Made Ice Cream

My great sister Katherine loved to make ice cream in the hot summer time. It was always fun to gather at their house and have a big freezer of this yummy confection to share and top with fresh summer fruits.

- 4 eggs
- 1 c. sugar
- 1 can sweetened condensed milk
- 1 c. evaporated milk
- 1/2 gal. whole milk
- 2-3 Tbsp. pure vanilla

Mix sugar, eggs, and some milk, put in freezer and add rest of milk, stir in freezer. Freeze according to freezer directions. Makes 1 gallon.

I know that some people do not like to eat the raw eggs, so you may want to pass on this recipe, or cook the ingredients and cool before freezing.

desserts & other sweet treats

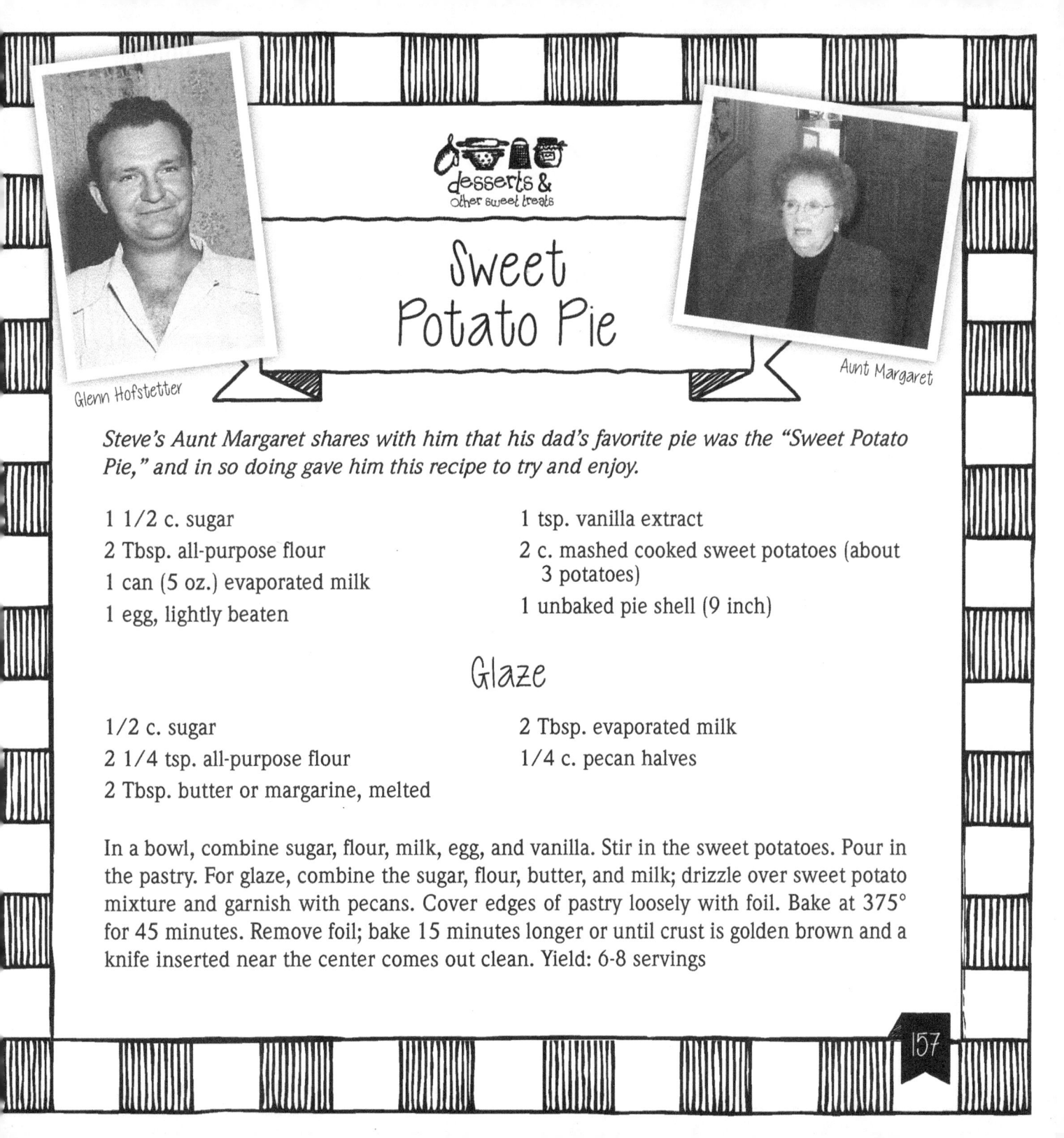

Sweet Potato Pie

Glenn Hofstetter

Aunt Margaret

Steve's Aunt Margaret shares with him that his dad's favorite pie was the "Sweet Potato Pie," and in so doing gave him this recipe to try and enjoy.

1 1/2 c. sugar
2 Tbsp. all-purpose flour
1 can (5 oz.) evaporated milk
1 egg, lightly beaten
1 tsp. vanilla extract
2 c. mashed cooked sweet potatoes (about 3 potatoes)
1 unbaked pie shell (9 inch)

Glaze

1/2 c. sugar
2 1/4 tsp. all-purpose flour
2 Tbsp. butter or margarine, melted
2 Tbsp. evaporated milk
1/4 c. pecan halves

In a bowl, combine sugar, flour, milk, egg, and vanilla. Stir in the sweet potatoes. Pour in the pastry. For glaze, combine the sugar, flour, butter, and milk; drizzle over sweet potato mixture and garnish with pecans. Cover edges of pastry loosely with foil. Bake at 375° for 45 minutes. Remove foil; bake 15 minutes longer or until crust is golden brown and a knife inserted near the center comes out clean. Yield: 6-8 servings

Jack Kennedy

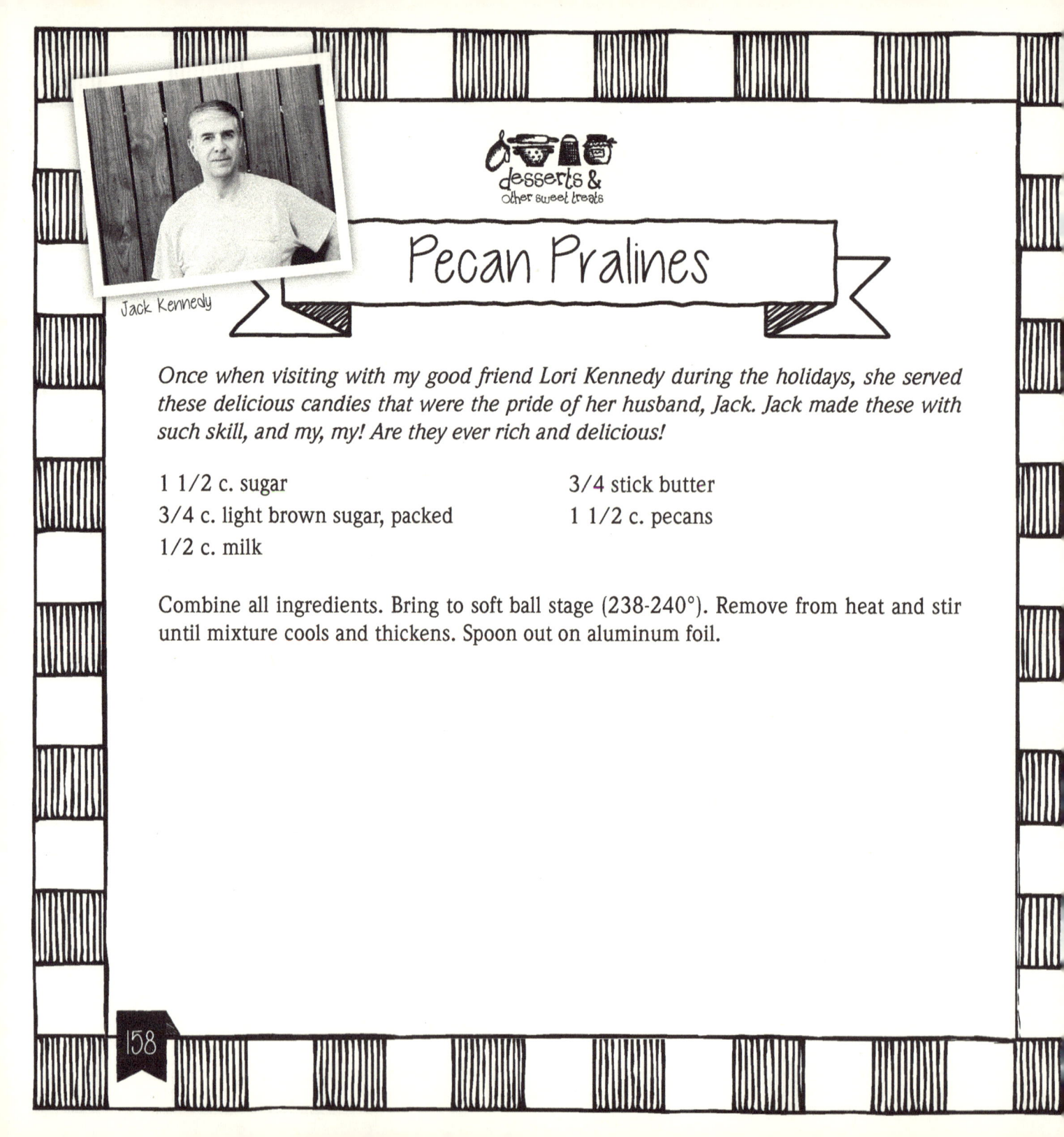

desserts & other sweet treats

Pecan Pralines

Once when visiting with my good friend Lori Kennedy during the holidays, she served these delicious candies that were the pride of her husband, Jack. Jack made these with such skill, and my, my! Are they ever rich and delicious!

1 1/2 c. sugar
3/4 c. light brown sugar, packed
1/2 c. milk
3/4 stick butter
1 1/2 c. pecans

Combine all ingredients. Bring to soft ball stage (238-240°). Remove from heat and stir until mixture cools and thickens. Spoon out on aluminum foil.

desserts & other sweet treats

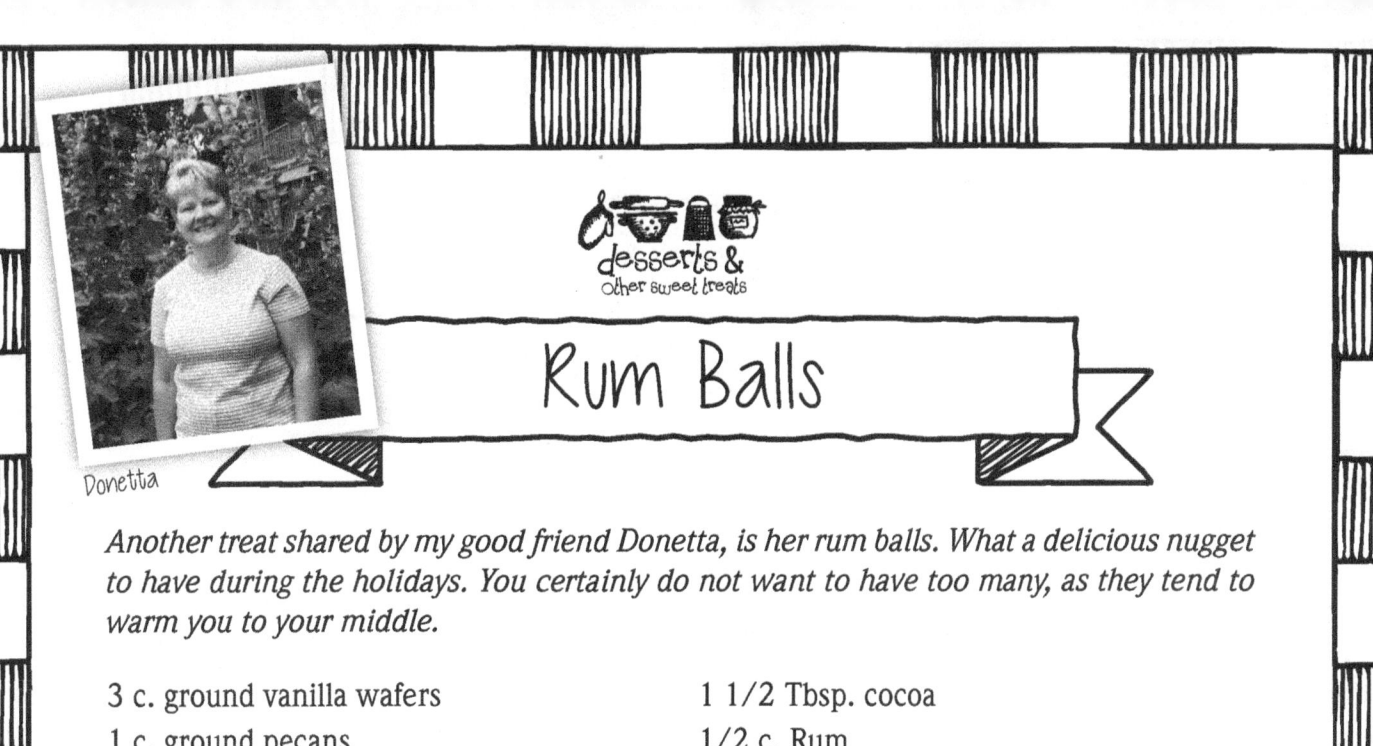

Rum Balls

Donetta

Another treat shared by my good friend Donetta, is her rum balls. What a delicious nugget to have during the holidays. You certainly do not want to have too many, as they tend to warm you to your middle.

3 c. ground vanilla wafers
1 c. ground pecans
3 Tbsp. white syrup
1 1/2 Tbsp. cocoa
1/2 c. Rum

Mix ingredients together. Break off enough to roll in shape of a cherry. Roll in powdered sugar.

desserts & other sweet treats

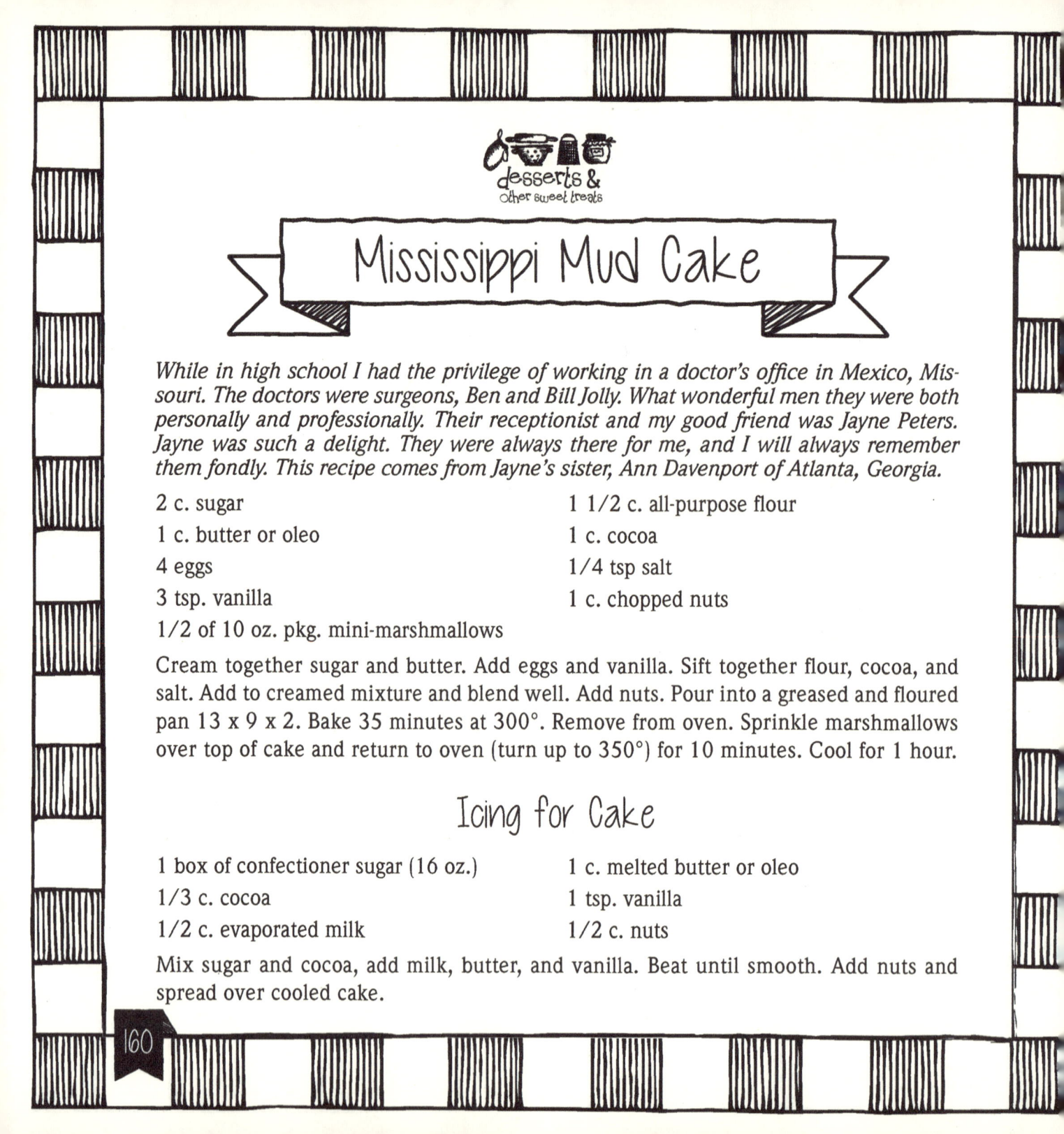

Mississippi Mud Cake

While in high school I had the privilege of working in a doctor's office in Mexico, Missouri. The doctors were surgeons, Ben and Bill Jolly. What wonderful men they were both personally and professionally. Their receptionist and my good friend was Jayne Peters. Jayne was such a delight. They were always there for me, and I will always remember them fondly. This recipe comes from Jayne's sister, Ann Davenport of Atlanta, Georgia.

- 2 c. sugar
- 1 c. butter or oleo
- 4 eggs
- 3 tsp. vanilla
- 1/2 of 10 oz. pkg. mini-marshmallows
- 1 1/2 c. all-purpose flour
- 1 c. cocoa
- 1/4 tsp salt
- 1 c. chopped nuts

Cream together sugar and butter. Add eggs and vanilla. Sift together flour, cocoa, and salt. Add to creamed mixture and blend well. Add nuts. Pour into a greased and floured pan 13 x 9 x 2. Bake 35 minutes at 300°. Remove from oven. Sprinkle marshmallows over top of cake and return to oven (turn up to 350°) for 10 minutes. Cool for 1 hour.

Icing for Cake

- 1 box of confectioner sugar (16 oz.)
- 1/3 c. cocoa
- 1/2 c. evaporated milk
- 1 c. melted butter or oleo
- 1 tsp. vanilla
- 1/2 c. nuts

Mix sugar and cocoa, add milk, butter, and vanilla. Beat until smooth. Add nuts and spread over cooled cake.

Cherry Fruit Cake

desserts & other sweet treats

Brent's great-aunt, Henrietta Beatty (she was a vice-president at 1st National Bank in Mexico, Missouri) had a wonderful recipe for a great fruit cake. Although some people do not care for this delicacy, this is one of the best. Even if you think you don't like this seasonal treat, you may want to give it a try.

- 1 1/2 c. sifted all-purpose flour
- 1 1/2 c. sugar
- 1 tsp. baking powder
- 1 tsp. salt
- 2 pkgs. (7.25 oz. each) pitted dates
- 1 lb. diced candied pineapple
- 2 jars (16 oz. each) maraschino cherries, drained
- 18 oz. (about 5 1/2 c.) pecan halves
- 6 eggs
- 1/3 c. dark rum
- 1/2 c. light corn syrup (save for last)

Grease 2 (9x5) loaf pans. Line with foil, allowing a 2-inch overhang and grease again.

Sift flour, sugar, baking powder, and salt in a very large bowl. Add fruit and pecans and toss until coated, (you will probably have to use your hands).

Beat eggs and rum thoroughly; pour over fruit mixture and toss until combined. Turn the mixture into the pans, pressing frequently to pack tightly.

Bake at 300° for 1 3/4 hours or until a toothpick comes out clean. Cool in pans for 15 minutes, then remove and tear off foil. Brush cakes with syrup while still warm. Cool thoroughly before serving or storing.

desserts & other sweet treats

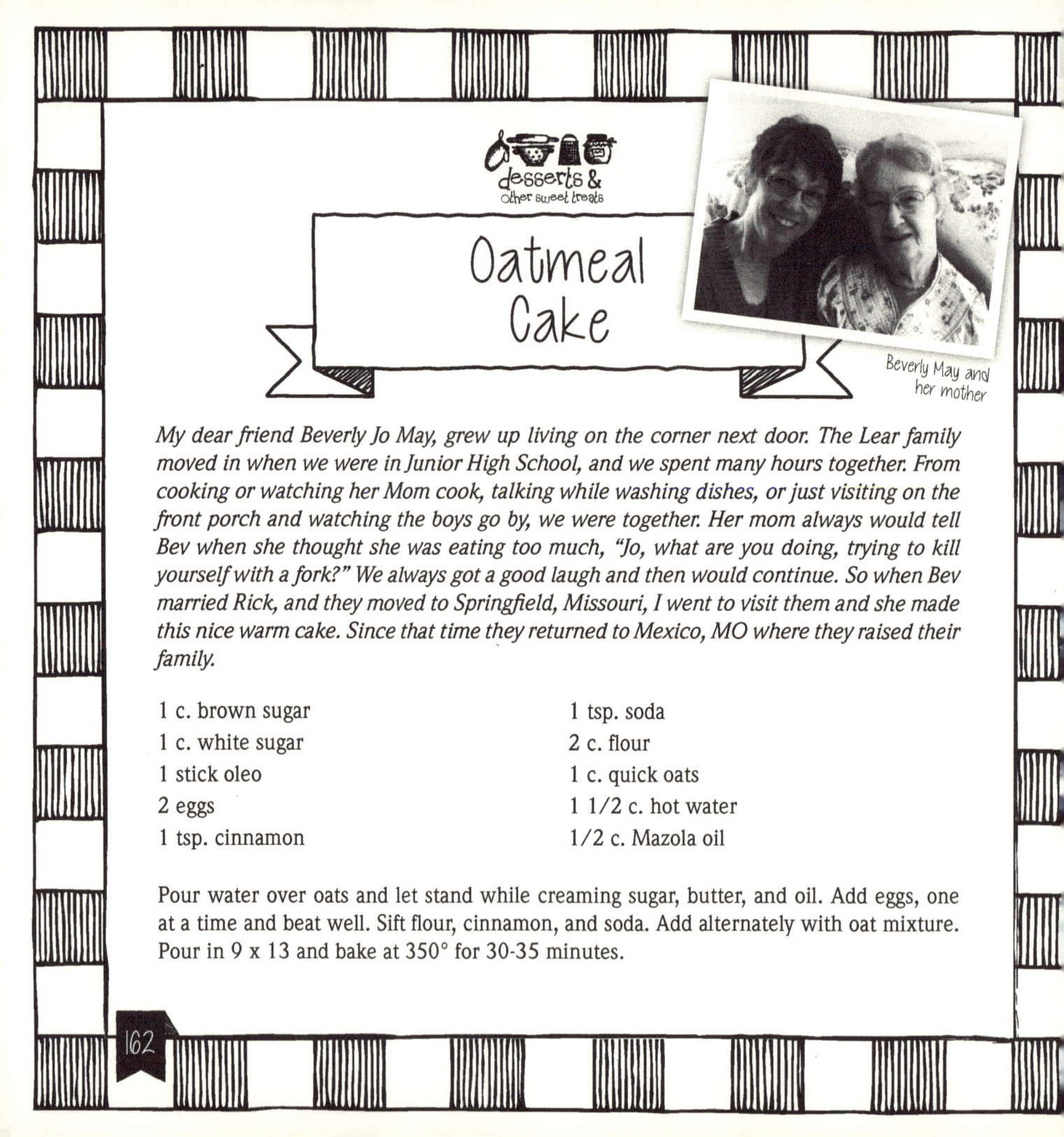

Oatmeal Cake

Beverly May and her mother

My dear friend Beverly Jo May, grew up living on the corner next door. The Lear family moved in when we were in Junior High School, and we spent many hours together. From cooking or watching her Mom cook, talking while washing dishes, or just visiting on the front porch and watching the boys go by, we were together. Her mom always would tell Bev when she thought she was eating too much, "Jo, what are you doing, trying to kill yourself with a fork?" We always got a good laugh and then would continue. So when Bev married Rick, and they moved to Springfield, Missouri, I went to visit them and she made this nice warm cake. Since that time they returned to Mexico, MO where they raised their family.

- 1 c. brown sugar
- 1 c. white sugar
- 1 stick oleo
- 2 eggs
- 1 tsp. cinnamon
- 1 tsp. soda
- 2 c. flour
- 1 c. quick oats
- 1 1/2 c. hot water
- 1/2 c. Mazola oil

Pour water over oats and let stand while creaming sugar, butter, and oil. Add eggs, one at a time and beat well. Sift flour, cinnamon, and soda. Add alternately with oat mixture. Pour in 9 x 13 and bake at 350° for 30-35 minutes.

desserts & other sweet treats

Oatmeal Cake Icing

(cook with low heat and stir carefully or it sugars)

1 stick butter
1 c. brown sugar

1/2 c. evaporated milk

Cook 10 minutes and remove from heat.

Add:
1 tsp. vanilla
1 c. pecans
1 c. coconut

Pour on hot cake and return to oven until icing bubbles.

Beverly May and granddaughter, Noelle

desserts & other sweet treats

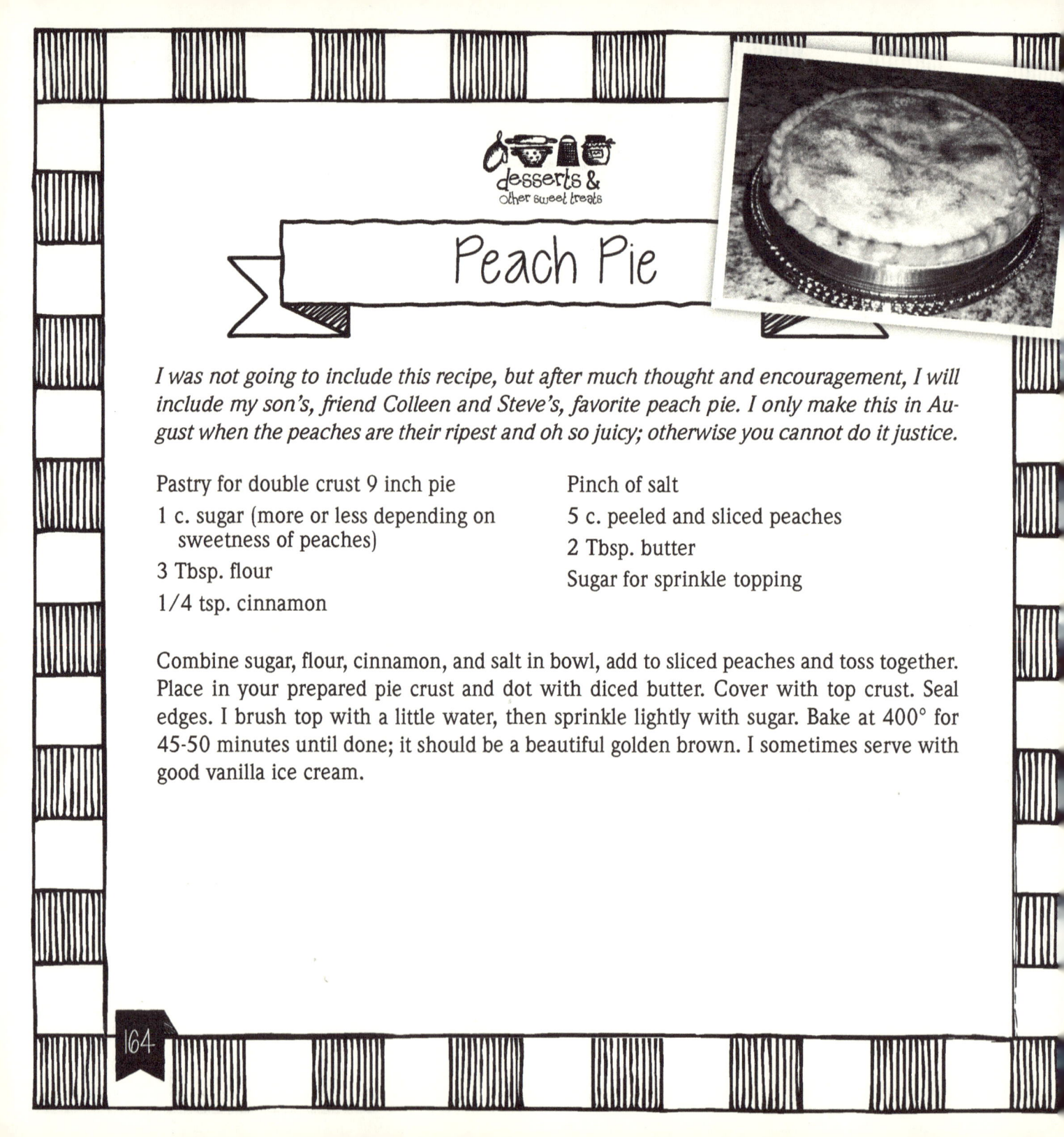

Peach Pie

I was not going to include this recipe, but after much thought and encouragement, I will include my son's, friend Colleen and Steve's, favorite peach pie. I only make this in August when the peaches are their ripest and oh so juicy; otherwise you cannot do it justice.

Pastry for double crust 9 inch pie
1 c. sugar (more or less depending on sweetness of peaches)
3 Tbsp. flour
1/4 tsp. cinnamon
Pinch of salt
5 c. peeled and sliced peaches
2 Tbsp. butter
Sugar for sprinkle topping

Combine sugar, flour, cinnamon, and salt in bowl, add to sliced peaches and toss together. Place in your prepared pie crust and dot with diced butter. Cover with top crust. Seal edges. I brush top with a little water, then sprinkle lightly with sugar. Bake at 400° for 45-50 minutes until done; it should be a beautiful golden brown. I sometimes serve with good vanilla ice cream.

Index

A
Angel Food Cake, 149
Appetizers
   Baked Cream Cheese Appetizer, 30
   Caramel Dip, 40
   Cheese Rolls, 33
   Cheese Tid-Bits, 41
   Cream Cheese Mints, 29
   Dill Dip, 23
   Frozen Fruit Cups, 32
   Fruit Dip, 40
   Hot Artichoke Augratin with French Bread Dippers, 31
   Korean Egg Rolls, 34
   Marcie's Spiced Pecans, 36
   Marilyn's Spiced Pecans, 37
   Meng Cheese, 38
   Party Fodder, 26
   Rainy's Meatballs, 42
   Reindeer Munch, 28
   Reuben Dip, 24
   Spicy Hot Pretzels, 25
   Sticky Wings, 27
   Summer Sausage, 39
   Yummy Sandwiches, 18
Apple Snicker Salad I, 67
Apple Snicker Salad II, 68
Asparagus Picnic Salad, 62

B
Baby Food Carrot Cake, 138
Baked Cream Cheese Appetizer, 30
Bar-B-Que, 102
Beef
   Bar-B-Que, 102
   Beef Brisket, 98
   Chuck Roast and Vegetables, 80
   Crock Pot Roast-Beef, 103
   Dalton's Prize-Winning Chili Con Carne, 108
   Deviled Beef Patties, 86
   Dorito Taco Salad, 54
   Ham Balls, 87
   Herbed Vegetable Beef Soup, 83
   Hofstetter's Prize Winning Chili Recipe, 110
   Korean Egg Rolls, 34
   Mom's (Me) Meatloaf, 114
   Plaza Steak Soup, 82
   Prime Rib, 99
   South of the Border Lasagna, 90
   Summer Sausage, 39
Beef Brisket, 98
Beverages
   Homemade Cappuccino, 22
   Mulled Cider, 19
   Raspberry Lemonade, 20
   Russian Tea, 21
Bread Pudding, 120
Breads
   Easy Dinner Rolls, 69
   Garlic-Cheese Biscuits, 63
   Whole-Wheat Bread, 64
Broccoli Cheese Soup, 85
Broccoli Salad, 51
Brown Sugar Dumplings, 146
Buttercream Frosting for Wedding Cake Cupcakes, 133

C
Cakes
   Angel Food Cake, 149
   Carrot Cake, 137
   Cherry Fruit Cake, 161
   German Apple Cake, 135
   Lemonade Cake, 125
   Low-fat Coffee Cake, 148
   Mississippi Mud Cake, 160
   Oatmeal Cake, 162
   Pineapple Upside Down Cake, 131
   Red Velvet Cupcakes, 154
   Salad Dressing Cake, 147
   White Wedding Cake Cupcakes, 132
Caramel Dip, 40
Carrot Cake, 137
   Baby Food Carrot Cake, 138
Casserole
   Corn Casserole, 44
   Hash Brown Casserole, 65
   Reuben Casserole, 104
   Yellow Squash Casserole, 70
Cauliflower and Broccoli Salad, 52
Cheese Rolls, 33
Cheese Tid-Bits, 41
Cheesy Zucchini Lasagna, 88
Cherry Crunch, 129
Cherry Fruit Cake, 161
Cherry Pie Filling Salad, 76
Chicken. *See also Poultry*
Chicken Enchiladas, 112
Chicken Enchilada Soup, 84
Chicken Hot Dish, 79
Chicken Pot Pie, 113
Chili. *See also Soups*
Chinese Coleslaw, 55
Chocolate Fondue, 124
Chuck Roast and Vegetables, 80
Cookies
   Ginger Snaps, 128

Grandma Linda's Baseball Cookies, 126
Grandma Witt's Sugar Cookies, 144
Joni's Mom's Cut-Out Cookies, 145
Kiddy Cookies, 116
Lost Snickerdoodle Recipe, 152
Russian Tea Cakes, 121
Snickerdoodles, 151
Springerle Cookies, 153
Corn Casserole, 44
Cranberry Salad, Linda's Version, 57
Cream Cheese Frosting, 139
Cream Cheese Mints, 29
Creamy Fettuccine Alfredo, 105
Crock Pot Roast-Beef, 103
Crustless Crab Quiche, 92
Cucumber and Onions, 58

D
Dalton's Prize-Winning Chili Con Carne, 108
Desserts
   Angel Food Cake, 149
   Baby Food Carrot Cake, 138
   Bread Pudding, 120
   Brown Sugar Dumplings, 146
   Carrot Cake, 137
   Cherry Crunch, 129
   Cherry Fruit Cake, 161
   Chocolate Fondue, 124
   German Apple Cake, 135
   Ginger Snaps, 128
   Glorified Brownies, 140
   Grandma Linda's Baseball Cookies, 126
   Grandma Witt's Sugar Cookies, 144
   Jan's Cream Cheese Frosting, 137
   Joni's Mom's Cut-Out Cookies, 145
   Katherine's Home Made Ice Cream, 156
   Kiddy Cookies, 116
   Lemonade Cake, 125
   Lost Snickerdoodle Recipe, 152
   Low-fat Coffee Cake, 148
   Low-Fat Key Lime Pie, 123
   Mississippi Mud Cake, 160
   Mom's Bread Pudding, 118
   Mother's Soft Pies, 142
   Oatmeal Cake, 162
   Oatmeal Cake Icing, 163
   Peach Pie, 164
   Peach Pie Dessert, 136
   Peanut Butter Bars, 141
   Pecan Pralines, 158
   Pineapple Upside Down Cake, 131
   Praline Sauce for Ice Cream, 155
   Raisin Pie, 130
   Red Velvet Cupcakes, 154
   Rhubarb Custard Pie, 117
   Rum Balls, 159
   Russian Tea Cakes, 121
   Salad Dressing Cake, 147
   Snickerdoodles, 151
   Snicker Pie, 122
   Springerle Cookies, 153
   Sweet Potato Pie, 157
   Toffee Bars, 150
   White Chocolate Cream Cheese Frosting, 134
   White Wedding Cake Cupcakes, 132
Deviled Beef Patties, 86
Deviled Eggs, 72
Dill Dip, 23
Dips
   Caramel Dip, 40
   Dill Dip, 23
   Fruit Dip, 40
   Hot Artichoke Augratin with French Bread Dippers, 31
   Reuben Dip, 24
Dorito Taco Salad, 54
Dressings
   French Dressing, 46
Drinks. See also Beverages

E
Easy Dinner Rolls, 69
Entrees
   Bar-B-Que, 102
   Beef Brisket, 98
   Broccoli Cheese Soup, 85
   Cheesy Zucchini Lasagna, 88
   Chicken Enchiladas, 112
   Chicken Enchilada Soup, 84
   Chicken Hot Dish, 79
   Chicken Pot Pie, 113
   Chuck Roast and Vegetables, 80
   Creamy Fettuccine Alfredo, 105
   Crock Pot Roast-Beef, 103
   Crustless Crab Quiche, 92
   Dalton's Prize-Winning Chili Con Carne, 108
   Deviled Beef Patties, 86
   French Toast, 81
   Ham and Beans, 93
   Ham Balls, 87
   Herbed Vegetable Beef Soup, 83
   Hofstetter's Prize Winning Chili Recipe, 110
   Jan's Pimento Cheese, 94
   Leo's Clam Chowder, 97
   Lobster House Flounder Parmesan, 91
   Mom's (Me) Meatloaf, 114
   Prime Rib, 99
   Reuben Casserole, 104
   Roasted Veggie Lasagna, 89
   Smoky Salmon Fillets, 96
   South of the Border Lasagna, 90
   Spicy Pimento Cheese, 95
   Spinach Pie, 78
   Steve and Linda's Chicken Noodle Soup, 101

Steve's Fra Diavolo, 106
Tortilla Soup, 100
White Chili, 111

F
French Dressing, 46
French Toast, 81
Frosting
   Buttercream Frosting for Wedding Cake Cupcakes, 133
   Cream Cheese Frosting, 139
   Jan's Cream Cheese Frosting, 137
   White Chocolate Cream Cheese Frosting, 134
Frozen Champagne Salad, 66
Frozen Fruit Cups, 32
Fruit Dip, 40

G
Garlic-Cheese Biscuits, 63
German Apple Cake, 135
Ginger Snaps, 128
Glorified Brownies, 140
Grandma Beckley's Cranberry Salad, 56
Grandma Linda's Baseball Cookies, 126
Grandma Witt's Sugar Cookies, 144
Grape Salad, 75
Greek Pasta Salad, 61

H
Ham and Beans, 93
Ham Balls, 87
Hash Brown Casserole, 65
Herbed Vegetable Beef Soup, 83
Hofstetter's Prize Winning Chili Recipe, 110
Homemade Cappuccino, 22
Hot Artichoke Augratin with French Bread Dippers, 31
"Hot" Macaroni, 73

I
Icing, 139
   Oatmeal Cake Icing, 163

J
Jan's Cream Cheese Frosting, 137
Jan's Pimento Cheese, 94
Jeane's Chicken Salad, 48
Joni's Mom's Cut-Out Cookies, 145

K
Karen's Creamy Macaroni Salad, 74
Katherine's Home Made Ice Cream, 156
Kiddy Cookies, 116
Korean Egg Rolls, 34

L
Lava Sauce, 119
Layered Salad, 53
Lemonade Cake, 125
Leo's Clam Chowder, 97
Linda's Version of the Cranberry Salad, 57
Lobster House Flounder Parmesan, 91
Lost Snickerdoodle Recipe, 152
Low-fat Coffee Cake, 148
Low-Fat Key Lime Pie, 123

M
Madison's Salad, 50
Main Dish. *See also Entrees*
Marcie's Spiced Pecans, 36
Marilyn's Spiced Pecans, 37
Meng Cheese, 38
Mississippi Mud Cake, 160
Mom's Bread Pudding, 118
Mom's (Me) Meatloaf, 114
Mother's Soft Pies, 142
Mulled Cider, 19

O
Oatmeal Cake, 162
Oatmeal Cake Icing, 163

P
Party Fodder, 26
Pasta
   Cheesy Zucchini Lasagna, 88
   Creamy Fettuccine Alfredo, 105
   Greek Pasta Salad, 61
   "Hot" Macaroni, 73
   Karen's Creamy Macaroni Salad, 74
   Roasted Veggie Lasagna, 89
   Steve's Fra Diavolo, 106
Pat Darnell's Creamy Hot Bacon Salad, 45
Peach Pie, 164
Peach Pie Dessert, 136
Peanut Butter Bars, 141
Pea Salad or Red Bean Salad, 59
Pecan Pie, 155
Pecan Pralines, 158
Pies
   Cherry Crunch, 129
   Low-Fat Key Lime Pie, 123
   Mother's Soft Pies, 142
   Peach Pie, 164
   Peach Pie Dessert, 136
   Pecan Pie, 155
   Raisin Pie, 130
   Rhubarb Custard Pie, 117
   Snicker Pie, 122
   Spinach Pie, 78
   Sweet Potato Pie, 157
Pineapple Upside Down Cake, 131
Plaza Steak Soup, 82
Plum Sauce, 47
Pork
   Bar-B-Que, 102
   Ham and Beans, 93
   Ham Balls, 87
Potato Salad, 71

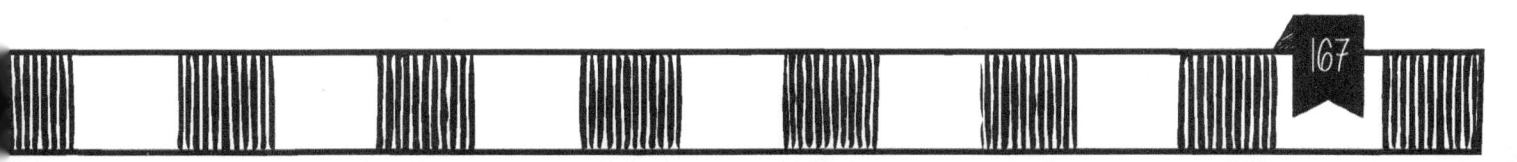

Poultry
- Chicken Enchiladas, 112
- Chicken Enchilada Soup, 84
- Chicken Hot Dish, 79
- Chicken Pot Pie, 113
- Jeane's Chicken Salad, 48
- Steve and Linda's Chicken Noodle Soup, 101
- Sticky Wings, 27
- Tortilla Soup, 100
- White Chili, 111

Praline Sauce for Ice Cream, 155
Prime Rib, 99

R
Rainy's Meatballs, 42
Raisin Pie, 130
Raspberry Lemonade, 20
Red Velvet Cupcakes, 154
Reindeer Munch, 28
Reuben Casserole, 104
Reuben Dip, 24
Rhubarb Custard Pie, 117
Roasted Veggie Lasagna, 89
Rum Balls, 159
Russian Tea, 21
Russian Tea Cakes, 121

S
Salad Dressing Cake, 147
Salads
- Apple Snicker Salad I, 67
- Apple Snicker Salad II, 68
- Asparagus Picnic Salad, 62
- Broccoli Salad, 51
- Cauliflower and Broccoli Salad, 52
- Cherry Pie Filling Salad, 76
- Cranberry Salad, Linda's Version, 57
- Dorito Taco Salad, 54
- Frozen Champagne Salad, 66
- Grandma Beckley's Cranberry Salad, 56
- Grape Salad, 75
- Greek Pasta Salad, 61
- Jeane's Chicken Salad, 48
- Karen's Creamy Macaroni Salad, 74
- Layered Salad, 53
- Linda's Version of the Cranberry Salad, 57
- Madison's Salad, 50
- Pat Darnell's Creamy Hot Bacon Salad, 45
- Pea Salad or Red Bean Salad, 59
- Potato Salad, 71
- Shrimp Salad, 49
- Vegetable Salad, 60

Sauces
- Lava Sauce, 119
- Plum Sauce, 47
- Praline Sauce for Ice Cream, 155
- Vanilla Sauce, 120

Seafood
- Crustless Crab Quiche, 92
- Leo's Clam Chowder, 97
- Lobster House Flounder Parmesan, 91
- Shrimp Salad, 49
- Smoky Salmon Fillets, 96
- Steve's Fra Diavolo, 106

Shrimp Salad, 49
Sides
- Chinese Coleslaw, 55
- Corn Casserole, 44
- Cucumber and Onions, 58
- Deviled Eggs, 72
- Easy Dinner Rolls, 69
- Garlic-Cheese Biscuits, 63
- Hash Brown Casserole, 65
- "Hot" Macaroni, 73
- Whole-Wheat Bread, 64
- Yellow Squash Casserole, 70

Smoky Salmon Fillets, 96
Snickerdoodles, 151
Snicker Pie, 122
Soups
- Broccoli Cheese Soup, 85
- Chicken Enchilada Soup, 84
- Dalton's Prize-Winning Chili Con Carne, 108
- Herbed Vegetable Beef Soup, 83
- Hofstetter's Prize Winning Chili Recipe, 110
- Leo's Clam Chowder, 97
- Plaza Steak Soup, 82
- Steve and Linda's Chicken Noodle Soup, 101
- Tortilla Soup, 100

White Chili, 111
South of the Border Lasagna, 90
Spicy Hot Pretzels, 25
Spicy Pimento Cheese, 95
Spinach Pie, 78
Springerle Cookies, 153
Steve and Linda's Chicken Noodle Soup, 101
Steve's Fra Diavolo, 106
Sticky Wings, 27
Summer Sausage, 39
Sweet Potato Pie, 157

T
Toffee Bars, 150
Tortilla Soup, 100

V
Vanilla Sauce, 120
Vegetable Salad, 60

W
White Chili, 111
White Chocolate Cream Cheese Frosting, 134
White Wedding Cake Cupcakes, 132
Whole-Wheat Bread, 64

Y
Yellow Squash Casserole, 70
Yummy Sandwiches, 18

A closing blessing to all:

Thank you God, for our food, friends, and family.

Amen

Recipe Publishers

WE ♥ COOKBOOKS

Springfield, Missouri
(417) 619-4939
www.RecipePubs.com

Copyright © 2013 by Linda Hofstetter

First Edition

Library of Congress Control Number: 2013947137

ISBN: 978-0-9898137-0-9

Author: Linda Hofstetter

Cover and Graphics Layout by: Amanda DeGraffenreid

Edited by: Pam Eddings

All rights reserved. This publication; *Mothers, Brother, Sisters, and Others - A Collection of Loved Recipes for You and Your Family* its content and cover are the property of Linda Hofstetter. This book or parts thereof, may not be reproduced in any form without permission from Linda Hofstetter or Recipe Publishers; exceptions are made for printed reviews and advertising and marketing excerpts.